BATTLE AT BULL RUN

Also by *William C. Davis*

DUEL BETWEEN THE FIRST IRONCLADS
THE BATTLE OF NEW MARKET
BRECKINRIDGE: Statesman, Soldier, Symbol

WILLIAM C. DAVIS

BATTLE AT BULL RUN

A History of the
First Major Campaign
of the Civil War

DOUBLEDAY & COMPANY, INC.
GARDEN CITY, NEW YORK

Library of Congress Cataloging in Publication Data

Davis, William C 1946–
  Battle at Bull Run.

  Bibliography: p. 279
  Includes index.
  1. Bull Run, 1st Battle, 1861.   I. Title
E472.18.D39   973.7'31
ISBN 0-385-12261-6
Library of Congress Catalog Card Number 76–42322

Contents

LIST OF ILLUSTRATIONS

PHOTOGRAPHS

Following page 58

Following page 106

Maps

ACKNOWLEDGMENTS

It is unfortunate that the acknowledgments in which historians thank those who helped them are not better read, for those who help deserve to be recognized. Theirs is a contribution of inestimable value, for they give of their time and expertise, with no recompense. A score and more of men and women have thus made their contribution to this work, and it is a happy duty to pay a small measure of tribute to their assistance.

With uniform courtesy and dispatch, aid with the manuscripts collections in their charge was lent by: M. H. Highes, Bowdoin College Library; Archie Motley, Chicago Historical Society; Eleanor S. Brockenbrough, Museum of the Confederacy; Kathleen Jacklin, Cornell University Library; Linda M. Matthews, Emory University Library; Charlotte Ray, Georgia Department of Archives and History; Harriet McLoone, Henry E. Huntington Library; Thomas L. Gaffney, Maine Historical Society; Dennis P. Kelly, Historian at Manassas National Battlefield Park; Richard J. Cox, Maryland Historical Society; Mary Jo Pugh, Michigan Historical Collections, University of Michigan; Ruby J. Shields, Minnesota Historical Society; Dwight Harris, Mississippi Department of Archives and History; Tom Dunnings, New-York Historical Society; Marylin Bell, Tennessee State Library and Archives; Howson W. Cole, Virginia Historical Society; John Dudley, Virginia State Library; Phyllis Burnham, Western Michigan University Archives, and Margaret Cooke of the Earl Swemm Library, College of William and Mary.

Beyond the efforts of those just named, a few individuals deserve a special portion of thanks for their contributions far above that expected of them. At Duke University's William R. Perkins Library, Winston Broadfoot, David W. Brown, and Sharon Knap lent every courtesy during my extensive research through the fine collections of that institution. A few miles away from Duke, at the University of North Carolina, Karen L. Jackson, Richard Shrader, and Everard Smith of the Southern Historical Collection were equally patient and helpful, pointing out several items that would otherwise have been missed. And at the South Caroliniana Library, University of South Carolina, Columbia, Allen H. Stokes and George Terry were very helpful in guiding research through the numerous manuscript collections which touch on First Bull Run and South Carolina's prominent part in the fight.

Friends, as always, provided not only moral support but also occasionally some good research aids. Robert J. Younger, of Dayton, Ohio, made available copies of the hard-to-find *Confederate Veteran* with its fund of indispensable articles by veterans of the battle. In addition, a number of rare out-of-print titles that might otherwise have been inaccessible were lent by him for the duration of the research. B. Franklin Cooling, John Slonaker, and Richard J. Sommers of the U. S. Army Military History Research Collection, Carlisle Barracks, Pennsylvania, allowed ample use of the excellent facilities and resources of that institution, and met repeated requests with helpful courtesy.

As for Pamela Davis, who managed to contend with several months of children, lawn, and seemingly endless restorations to an ante-bellum house that yet remains to be completely explored, all without much help from the great American historian, now she can take a much deserved rest. Her labors, for a time, may let up. Mine, I fear, are just beginning.

INTRODUCTION

At noon on July 10, 1861, Major W. P. Butler stepped into the headquarters of the First Brigade, of the newly designated Confederate Army of the Potomac, at Fairfax Court House, Virginia. There was, he said, a young lady outside who wished to see the general.

Brigadier General Milledge L. Bonham at first refused to see her. Indeed, he was under orders not to allow women to pass through his lines. Fairfax Court House stood barely twenty miles west of Washington, and he and his superiors had information that female spies from the Federal capital had attempted to pass in disguise on several occasions. The main Confederate army lay posted in and about Manassas Junction just ten miles southwest of Bonham's position. There was much the enemy in Washington would like to know of its strength and intentions. Justifiably, Bonham was cautious.

But the young lady insisted, said Provost Marshal Butler. She had vitally important information which she must deliver to Bonham, and to no other. The general relented, his capitulation softened somewhat by Butler's admission that the young woman was "very pretty."

Bonham soon agreed. "I was very much startled," he wrote, "at recognizing the face of a beautiful young lady, a brunette, with sparkling black eyes, perfect features, glossy black hair." He had seen her before. Sitting as a congressman from South Carolina in the House of Representatives in Washington, he had seen her face more than once among the spectators in the House gallery. That, however, was seven months ago, in what seemed another world.

Now the young lady introduced herself as Bettie Duval of Washington. She had left that city the day before, dressed in a farm woman's costume, riding across the Potomac River via the Chain Bridge in a market cart. Once in northern Virginia, she spent the night at the home of a friend, and there traded her humble clothing and cart for a neat riding dress and a horse. Escorted by a cousin, she rode the next morning toward Bonham's cavalry pickets near Vienna, several miles north of Fairfax Court House, and from there proceeded with a cavalry escort to the general's headquarters. In all, she had ridden fourteen dusty miles on an unusually hot and humid morning. Yet, she said, she stood prepared to ride on to the main army at Manassas unless Bonham agreed to take her information and forward it to his commander. For weeks now would-be heroines had been coming into Confederate camps, the bearers of "vital information" which proved to be worthless. Consequently Bonham was skeptical of Miss Duval but in the end he agreed to pass her dispatch along to his superior.

"Upon my announcing that I would at once have it safely forwarded," the general later recalled, "she took out her tucking comb and let fall the longest and most beautiful roll of hair that I have ever seen on human head. Flushed from the morning's ride, with the glow of patriotic devotion beaming from her bright face, she looked to the Confederate General radiantly beautiful. She took from the back of her head, where it was safely tied, a small package not larger than a silver half dollar carefully sewed up in black silk, which she said contained the important information . . . to the effect that the enemy would advance the day he did."

The whole scene so reeked of penny romance that it bordered on the ludicrous. A beautiful heroine, disdaining to sweat—or even glisten—from her hot, perilous ride, unfolds her raven tresses before the chivalrous general of the Confederacy to deliver a message of vital importance to the infant Southern nation. It was all really happening, but more like fiction come to life, a Waverley novel gone mad. Years later, Mark Twain would only half in jest propose that the American Civil War was to be blamed on Sir Walter Scott, that the people of the South had somehow persuaded themselves that the mythical era of gallant knights and fair damsels of *Ivanhoe* had come to life in Dixie. An entire nation, like this small group in Bonham's headquarters, seemed to be playing a role from a romance. Only here the stake was not a maiden's hand, the chivalry would be absent from the stage all too quickly, and the end of the drama just begun lay farther in the distance than any of the players imagined.

But for General Bonham in the immediate moment there were other matters to consider. Miss Duval's message came from a reliable source, and its import was unmistakable. "McDowell has certainly been ordered to advance on the sixteenth," it read. Even as Bonham watched Miss Duval put her hair back in place, he knew that in less than a week a Federal army would be on the move toward Manassas. Somewhere there or among the positions along the gentle stream called Bull Run, a major clash of arms was inevitable.[1]

CHAPTER 1

AN ARMY IN THE MAKING

America, it seemed, had gone mad and gone to war with itself. Four decades of compromise between the sections of the country had come to naught, largely because the lawmakers of Washington repeatedly chose to treat the symptom rather than the illness. Missouri might be admitted to the Union as a slave state in 1821 and California admitted as a free state in 1850, but still the bare fact of slavery in America remained. It was a sickness that tore at the Republic's very being and one that could only be dealt with in violence and in pain.

In 1860 it seemed that the crisis had come. November saw the election of Abraham Lincoln to the Presidency. The reaction in the South was instantaneous. Grown paranoid over its ever-dwindling minority status in population and representation in Congress, and further excited by the relatively small but extremely vocal abolition movement in the North, the Southern states and their leaders saw no choice ahead but to forfeit slavery and the shadow issue of state rights, or else attempt to leave the Union. Their right of secession seemed unquestionable, and their ability to defend that right—with the certain aid of the Almighty —against a mob of Yankee shopkeepers, was a foregone conclusion. On December 20, 1860, South Carolina formally adopted an ordinance of secession, and the next day her legislators in Washington, Bonham among them, withdrew from Congress.

Within days other states passed similar ordinances. By February

1, 1861, seven Southern states had withdrawn from the Union. A week later a constitution for the newly formed Confederate States of America was adopted, and on the following day, February 9, Jefferson Davis was chosen provisional president. In a few days Davis would intimate that secession *might* result in war with the North, but he did not expect it. Meanwhile, Lincoln, while en route to Washington for his inauguration, stated repeatedly that there was no real crisis, only an "artificial" one.

But the new Confederacy was doing little to avoid a crisis. Indeed, the "fire-eaters" of the South encouraged it. Federal property in all of the seceded states was seized, a United States garrison at Pensacola, Florida, was forced to fortify itself on offshore Fort Pickens, and Major Robert Anderson's command at Charleston, South Carolina, lay bottled up in Fort Sumter out in the harbor. On January 9, when the relief ship *Star of the West* tried to bring men and supplies to Anderson, Confederate shore batteries opened fire and forced her to abandon the attempt. As yet no blood had been shed. The almost daily incidents that occurred in the first months of 1861 were of a minor character and were well contained. Neither Davis nor Lincoln wanted open conflict. The former hoped for a peaceful separation, the latter a peaceful reconciliation.

Part of the reason that both hoped to avoid war was that neither was fully prepared for it. At the beginning of 1861, the United States Army numbered barely over 16,000, the majority of them thinly spread throughout the Western states and territories as an Indian deterrent. The new Confederacy, of course, had no standing army when created, but it did have the benefits of a militia tradition that dated back to colonial times. Indeed, the local militia company often served as the center of society and entertainment. In major cities throughout the South young men of the finest families vied for membership in an elite company. Some groups like New Orleans' Washington Artillery and the Richmond Howitzers had been in existence for years. Scores of others came into being in 1859, when John Brown's raid on the Federal arsenal at Harpers Ferry, Virginia, sent a jolt through the slave states. From this nucleus Davis might expect to draw the core of an army, but it would take time.

Equally important was the uncertainty, felt by both sides, over the course that the border states would pursue. Virginia, Maryland, North Carolina, Kentucky, Tennessee, Missouri, and Arkansas were all slave states, yet each harbored a powerful quotient of Union sentiment. Should they all remain neutral—which seemed to be the inclination of Kentucky—then Union and Confederacy would be, at their nearest point, over 150 miles apart. An overland conflict would be impractical if not impossible. Should they side with either of the contending parties, however, victory for that side seemed almost assured.

Knowing this, Lincoln took from the first a cautious stance toward the border states, and a conciliatory tone toward the Confederacy. In his Inaugural Address on March 4, 1861, he made it clear once more that he sought not the destruction of the institution of slavery as it then existed in the slave states, and neither did he wish to interfere with any of the other legitimate business of the states under the Constitution. Thus, he said, if war should commence, it could only be precipitated by the South. "In *your* hands, my dissatisfied fellow countrymen, and not in *mine*, is the momentous issue of civil war." He would not use force to reunite the severed states unless they forced it upon him. "The government will not assail *you*, unless *you* first assail *it*. You can have no conflict, without being yourselves the aggressors." It was more than a message to the Confederacy. It was a declaration of intent for the border states, and particularly Virginia. The least hostile act might drive her into the secessionist camp, and with her could go most of the others.[1]

What Lincoln might take for aggression, however, Davis regarded as self-defense. Now that the "sovereign" states had withdrawn and formed their own nation, the presence of Federal armed forces at Forts Pickens and Sumter was not only an affront, but also in the case of the latter a threat to the peaceful commerce of South Carolina. While he tried for months to persuade Washington to evacuate Sumter peacefully, Davis and South Carolina Governor Francis W. Pickens steadily built up the batteries in and around Charleston. They hoped to starve Anderson into leaving. But then came notification from Lincoln on April 8 that he was sending supply ships to Sumter. If no hostile action were taken, as with the *Star of the West*, then he promised to land food only, and not reinforcements.

With their plan of starving Anderson thus threatened, Davis authorized the Confederate commander at Charleston, Brigadier General P. G. T. Beauregard, to demand the fort's immediate surrender. If Anderson did not comply, Beauregard was to open fire. Anderson tried to play for time, but for him it ran out at 4:30 A.M., April 12. Confederate batteries opened fire. Thirty-four hours later Anderson surrendered.

Now it was done. The Confederacy had assailed the Federal Government. Armed insurrection had begun, and Lincoln had a solemn duty to put it down. On April 15 he issued a call on the remaining states to raise 75,000 volunteers for three months' service to defend the Union. This was too much for Virginia. With her Southern sentiments already stirred by the success in Charleston, she voted for secession two days later. During the next month Arkansas, Tennessee, and North Carolina would follow. Maryland, Kentucky, and Missouri, would maintain, though tenuously at times, their ties with the old Union. Thus the battle lines were drawn but no blood had been shed. There was still hope for peace, though whether it could come by reconciliation or separation no one could say. But events were beginning to shape themselves. Threats and pressures on leaders were accelerating, promising to jump entirely out of control and hurtle North and South toward catastrophe.

The next move was up to Washington. Even as the order for the volunteers went out, Lincoln consulted with his chief military adviser, Lieutenant General Winfield Scott. The immediate problem facing them was the defense of the capital, the removal or destruction of important Federal property and military goods in danger of falling into Confederate hands, and the formation of an army to protect Washington, prevent Maryland from joining her Southern sisters, and eventually put down the rebellion by force if necessary.

Scott, as it happened, was older than the United States. He was born a Virginian in 1786, but there had never been any question that his allegiance to the Union stood above all else. He was a military legend. A hero in the War of 1812, he went on to become a brigadier general in the Regular Army and, by 1841, a major general and general-in-chief of the United States Army. In this capacity he became the chief architect of the victory in the war with Mexico, and emerged from the conflict with sufficient stature to obtain the Whig nomination for the Presidency in 1852. But in the subsequent election, Franklin Pierce dealt him a smashing defeat.

He had always been a moderate man, given to conciliation where possible, loath to use force unless necessary. By 1861, however, much of the public confidence in him had dwindled. He was seventy-four years old, his six-foot-five-inch frame made almost comical by obesity. He could not ride a horse, walked with difficulty, lost his temper more and more easily, and seemed at times to let his pride cloud his judgment. But behind the lumbering façade still worked a brilliant mind and a loyal heart. "I have served my country, under the flag of the Union, for more than fifty years," he declared. "I will defend that flag with my sword, even if my native State assails it."[2]

Scott regarded the defense of Washington as his first priority. With Virginia now seceded and actively raising troops for her own defense, only the Potomac separated the capital from the hostile camp. Troops were needed at once to garrison the Federal city, but getting them there presented a difficult problem. The only overland routes passed through miles of Maryland soil in which the sentiment for secession ran high. The best and quickest avenues involved passage through Baltimore, perhaps the most rabidly pro-Southern section of the state. On April 19 the citizens of Baltimore provided a vivid portent of the difficulty Scott would have moving troops through Maryland. On that day the 6th Massachusetts Infantry arrived in Baltimore on its way to Washington. Here their rail cars had to be pulled by horse across the city to the Washington station. An angry mob began to gather, taunting the soldiers with insults, then throwing bricks and paving stones. Finally shots were fired, and by the time the 6th Massachusetts was again on its way, at least four soldiers and nine civilians lay dead in the streets of Baltimore. Worse yet, the incident so inflamed secessionist passions in the city that this rail route could not safely be used again by troops bound for Washington. The capital, in effect, lay isolated from the rest of the Union.

For a solution to the immediate problem of reinforcing Washington, Scott turned to an old friend who, like himself, had been born before the turn of the century. Robert Patterson was a na-

tive of Ireland, born in 1792. Because of political difficulties, the
family moved to Pennsylvania in 1798, and young Patterson grew
up in the Quaker state until, at age twenty, he entered the Army
in the War of 1812, rising to the rank of colonel. At war's end he
remained in the Pennsylvania militia, eventually winning a major
generalcy. When war with Mexico broke out, he was commissioned in that rank in the United States Army, and subsequently
accompanied Scott in his march to Mexico City as his second-in-
command. By 1861, Patterson was the only battle-experienced
officer other than Scott himself who had exercised high command
in the headquarters and the field. The very same day that the 6th
Massachusetts encountered trouble in Baltimore, Scott had Patterson commissioned once again a major general and placed him
in command of a military district comprising the states of Delaware, Maryland, and Pennsylvania, as well as the District of Columbia. Now it was up to Patterson to organize the three-month
troops being raised and to get as many of them as possible into
Washington without delay.

Patterson was not a happy choice. He had never held independent command or the sole responsibility that went with it.
Now he vacillated, unsure of himself. He saw difficulties and pitfalls in every move, found delays in the slightest happenstance,
and consistently refused to make his own decisions. Instead, he
consulted his subordinates, apparently in hopes of finding an
overwhelming consensus that would force him into an obvious
course. Alas, his staff officers were, for the most part, just as in-
decisive as he.

Consequently, while Patterson and Scott had a plan for opening a route through Maryland, nothing was immediately done
about it. The general-in-chief, perhaps sensing that he had given
Patterson more than he could handle, broke up the department
on April 27. The District of Columbia and part of northern Maryland were placed under another of Scott's favorites, Colonel
Joseph K. F. Mansfield, while Brigadier General Benjamin F. Butler, a Massachusetts politician, received command of that part of
Maryland lying between Washington and Annapolis.

Now, it was hoped, Patterson could concentrate all his energies
upon opening a route through Maryland to the capital in order to
reinforce the city. Scott devised a plan to move troops to Phila-

delphia, transport them by train to Havre de Grace, thence by ship to Annapolis, and from there once again by rail to the District of Columbia. At the same time, he ordered Patterson to prepare for a march on Baltimore. The city must be occupied by Federal forces before rebellion had a chance to spread any farther. Patterson, as usual, offered only excuse and delay, even though he had twenty-six regiments in various stages of readiness at his command. Finally he promised to move on Baltimore on May 8. Five days later he still had not moved, when unexpected news came from Butler that he had marched without orders, entered Baltimore quietly by night, and occupied the city unawares. Scott was understandably displeased with Butler, and replaced him immediately with another officer, but the fact remained that Baltimore was now safely in Federal hands, and the movement of Union troops through it to Washington could proceed without serious hazard. As for the state of Maryland herself, ties with the Union remained somewhat tenuous for the next four months until Lincoln arrested disloyal members of the state legislature. Thereafter, despite much continued sympathy for the Confederate States, Maryland remained a loyal state.

Even while agonizing over the relief of Washington, Scott addressed himself to the other pressing needs in the current emergency. On April 18, the day after Virginia voted to secede, the Federal armory at Harpers Ferry was burned and abandoned under imminent threat of being attacked and seized by Virginia state forces gathered nearby. Some 15,000 stands of arms were destroyed or seriously damaged, as well as machine and carpenter shops. Nothing, it was hoped, had been left intact to aid or arm the rebels. Two days later the United States Navy shipyard and drydock facilities in and around Norfolk, Virginia, were fired, and those ships that could not be taken away were scuttled or burned. This was the last remaining United States property in Confederate-occupied territory, or at least the last that Scott could reach to damage or destroy.

Now he could turn his attention to fortifying Washington and, it was hoped, to occupying enough of the Virginia side of the Potomac to give the city some breathing space, and make it secure from artillery bombardment. As soon as Baltimore was secure, volunteer regiments began pouring into Washington at a steady rate, and just as steadily Mansfield put them to work building defenses, drilling, slowly turning the city into an armed camp.

As soon as possible, Scott wanted to cross to the Virginia side of the Potomac and turn the rebels out of Alexandria. It would afford somewhat of a relief from the tension of having an armed enemy just across the river, give Scott a base in Virginia from which to launch any further operations in putting down the rebellion, and finally it would remove from the eyes of the capital the insulting sight of Confederate flags flying from Alexandria's rooftops.

Actually, the Confederate commander in Alexandria, Lieutenant Colonel A. S. Taylor, beat Scott by some three weeks. He was under orders from his superior, Colonel Philip St. George Cocke, not to abandon Alexandria without fighting, even against overwhelming numbers. If forced out, Taylor was to retire slowly, breaking up the railroad tracks as he went, falling back toward Manassas Junction. Only if in danger of "uselessly sacrificing your command" was he to fall back, and even then Cocke expected of him a "gallant and fighting retreat."

But Taylor could see what Cocke could not. His troops were few and inefficient. Some were armed with antiquated flintlock muskets, while others were barely armed at all, and many had no cartridges or musket caps. Worse yet, all but one company of infantry consisted of local men, with homes in the city. Consequently, they were spread out all around the town, and it would be almost impossible to call them all together at the point of attack, for each man would want to defend his home. Taylor doubted that he could put up any fight at all other than "a disastrous and demoralizing retreat in the face of an enemy." An orderly withdrawal would be far more beneficial to his command's morale. Finally, he received information which indicated that Scott would try to occupy Alexandria on May 6 or 7 by a movement from Washington and a flank march by troops he believed to have been landed a few miles downriver at Mount Vernon. Under these circumstances, Taylor felt he had no choice but to evacuate Alexandria, which he did on May 5. Cocke wanted him arrested, but was persuaded otherwise, while Alexandria and a foothold on the Virginia shore lay open to the Federals without resistance.[3]

Not until the morning of May 24 did Scott move. Since most of the troops in Washington by this time were New York volunteers, he felt it politic to place them under the command of a New York militia major general, Charles W. Sandford, though Mansfield had' over-all responsibility for the operation. It was all accomplished quietly. Bridges were crossed and secured before they could be fired, and the only Confederate troops in the city, a company of thirty-five cavalry, were taken without a shot. Indeed, the only unfortunate occurrence of the operation was the murder of Colonel Elmer E. Ellsworth of the 11th New York. A special friend of Lincoln's, he had seen a rebel flag flying from the roof of the Marshal House in Alexandria. Personally he entered the house, climbed up to the roof and took down the offensive banner, only to be shot dead by the proprietor of the place.

The movements of May 24 were not confined solely to Alexandria. Sandford also occupied Arlington, and with it the Custis-Lee mansion overlooking the Potomac. Built by George W. P. Custis, adopted son of one of America's greatest soldiers, George Washington, it was then the residence of Custis' son-in-law, Robert E. Lee of the Virginia state forces, and a brigadier in the new Confederate Army. Sandford made the home his headquarters in order to protect it from possible vandalism.

With Alexandria secured, the Federal authorities now faced a new problem. Virginia was outside the departmental limits of Mansfield's District of Columbia command. A new department must be created to encompass this part of Virginia and any other ground that ensuing events might bring under Federal control. Because he was a state militia general and not a Regular Army officer, Sandford was regarded as unsuitable for the command. Scott had his own choice, Mansfield, but others soon took the matter almost entirely out of his control. Against his preferences and better judgment, Scott was forced to appoint to the command a man who had never led even a company of men in battle, and who just two weeks before had been a mere major in the office of the adjutant general.

Irvin McDowell never in his life expected to be where he found himself in May 1861. He was forty-two years old, an Ohioan who, after graduating from the United States Military Academy at West Point, went on to become an instructor in tactics at the

Academy. When war came with Mexico, he served on the staff of Brigadier General John E. Wool, and comported himself with such gallantry at the Battle of Buena Vista that he was given a brevet promotion to captain. The remainder of the war he spent on Scott's staff, and a warm friendship grew between them. After the war, McDowell remained on Scott's staff, apparently content with a career that was bound nowhere.

Personally he was something of an enigma. A large man of robust physique, he was not handsome but did have, thought some, a "congenial face." Blue-eyed, square-jawed, bearded, and quite heavy-set, he did at least give the appearance of self-confidence. In his personal habits he seemed a puritan. He neither drank nor smoked, even disdaining tea and coffee. But he more than made up for this abstinence by his eating habits. "At dinner he was such a Gargantuan feeder and so absorbed in the dishes before him that he had but little time for conversation," wrote a fellow officer. "While he drank neither wine nor spirits, he fairly gobbled the larger part of every dish within reach, and wound up with an entire watermelon, which he said was 'monstrous fine!'"

Beyond this there was a certain lack of humor coupled with a stiff formality or aloofness that separated him automatically from his subordinates and superiors. A bad listener, he frequently lost himself in thought while others were speaking. This, combined with a rare ability to forget names and faces, failed to endear him to many. Sometimes rude, he often let his temper flare out of control. A good friend, Lincoln's Secretary of the Treasury Salmon P. Chase, found that McDowell was "too indifferent in manner, and his officers are sometimes alienated by it. . . . There is an apparent *hauteur*: no, that is not the word—rough indifference expresses better the idea—in his way toward them, that makes it hard for them to feel any very warm personal sentiments toward him."

McDowell had attracted some little attention to himself during April when he aided in the organization of Washington's defenses. He was an outspoken Unionist, and was well known to Chase, himself a former governor of Ohio. Chase, Governor William Dennison of Ohio, and even Secretary of War Simon Cameron all hoped to advance McDowell as soon as possible. The opportunity came early in May when Lincoln called for the expansion of the Regular Army by 22,714 men of all arms. Such an enlargement would require several new brigadiers and major generals. When the Cabinet met to discuss appointments, Chase was determined that McDowell should be one of those selected. He wanted a major generalcy for him, and during the meeting had called McDowell to the Executive Mansion to inform him of his plans. When Chase left the meeting briefly to talk with him, a dumfounded McDowell observed that such a promotion would certainly cause bad feeling toward him among those officers superior to him who would be passed over in the act, and suggested that he would be more than content as a brigadier.

With no difficulty, McDowell was appointed a brigadier general in the Regular Army to date from May 14, 1861. The only real opposition to the appointment came from Scott. Besides the fact that it jumped McDowell over many other officers who were his senior in rank and length of service, it also elevated him over Scott's old friend Mansfield. Consequently, Scott insisted that Mansfield be made a brigadier to date from May 14 as well. Lincoln complied, and Scott took some relief from the fact that Mansfield, formerly a colonel, would still at least outrank McDowell, who had been only a brevet major.

The satisfaction proved of short duration. Now that the new brigadiers stood ready for assignment, Scott was given his choice between Mansfield and McDowell for the Virginia command. He did not wish to send either, wanting to keep Mansfield in command in the District, and having other plans for McDowell. But since Sandford was not considered suitable, Scott reluctantly chose McDowell to replace him. Soon afterward he sent two of his aides to McDowell to suggest that he ask the Secretary of War not to assign him to the Virginia post. Scott's motives are somewhat obscure, though he would declare that he did not want to invade Virginia. Perhaps it was because of his own ties to the Old Dominion. He did say that he favored a large-scale movement down the Mississippi instead, thinking it would end the conflict if successful. A march into Virginia would affect only the one state, whereas capture of the Mississippi would split the Confederacy in two.

Whatever the case, McDowell declined to accept Scott's suggestion. "I said I could not do that," declared the new brigadier.

"Just appointed a general officer, it was not for me to make a personal request not to take the command which I had been ordered upon. I could not stand upon it. I had no reputation, as he had, and I refused to make any such application." Consequently, on May 27 the Department of Northeastern Virginia was created by the War Department, and Brigadier General Irvin McDowell received command. It was a heady moment for the new general, but one clouded by a brooding lieutenant general in Washington who had been used to having his way. Scott did not appreciate McDowell's refusal, and would not forget it. "The general was cool for a great while," McDowell would recall, and it would have a material effect upon the coming operations in Virginia.[4]

McDowell rode across the Potomac on the afternoon of May 27, but arrived too late to take formal command. Instead, he conferred with Sandford on the situation in and around Alexandria, spent the night, and the next morning rode into the city well before 5 A.M. He spent the rest of the day examining his troop positions and reviewing the condition of his soldiers. What he found demanded immediate action. No defensive works at Alexandria had yet been started or even planned, besides which no one had sent over tools to do the work. Worse, the men complained of inadequate supply. There were no wagons to haul commissary goods, most officers did not yet possess enough experience to organize adequate supply services for their men, and communications were so bad between the Virginia and Washington sides of the river that orders for food, when sent, were not received. Indeed, one of the regiments actually hired its own private freight wagons to procure supplies.

McDowell immediately requested more wagons from the War Department, and as well asked to have a number of Regular Army officers assigned to him for staff and other duties involved in getting the small army running more efficiently. In one instance, the general actually feared a violation of the Constitution. Troops in his command were quartering themselves in private homes and fields, not necessarily with the owners' permission. He immediately asked for funds, if necessary, to pay rent and recompense for wood taken for fires.

Indeed, this matter of abusing the private property of Virginia citizens proved of great concern to McDowell. He knew that, even though the state had seceded, there still dwelled within the Old Dominion a substantial Union sentiment. Abuses of her citizenry could only undermine that support, thereby endangering the ultimate success of any military movement that might require some degree of local sympathy. "I am aware we are not, theoretically speaking, at war with the State of Virginia, and we are not, here, in an enemy's country," he wrote. Thus, outrages against the persons and property of Virginia's citizens by his soldiers, even under the excuse that the victims were secessionists, could not pass unpunished. He proposed that he set up a military commission to try offenders, since local civil justice had broken down. The whole subject may have been on his mind thanks to his own somewhat unconstitutional occupation of the Custis-Lee mansion. Mrs. Lee wrote to him on May 30 to protest the use of her home as Federal headquarters, and the same day McDowell hastened to reply. He told her that he was staying outside the house in a tent on its grounds, "preferring this to sleeping in the house, under the circumstances which the painful state of the country places me with respect to its proprietors." He promised to have such care taken with the house that whenever Mrs. Lee returned she should find nothing out of place. Meanwhile, McDowell gave orders forbidding his officers and men to arrest or detain any Virginian solely because of Confederate sentiments, and warning them not to enter forcibly or search a home without orders. At the same time he asked that careful accounts be kept of all crops destroyed, the number and size of buildings occupied, and the value of lands used for troop encampments or earthworks. Authorization was given to the public to make application for restitution of any damages incurred to their property. So far McDowell was waging a very civil war indeed.[5]

McDowell formally took command on May 28, and at once began the work of making an army of the disparate group of officers and regiments at hand. An important appointment was that of Captain James B. Fry to the duties of assistant adjutant general, the chief officer through whom the general's orders would be promulgated, and by whom he would communicate with headquarters in the War Department. Fry, a thirty-four-year-old Illinoisian, possessed one quality that stands pre-eminent in a staff officer—complete loyalty and devotion to his superior. McDowell would need that in the days ahead.

Brigades had to be organized, and commanders appointed for them. McDowell wanted only Regular officers for this task, and he found them in Colonels Charles P. Stone, Samuel P. Heintzelman, and David Hunter. To Stone he gave the 1st Michigan Infantry, the 11th New York, and the 5th Massachusetts. Heintzelman's brigade contained the 8th, 12th, and 27th New York regiments, and Hunter's the 5th, 28th, and 69th New York. This, with a few companies of cavalry and sections of artillery, made up his command for the moment. It was a modest beginning for what would become one day one of the greatest armies in military history.[6]

CHAPTER 2

THE "SOUTHRONS" GATHER

As soon as Virginia's intention of seceding was announced, the Confederate Government, then operating in Montgomery, Alabama, sent Vice President Alexander H. Stephens to Richmond in order to smooth the state's road into the Confederacy. Stephens encountered no difficulty, and indeed had little to do, for Virginia's mind was settled. Immediately thereafter, on April 20, Governor John Letcher issued a call for volunteers to defend the state against Federal invasion, and in it invited any Virginia officers in the United States Army and Navy to resign their commissions and accept appointments of similar or higher grade in the state service. The very next day he elaborated upon his decree, ordering that all companies then raised between Richmond and the Blue Ridge and in the Shenandoah Valley should rendezvous as quickly as possible and hold themselves ready for action. Sensing immediately that Virginia must first defend her northeastern border along the Potomac, Letcher immediately ordered Cocke to defend "the line of the Potomac."

Cocke was an old soldier from one of Virginia's finest families. A West Point graduate, he nevertheless left the service in 1834, and for the next twenty-seven years devoted himself to managing plantations in Virginia and Mississippi. He became an eminent agriculturalist, publishing frequent articles in journals and writing a book on farm management. A slender, handsome, yet somehow sad-looking man, he accepted an appointment as brigadier in the state service on April 21.

Even as Cocke moved to Alexandria to take command, other officers began to tender their services to Letcher. One of them was Colonel Robert E. Lee. There is little doubt that, on April 18, Lee was called to Washington and offered the command of the army which would be raised to put down the rebellion. It would have been the greatest assignment of his already distinguished career, but he declined. The son of a Revolutionary War hero, "Light-Horse Harry" Lee, he compiled an unexampled record at West Point and thereafter spent thirty-two years in the Army. During the Mexican War, serving on the staffs of Wool and later Scott, he repeatedly won plaudits, and promotions, for his daring in battle and his efficiency in the field. In 1852 he took over the superintendency of the Military Academy, and seven years later, now an officer in the field, commanded the troops which captured John Brown and his raiders at Harpers Ferry. He was a great favorite of Scott's, and it was a sad moment for all parties concerned when, on April 20, 1861, Lee resigned his commission. Two days later Letcher made him a major general in command of all state forces.

Immediately Lee conferred with Cocke on what could be and should be done on the Potomac line. The outlook was not encouraging. On April 23, Cocke had but 300 men fit for duty, no artillery and ammunition, no staff, and no engineers to erect defensive works. He was virtually powerless to resist any movement across the river from Washington, particularly when he thought he could see as many as 10,000 Federal troops in the capital. In a failing as old as warfare itself, Cocke was greatly exaggerating his opponents' numbers.

All he could do, Cocke reported, was to "act for the present absolutely on the defensive; to watch the enemy; to keep you informed of his movements; to rally to my aid the whole country in the rear; to organize, and await re-enforcements from every possible quarter." Immediately Lee began to send Cocke what he could—two cannon here, an engineer officer there, small arms and ammunition. A few days later Cocke removed his personal headquarters some distance to Culpeper Court House, well into the interior of the state. Here he could begin his stated task of rallying to arms the young men of the state, setting up camps to train them, and better directing the over-all defense of the long line of the Potomac, from Alexandria to Harpers Ferry. Meanwhile, he left a small command behind at Alexandria, more to observe than defend. Had Cocke known how long it would take Scott to mount a movement across the Potomac, the Confederate might have been a little less fearful of his position. It seemed not to occur to him, or to others including Lee, that the Federals were just as unprepared to attack as they were to defend.[1]

While Lee and Cocke fretted over their weakness in troops, the process of commissioning more generals went on. Virginia was among the largest of the Confederate states, and her defense would require several regional commands and commanders. Major General William B. Taliaferro was ordered to take charge of Virginia forces in and around Norfolk. Colonel George A. Porterfield was assigned to command forces in northwestern Virginia. And to organize the motley assemblage of militia and volunteers who had swarmed into Harpers Ferry after the Federals set their fires and evacuated, Letcher and Lee appointed Colonel Thomas Jonathan Jackson.

Even as the Federals were marching away from a burning Harpers Ferry on April 18, two companies of Virginia militia raced into the little town to begin putting out fires. As many guns as could be saved soon found themselves in the hands of enthusiastic Southerners. And when word of the capture spread, other companies from throughout the Shenandoah Valley and the hills of western Virginia began to flock to the arsenal town. Even without an acknowledged commander, the various groups of soldiers, clothed like a patchwork and armed with every description of new and ancient weapon, began to drill and train. Within a week after the occupation, Captain William Baylor, commanding the West Augusta Guards—soon to be Company L, 5th Virginia Infantry—wrote home that "The men work willingly, eat heartily, and sleep as soundly on the ground, as a prince in a palace. They are ready for a fight, and I believe are eager to show their courage in driving back any invading force."[2]

There was no question that Harpers Ferry would be a point of attack in any Federal attempt to regain Virginia. Resting as it did at the very northern tip of the Shenandoah, it commanded the entrance to the valley. Who controlled that valley, in turn, held

the fate of Virginia. The state fed on the Shenandoah's grain, and
the valley itself split the commonwealth in half. The Shenandoah
had to be held if Virginia were to remain intact, and the way to
hold it was to hold Harpers Ferry.

After a few days of directionless drilling among the volunteers
gathered there, it was obvious that a commander had to be sent to
make order, organize the troops into regiments, and set up defenses against attack. Hence the appointment of Jackson.

And an odd appointment it was. Jackson was thirty-seven now,
a native of western Virginia, and an undistinguished graduate of
West Point. His service in the Mexican War won him two brevet
promotions but little notice, and in 1852 he resigned his commission to become an instructor at Lexington's Virginia Military In-
stitute. Here it was that many of the stories about Jackson started,
for the combination of eccentric professor and imaginative boys
was bound to strike sparks. They called him "Tom Fool" and
"Old Blue Light," the latter because of his eyes. Few if any of the
boys liked the punctilious disciplinarian, and at least one resolved
to kill him someday. Twice cadets challenged him to duels. When
not damning him, they privately subjected him to ridicule for his
quaint habits. He sucked lemons at every opportunity, to relieve a
stomach disorder. He would not touch pepper for fear it would
make his leg ache. His high-pitched voice sounded totally incon-
gruous coming from his six-foot, robust frame. He rarely laughed,
and when he did his head fell back, his mouth opened wide—and
no sound whatsoever came out. He was such a stickler for obeying orders that, on the day he was to lead a column of cadets
to Richmond after he had been commissioned, he sat motionless
on his horse until the courthouse bell rang the hour of noon. He
and the column were ready to go five minutes earlier, but his orders called for him to leave at noon, and that was when he would
leave.

Once in command at Harpers Ferry, Colonel Jackson lost no
time in whipping his men into shape—literally, thought some. He
drilled them incessantly, regardless of the weather, and denied
them any of the luxuries that the volunteer of 1861 thought necessary. One angry private complained that Jackson "considered a
gum cloth, a blanket, a tooth brush and forty rounds of cartridges
as the full equipment of a gentleman soldier." At first he proved

to be just as unpopular with the men as he had been with the boys. But in time they came to understand and respect the man. For all his peculiarities, there was a rock-hard strength to him. He brought them order out of confusion, and he surprised them by showing them what they could achieve with discipline. As for the other requisites of the soldier, bravery and fighting spirit, they brought that with them to Harpers Ferry. "A fierce spirit animates these rough-looking men," wrote a Confederate officer, "and if called upon, even now, to meet the enemy, I have no fear of the result of the battle."

In time Jackson organized them into regiments. They came with such colorful appellations as the "Grayson Daredevils," "Montgomery Fencibles," "Ready Rifles," "Hamtranck Guards," and "Hedgesville Blues." Jackson gave them, instead, more prosaic designations as the 2d, 4th, 5th, and 27th Virginia Infantries. A few weeks later the 33d Virginia would be added to these regiments, along with the Rockbridge Artillery, to form the First Virginia Brigade. Not to be denied their little sobriquets, the men in the ranks quickly dubbed themselves "The Innocent Second," the "Harmless Fourth," the "Fighting Fifth," and the "Fighting Twenty-Seventh." Later, when the 33d Virginia joined the brigade, and came down with an infestation of lice, their comrades immortalized them as the "Lousy Thirty-third." But Jackson did not mind. "I am very thankful to our Heavenly Father for having given me such a fine brigade," he wrote to his wife. In time he would believe the brigade to be an instrument of the Almighty himself.[3]

Other officers came to Harpers Ferry in the days ahead. One of them was James Ewell Brown Stuart, formerly a lieutenant in the United States Cavalry, and now the leader of several companies of Confederate horse. Stuart had been at Harpers Ferry before, in 1859, when he served as Lee's aide in the capture of John Brown. Now he was a Confederate lieutenant colonel, and his first order of business was the organization of his companies into a regiment, the 1st Virginia Cavalry. A merry, bearded, handsome man, he had all the flair and dash that typified the romantic *beau sabreur* of romantic fiction. Complete to the panache in his hat, he was a cavalryman's cavalryman.

And it is here, at Harpers Ferry, so often a stage for great drama in the coming contest, that one of the principal actors enters from the wings. On May 15, 1861, the War Department assigned command at Harpers Ferry to a new brigadier general, Joseph Eggleston Johnston. He was a small, slight man, wispy hair receding back from a high forehead, his small goatee so projecting from his slender, hollow-cheeked face as to give him a rodent-like appearance. There were few indeed who came to the Confederacy from the old Army with a better reputation. He attended the Military Academy with Lee, and thereafter served in campaigns against the Seminoles in Florida, and in the Mexican War. He seemed to have a natural attraction for bullets, being wounded repeatedly. But just as often he won compliments and promotions. Eventually he wound up in Washington, surpassing Lee in rank, to become a brigadier general in the Regular Army, and quartermaster general. It was a long way to have come, the capstone to a fine career. But Johnston was from Virginia, and immediately upon her secession he resigned his commission and accepted one, first as a major general in Virginia's state troops, and later as a brigadier in the Confederate service. He was fifty-four, in his prime, conscious of his reputation. Indeed, as events would show, he was perhaps too conscious of it.

Besides the brigade that would be given to Jackson, Johnston found several other regiments at Harpers Ferry that were either formed or ready to organize. Virginia provided the 10th and 13th Infantries, Mississippi her 2d and 11th, and Alabama the 4th. In addition, the nucleus of the 1st Maryland Infantry was there, known as the Maryland Battalion. Southern sympathizers, some of whom had stoned the 6th Massachusetts on its march through Baltimore, these men were almost exiles from their native state, whose soil lay in their sight, just across the Potomac. Other exiles, from Kentucky, formed a battalion led by Blanton Duncan.

In all there were about 5,200 men. "These troops were undisciplined, of course," wrote Johnston—surely he was not including Jackson's regiments!—"and, like all new troops assembled in large bodies, they were suffering very much from sickness; nearly forty per cent. of the 'total' being in the hospitals there or elsewhere, from the effects of measles and mumps."

As for the troops themselves, these early days of learning and enduring were not much different from similar days for soldiers throughout the ages. Liquor was always a problem. When Jackson arrived he ordered that all of the town's spirits be destroyed. "The barrels were brought forth," wrote a private of the 5th Virginia, "the heads knocked in, and the contents poured into the gutter; but the men dipped it up in buckets, and there was a sound of revelry by night." When Jackson ordered the whiskey poured into the Potomac, soldiers stood around with buckets tied to ropes and, lowering them, caught much of the nectar just as it was about to pollute the river. It was noticed that the Kentuckians showed a particular fondness for the stuff.

The 11th Mississippi was particularly hard hit by the measles. "For the last ten days we have had an average of forty cases per day," wrote a member of the "Noxubee Rifles"—Company F, 11th Mississippi. Eventually every member of the company suffered it, some looking "as spotted . . . as a Leopard. . . . We are in a bad condition for a fight," he wrote "with nearly half our Regiment sick with the measles."[4]

At least a contributing factor to the high disease rate was the constant weariness of the men under first Jackson's, and then Johnston's, regimen of training. A worn-out Mississippian confided the daily routine to his diary: "5 A.m. Reveillie—5½ A.m. squad drill—6 Surgery call—6 Breakfast—7 first Guard Mounting—7½ Guard Mounting—8 Squad drill—10½ Camp drill —1 P.m. dinner—3 P.m. camp drill—6 P.m. Dress parade." It was a grueling pace. On one day, the 2d Mississippi could muster only thirty-four healthy men on the parade ground.[5]

Even when healthy, the men had problems drilling, thanks to the haphazard character of their weapons and equipment. It was the first thing Johnston noted on his arrival. Some regiments were well armed. Others carried antiquated muskets almost as dangerous to the shooter as to the target. And some units had no weapons at all. The 1st Maryland needed rifles desperately. But if they did not have guns, they did have Jane Claudia Johnson.

The wife of Major Bradley T. Johnson, she decided that her place was not back home in the comfort of Maryland while her husband suffered the privations of an officer's life. She decided to join him in Harpers Ferry. The first thing she saw on her arrival— after her husband, presumably—was that his regiment had no arms. At once, on May 24, she left, bound for North Carolina and influential friends who could raise the money to supply rifles. Instead of raising money, however, she raised the governor. After presenting her case to him, Jane Johnson had the satisfaction of being presented with 500 .54 caliber rifles, 10,000 rounds of ammunition, and 3,500 musket caps. Not about to pass up the opportunity of the moment, a gathering of distinguished men of Raleigh, North Carolina, met to pay tribute to her before her departure. "If great events produce great men," said the speaker, "so, in the scene before us, we have proof that great events produce great women." With this said, Mrs. Johnson promptly left for Richmond. Stopping there, she picked up some blankets, tents, and other camp equipment from Governor Letcher, and then delivered it all to Harpers Ferry on June 3. And when she noticed on her arrival that the Maryland men stood ill-clad, she arranged neat gray uniforms for them as well. In all she proved a rather efficient quartermaster.[6]

As for the Kentuckians, they proved to be troublesome, difficult for their officers to handle, even insurrectionary. They were ill-armed and badly clothed, though Duncan asserted that they were eager for a fight and "will do good service." Perhaps the trouble with them was really too much of that "destroyed" whiskey.[7]

And so Johnston and Jackson molded their small army. Cocke had been hard at work as well, and as every week passed other states of the newborn Confederacy sent their sons to Virginia. On May 3, Letcher authorized Cocke to call out and muster into the service volunteers from eighteen counties, ordering him to organize them into no more than ten regiments of infantry, two of cavalry, and eight companies of artillery. Being conscious of the important role that local pride and relationships would have in building up morale, Letcher recommended that if possible regiments be made up of men from the same areas. By May 8, Cocke had sixteen companies of all arms, not yet regimented, and indeed he seemed to drag his feet somewhat in the task. Slowly, however, they took shape. And what Cocke did not organize himself others raised elsewhere in the interior of the state. Colonel Jubal A. Early was sent to Lynchburg to raise volunteers there and form them into regiments. Working diligently at the task, Early built the 24th Virginia, which would be his own regiment, the 28th Virginia, and the 30th, later to become a cavalry unit. Their muskets were mostly old smoothbores, they had no belts or bayonet scabbards, and impromptu cloth pouches for ammunition were made for them by local ladies. The cavalry carried mostly double-barreled shotguns, while their sabers were old ones collected from veterans of earlier wars.

Working from his headquarters, Cocke managed to form the 7th Virginia in May, a regiment that counted among its companies the Washington Volunteers, men actually hailing from the District of Columbia. He used three companies of the 6th Battalion to form the nucleus of the 17th Virginia Infantry, three companies enlisted in Alexandria over a week before Virginia seceded. Sent to Cocke from the southwestern counties of the state were the companies that would become the 11th Virginia.[8]

But Virginia would not furnish the stuff of this contest alone. Virtually every state of the Confederacy but Texas and Florida sent regiments to the Old Dominion, or were organizing them for the coming struggle. Everywhere the process of enlisting was accompanied by an almost carnival atmosphere, the young men rushing to get into the service before the fun was all over. "Nothing would do me but to enlist," wrote a young Mississippian. "My parents pleaded with me, saying I was too young to go to war, too young and too delicate. I should at least wait until I was eighteen. But nothing could shake my resolution to be a soldier."

In Mississippi they raised the 2d, 13th, 17th, and 18th Infantries. It was hot work as spring inevitably wore on toward summer. "Drilling is warm work," wrote a private of the 18th Mississippi. "We would get pretty tired before our day's work ended. We were, however, learning our lessons in soldiering, and the drill was an important part of them. It is this mainly that makes the difference between trained soldiers and a mob." When the time came to leave for the front, most of the Mississippians had to steam upriver to Vicksburg to meet the railhead. Departure for them was a festive occasion. "I shall never forget that beautiful day, and how elated I was, marching down the street while the band played 'The Bonnie Blue Flag' and 'Dixie.' Thousands were on the sidewalks, cheering and waving handkerchiefs. Some were crying, and of course it never occurred to me that many of us would never see those dear friends and neighbors again." Of course there were pompous, patriotic speeches. Boat whistles blew and bells rang,

and the people on shore laughed, sang, shouted, or cried. Then
the steamboats drew in their planks, swung out into the river,
"and were off for the war." Despite the exhilaration of the adven-
ture to come, there were those—especially the young ones—for
whom leaving home hurt terribly. "I was a small, delicate boy,"
wrote Private George Gibbs of the 18th, "had never been away
from my father and mother, and I was anything but happy in
parting from them. I hid from the other soldiers and had a big
cry."[9]

The same scene was repeated in New Orleans, down the river.
There the Washington Artillery, which dated back to 1840, had
been ready for the call long before the Confederate States organized themselves. When Secretary of War Leroy P. Walker accepted the command into the Confederate service, the city went
wild with joy. Money poured in from contributors who wanted
the men well outfitted. Each man provided his own uniform and
sidearms, officers their own horses. On May 26, a brilliant Sunday
morning, the four immaculately clad companies of the unit
marched behind their bright banners to form in Lafayette Square
to be mustered into the service. Surrounded by thousands of
onlookers, they then proceeded to Christ Church. There the
unit's colors were placed against the chancel rail while a stirring
sermon enjoined them to fight well and "remember that they
were educated to be gentlemen, and it behooved them to bring
back their characters as soldiers and gentlemen unblemished." As
if it were Guinevere blessing the sword of Lancelot, they held
their banners up before the altar for the benediction. Then they
marched to the train for Virginia; a special train, incidentally.
These were the finest sons of the Crescent City. No common soldier accommodations for them. A special twenty-one-car train had
been chartered, with passenger cars for the officers and men, boxcars for the animals, and open flatcars for their cannon. War was
one thing—comfort quite another.[10]

From across the river, the 1st Arkansas came with somewhat
less fanfare. These were simple Westerners coming for a fight. No
frock coats and epaulets with them—just rifles. More murderous-
looking was another Louisiana unit, the 1st Louisiana Battalion,
dressed in French Zouave fashion with baggy blue and white
striped trousers, short brown jacket, and a small cap with a long

red tassel. At their waists they carried the most vicious-looking knives, shaped like a bowie but longer than a South American machete. The 1st, 2d, and 3d Tennessee formed for the trip to Virginia as well. Nothing fancy about them. They were mountaineers for the most part, used to a hard life and a hard fight.

Alabama, too, sent her sons, the 4th, 5th, and 6th Regiments. They formed and left for the front amid the same general elation. With names like "Raccoon Roughs," these hardy Southerners banded together in haste, and not always with the most appropriate equipment. The 6th Alabama had men wearing coonskin caps, and its officers wore double-breasted frock coats made of brilliant green cloth "more suited to Irishmen than to Americans," thought one captain. Even more unsuited to these Confederates were the buttons on their coats—leftover brass buttons from the United States Army.

Like the other regiments from Louisiana, Mississippi, Arkansas, and Tennessee, these Alabamians had to face a special danger before ever reaching Virginia. Eastern Tennessee was a hotbed of Union sympathy. Militant tories there vigorously opposed secession and, once it was a fact, continued to harass Confederate efforts at recruiting and movement of troops. The Virginia & East Tennessee Railroad, the major avenue into Virginia from the Deep South, ran through several score miles of this Unionist territory. "At the depots crowds of men were gathered, some cheering, some jeering, my troops as they passed," wrote John B. Gordon of the 6th Alabama. The Stars and Stripes floated over houses on one side of the tracks, while various Confederate banners fluttered on the other. It was a tense passage for all, but fortunately little or no violence took place. But there were hints of sabotage, as when the locomotive "Sam Tate" burst a boiler, killing four Mississippians and injuring several others.[11]

In Georgia the state raised the 6th, 7th, and 8th Infantries. Here the Oglethorpe Rifles of Savannah had seized Fort Pulaski at the outbreak of rebellion, and here they became part of the 8th Georgia, led by a dashing Colonel Francis Bartow. In North Carolina the 5th, 6th, and 11th Regiments formed for the war. The Old North State, the last to leave the Union and join the Confederacy, was well on her way to being the state that would furnish more men for the Southern cause than any other.

For now, however, the state that would send more regiments to
Virginia than any other was, predictably, the seedbed of secession,
South Carolina. Seven units regularly raised and one private com-
mand would form and find their way to the Old Dominion.

Most of the men in these regiments enlisted before the firing
on Fort Sumter in the first wave of patriotic enthusiasm. Only
after the capture of the Federal stronghold did the state formally
organize them into the 1st, 2d, 3d, 4th, 5th, 7th, and 8th South
Carolina Infantries. Their confidence knew no bounds. "It is
firmly believed that we will have Washington in less than a
month," a man of the 7th Regiment wrote on learning of Virginia's secession. "We are upon the eve of great events," wrote a
man of the 3d South Carolina, "and what the results will be
heaven alone can tell."

The companies and regiments went into camp at Charleston
for drill and outfitting, and for the formality of transferring themselves from the state service into that of the Confederacy. There
were those who welcomed the change, since it would mean new
officers. Almost all of these Confederate regiments were electing
their own company and field officers, with the result that leaders
as often as not had no military talent but a lot of whiskey at election time. It was hardly a desirable system, but one which at least
quickly provided officers for an infant nation with no standing
army. It also contributed to regimental *esprit*. Unfortunately, the
practice inevitably put blunderers in high places. "I would rather
risk my life for three years under an educated military man,"
wrote one soldier, "than one year under an illiterate man."

In an attempt to bring a professional competence to the new
regiments, cadets from the Citadel, a fine private military academy, came to the regiments to drill them some six hours every
day. It was no easy task to turn farmers, shopkeepers, and indo-
lent sons of rich planters into soldiers. Private donation uni-
formed them; captures from Federal arsenals, mixed with state
and private purchases, armed them. Camp life proved a hardship
for some, yet others thrived. For most, however, "the incidents of
camp life are not amusing." The prevailing feeling was one of
"dullness and monotony." Worse yet for these men was the separation that a move to Virginia would cause. Like the soldiers from
the rest of the Deep South, once in the Old Dominion, they

could expect few if any visits to home until the unpleasantness was over. A brief furlough from camp, then, was a prize. "I have had the blues for the last two or three days," wrote one officer who missed his last opportunity for a visit home; "the time we stay when we go home is so short that it does us no good. Of course we love to go, but then the separation comes so hastily that we cannot enjoy it much." When finally the time did come for the regiments to board the cars for Richmond, the trip proved to be less than a lark. The coaches were dirty and, perhaps to forget their sorrow at leaving home, a great number of the men were drunk or insubordinate. "Every man in the regiment mistook himself for Commander-in-Chief," wrote a man of the 4th South Carolina. Much of the confusion could be blamed on a potion inauspiciously dubbed "rot-of-pop-skull."[12]

The one privately raised outfit was one of particular note, both for the caliber of its men and the character of its benefactor, financier, and commander. The Hampton Legion was the personal project of Wade Hampton, regarded by some as the biggest landowner in all the South. He was, in turn, the grandson of a man reputed to be the richest planter in the nation. Living his entire life in the most splendid luxury, Hampton moved easily into the South Carolina legislature, where he was an ardent Southern nationalist. When war came, however, his every possession was at the command of the new Confederacy. He offered his cotton for purchase of European arms and supplies, and he freely diminished his fortune in recruiting, training, and equipping splendidly his own little army, the Hampton Legion. Not just an ordinary regiment, the Legion had its own cavalry company and its own battery of artillery. No less than four of its officers would eventually wear the stars of Confederate generals.

The men developed a fierce attachment to Hampton. "He seemed to me a young man," wrote a private, "fully grown up, to be sure, but still young. His bearing was distinctly military, but without pompousness or egotism. His hair and beard were dark, and so were his eyes, which had a peculiar natural snappy motion that attracted attention."

Hampton trained his Legion a few miles outside Columbia, South Carolina, at "Camp Hampton." There on a spacious parade ground, surrounded by shady oaks and fed by a cool natural spring, the high tenor voice of Hampton put the men through their paces. In a spirit of equality not entirely customary among other such units raised from the well-born "chivalry" of the Palmetto State, officers and men ate at the same tables and of the same bread. Black slaves brought along by some of the men cooked the beef stew in great kettles. There was no cream for the coffee, but sugar in abundance, and a Columbia baker supplied the bread. Hampton paid for everything. At dress parade every evening, Hampton personally inspected and drilled the Legion, while scores of fine ladies and gentlemen from Columbia gathered to watch. It was altogether a grand way to go to war.[13]

From all over the South men were coming to Virginia. Throughout May and June and into July they would come. On their arrival they found a situation marked by little movement but almost constant change, and over-all a sense of confusion generated by a new government trying to organize itself, an officer corps, an army, a plan of defense, and means of offense, all at the same time. Considering the difficulties of the occasion, the success achieved is truly remarkable.

One of the first changes involved General Cocke. He became Colonel Cocke. The Virginia authorities decided that they had too many high-ranking officers in the state volunteer service. The result was the demotion by one grade of a number of generals who, like Cocke, now became colonels. At the same time, several officers in the Provisional Army of the Confederate States, the national army, were promoted a grade. It was a move toward centralization of military authority, and a sound one.

Meanwhile Cocke had not been standing still. Not long after he removed his headquarters to Culpeper Court House, he acted on orders from Lee to establish at Manassas Junction a force sufficient to defend it in case of attack. It was a move that should have been undertaken much earlier, for at Manassas lay the key to a successful defense of northern Virginia.

Virginia's railroads were her lifeline. Besides the Virginia & East Tennessee line running through the southwest part of the state, there was the Virginia Central, which met the East Tennessee line at Charlottesville and ran east across the Blue Ridge, through the Shenandoah, and terminated in the Alleghenies. Both were vital for bringing supplies—and troops—into the heartland of the state. For from Charlottesville, the Virginia Central ran northeast to Gordonsville and there met the southern terminus of the Orange & Alexandria, a line which ran northeast straight across the heart of northern Virginia to Alexandria. Any Federal movement from Washington would, by natural geography, move right along the line of the Orange & Alexandria. This alone made Manassas Junction an important point on the railroad, but it was that word "junction" which really determined the vital necessity of holding it. Here at Manassas, the Manassas Gap Railroad joined the Orange & Alexandria. Running due east from the junction, the Manassas Gap passed through the Bull Run Mountains at Thoroughfare Gap, crossed the Blue Ridge at Manassas Gap, bridged the south and north forks of the Shenandoah River, and came to a railhead at Strasburg, forty-five miles southwest of Harpers Ferry, right in the heart of the Shenandoah.

The strategic value of the Manassas Gap line escaped no one. It neatly connected the two major avenues by which Virginia might be invaded. Thus, should the Federals make an advance through Harpers Ferry via the Shenandoah, reinforcements might quickly be sent to Johnston from Cocke's command in the east. Conversely, if Cocke should be threatened by an advance from Washington, Johnston could get regiments to his aid almost overnight. Use of this rail line could almost double the available force of both commanders, unless, of course, both should be attacked at the same time. Never before in warfare had such an opportunity for rapid movement of troops presented itself. It was a novel approach to strategy that, once inaugurated here in northern Virginia, would become a basic tool of warfare.

Lee ordered Cocke to establish a defense force at Manassas on May 6, and Cocke acted immediately, sending a company of cavalry and a section—two guns—of artillery to join "two (raw, undrilled, ununiformed, and armed with the altered musket) Irish companies" already there. He ordered that all other companies then armed and organizing throughout his command proceed to Manassas as soon as possible. Lee sent the 11th and 28th Virginia —which Cocke had helped raise—to Manassas, and also dispatched several officers who were to take over the training of the as yet unorganized companies.

On May 9 Cocke went in person to inspect the possibilities for defense at Manassas. He concentrated his observations on the northern outskirts of the place toward Washington, and found the country "quite favorable for defensive operations," being heavily forested, with occasional cleared farms and fields, and narrow, winding roads—"mere ditches"—which would hamper any enemy cavalry or artillery maneuver. "The cover of forests, hills, and ravines make a fortress for brave men and riflemen in which to carry on the destructive guerrilla warfare upon any marching columns." Undoubtedly, in the back of his mind Cocke saw his command re-enacting the terrible destruction wrought upon the British column marching back to Boston by the militiamen of Lexington and Concord.

To wreak such havoc, Cocke had only 918 men of all arms at Manassas by May 14, but that number would grow steadily over the next several weeks. Cocke was disturbed by the weakness of his force, particularly since the Confederate Congress had formally acknowledged that a state of war existed between North and South. Now the Federals were sure to advance into Virginia, and Cocke was convinced they would do so via the Alexandria line. "The time appears to be at hand when we may expect the enemy to make some strong demonstration upon this line, a line so vitally important to our cause and a line at this moment unprepared to meet such odds, but which we desire to move heaven and earth to keep in a state of readiness for any emergency." Cocke, perhaps out of pique at being demoted, was venting rather openly his displeasure that Harpers Ferry was being reinforced into a force of several brigades, as were Norfolk and Richmond, while Manassas and, worse yet, Alexandria were left to their own devices entirely. He could not understand why the Orange & Alexandria and the Manassas Gap, as well as the junction, should be so ignored in the defensive build-up, "thus laying bare the very vitals of the State to a deadly attack or to a stunning blow." "*Verbum sap*," he told Lee's adjutant, implying that he should have to say no more to convey the foolhardiness of the situation. Why, he wanted to know, could not those regiments being sent from outside Virginia come to him?

Lee showed considerable patience with his rather self-important subordinate, explained that earlier threats at Norfolk and Harpers Ferry had seemed more imminent than along the Alexandria line, and now promised that Cocke's command would be strengthened with as much speed as possible. Indeed, Cocke's had been a thankless task, performed in spite of great obstacles, and yet he had molded the nucleus of a force to protect the line of the Orange & Alexandria almost without assistance. As a result, Lee was not only patient with Cocke, but receptive to his suggestions, and on May 15 the colonel proposed a bold plan of action for the coming campaign. He suggested massing troops in two places, Manassas and Winchester, near Strasburg, with the larger body in the latter place. At the same time, adequate transportation must be maintained on the Manassas Gap road at all times. These two small armies, he wrote, "being connected by a continuous railway through Manassas Gap . . . could readily cooperate and concentrate upon the one point or the other" to stop threats at either end. Thus Cocke became perhaps the first to put into words the strategy that would be used to meet the inevitable invasion whenever it came.[14]

Cocke would never get credit for his strategic conception. Indeed, at the moment his only reward would be to lose his command to another. With Cocke's demotion to colonel and the promotion of others in the Provisional Army to brigadier, there was no way to leave command of the Alexandria line in the Virginian's hands. The position must be assigned to one of the new generals. As it happened, at this time Brigadier General Milledge L. Bonham had arrived in Richmond with a small brigade consisting of the 1st and 2d South Carolina Infantries, the first of several units he was organizing in his home state. Bonham reached Richmond on May 11, and Lee immediately assigned his troops to the force being built up at Manassas. This effectively placed him over Cocke, and on May 21, Bonham formally received command.

Bonham was a handsome man, smooth, graying hair flowing gracefully about his head. He wore an immaculately kept mustache and chin beard and possessed, over-all, the look of one born to command. Not a graduate of West Point, he was, instead, a lawyer, a close friend and confidant of high-placed people in South Carolina, including Governor Pickens. He did possess some military experience, fighting in both the Seminole and Mexican Wars, but his forte was politics. The outbreak of secession found him sitting in Congress at Washington, but upon his resignation from that body Bonham accepted his friend Pickens' appointment as commander of South Carolina's army. On April 23, 1861, Bonham was appointed a brigadier in the Provisional Army.

Lee's instructions to Bonham were full and relatively comprehensive, perhaps because he had little confidence in the unschooled new general. He must avoid any injury to citizens or their property. He was to act strictly on the defensive, erect earthworks at Manassas particularly, and remain vigilant to all Federal approach. Special danger was apprehended from the direction of Alexandria, and as soon as Bonham's forces were sufficiently built up to warrant the move, Lee wanted him to reoccupy the city and defend it.

Bonham would do what he could toward erecting defenses at Manassas, but the situation at Alexandria was already out of his hands. Bonham reached Cocke's headquarters near Culpeper at midnight on May 23. The very next morning they received word that Sandford's Federals had crossed the Potomac and occupied Alexandria. Cocke telegraphed Bonham at Manassas with a description of all the available forces within the command, and that evening the general ordered all of the men with Cocke to move forward to the junction. Meanwhile, Colonel George H. Terrett, commanding the small group of defenders at Alexandria, fell back toward Manassas.

It was not an auspicious way for Bonham's incumbency to start, though no one blamed him. Pickens of South Carolina put that onus on Lee. "If Lee had been the man his reputation makes him, he never would have allowed them to cross the long bridge without a fight." The truth, thought Pickens, "is Lee is not with us at heart, or he is a common man, with good looks, and too cautious for practical Revolution."[15]

But blame was of little immediate importance. Manassas must be fortified before the Federals could move again. The same day that Alexandria fell, Lee sent the 1st Virginia to Bonham. The next day several engineer officers left Richmond to help Bonham with the construction of the defenses, and more arms and ammunition went the same way. At the same time Lee issued instructions that the Loudoun & Hampshire Railroad, running northwest along the Potomac from Alexandria to Leesburg, thirty-five miles distant, be destroyed as much as possible. This would prevent the enemy from steaming up that line to attack a small command at Leesburg guarding the center of the line between Manassas and Harpers Ferry.

By May 27, Bonham's command was estimated at 7,000, including a new cavalry battalion of four companies. Another estimate, two days later, placed it at 6,000. This was still hardly enough to meet the Federals now under McDowell, but almost every day more regiments would arrive.

In these last days of May it seemed that finally the Federals were launching their invasion. Grafton, in western Virginia, was occupied, Newport News in Hampton Roads was seized, Confederate batteries on Aquia Creek were attacked by gunboats, and on May 31 a scout left Alexandria to feel out Confederate positions around Fairfax Court House on the line to Manassas. Here, finally, there came a clash.

Lieutenant Charles Tompkins, commanding Company B of the 2d United States Cavalry, left his camp late on May 31 with a detachment of fifty men from his company under orders to reconnoiter the country leading up to Fairfax Court House. Bonham, anticipating some kind of movement toward Manassas, had so disposed his forces that it would be very difficult for enemy scouts to penetrate close enough to Manassas Junction to feel out his real force. He placed himself and the 1st South Carolina at Centreville, five miles in advance of the junction, put the 2d South Carolina in position at Mitchell's Ford on Bull Run, midway between Manassas Junction and Centreville, and sent an advance party to Fairfax. Thus any Federal reconnaissance would have to penetrate three enemy positions, each successively stronger than the one before it, to reach the vicinity of Manassas.

At Fairfax, Bonham had the Warrenton Rifles, a company soon to become part of the 17th Virginia', under Captain John Q. Marr, and two companies of cavalry from Rappahannock and Prince William Counties. In over-all command of the outpost was Lieutenant Colonel Richard Stoddert Ewell.

Lieutenant Tompkins approached Fairfax Court House about 3 A.M., June 1, and captured Ewell's advance picket post, though not before some Confederates got away to warn the colonel. When Tompkins rode into the small town, he thought he was fired upon by Confederates placed at the windows of a hotel and

some houses along the streets, and he and his men rode through
firing back. Ewell, in fact, posted no one in the town, and it was
probably civilians who fired on the Federal cavalry. Ewell had
pulled his company of infantry—the cavalry was badly armed and
took no part in the fight—back on the road leading from Fairfax
to Germantown, a mile or two to the north.

When Tompkins passed through Fairfax Court House, he
turned his command onto the road to Germantown, but soon retraced his route and on returning ran into Ewell with Captain
Marr's company posted squarely across the road. Tompkins
charged and was repulsed, re-formed, charged again, and was
driven back once more. Tompkins had two horses shot out from
under him, and suffered a badly contused foot when one of them
fell on him. One Federal was killed and three others captured.
Ewell lost in the skirmish five men captured, and suffered a minor
shoulder wound himself. Captain Marr was killed, shot through
the heart. Tompkins, thinking himself outnumbered by nearly a
thousand Confederates, withdrew and soon raced back for Alexandria with two lately arrived companies of armed rebel cavalry
on their heels. In fact, Ewell's combatants in the fight numbered
barely more than fifty, roughly equal to Tompkin's.

It was a fight of no great consequence. Tompkins was scolded
by McDowell for getting into a fight when not ordered to do so,
and Ewell won Bonham's compliments. It did preserve the country between Fairfax and Manassas for the Confederates, and
thanks to the small victory McDowell learned nothing of Bonham's numbers or dispositions. It would be over two weeks before
another Federal armed party tried to penetrate any distance into
northern Virginia. Perhaps Tompkins' overestimate of Ewell's
numbers played a part in this.

Regardless of the effects of the fight, it was the only shooting
that took place while Bonham was in command. Indeed, techni-
cally Bonham was not in command of the Alexandria line when
the fight occurred. The day before, May 31, Lee assigned a new
commander to replace Bonham, and the man was on his way to
Manassas even as the rifles fired. Much was expected of the new
general, for he was the hero of Fort Sumter, a Confederate Napoleon, Brigadier General Pierre Gustave Toutant Beauregard.[16]

"THREE YEARS OR THE WAR"

Poor McDowell, largely the victim of a situation not of his making, paid dearly for standing by his orders to take command of the troops in Virginia. Scott and Mansfield were never again co-operative, beyond those official expressions of anxiety to help and so forth with which military men can often cover their dealings. "I got everything with great difficulty," McDowell would complain. "General Mansfield felt hurt," the brigadier would say further, and he made McDowell pay for his pique.

Regiments were slow in coming across the river to take their assigned places with the Army of Northeastern Virginia. Scott or Mansfield had to approve each such assignment, and they took their time about it. When McDowell went personally to Mansfield to ask for more men, and more speedily, Mansfield just shook his head and replied, "I have no transportation." Without the necessary wagons to carry field equipment and supplies, a regiment could not move. McDowell went to Brigadier General Montgomery C. Meigs, quartermaster general of the Union Army. Yes, said Meigs, he had transportation, but he understood that Mansfield did not want any transportation assigned until McDowell's army was ready to advance into Virginia. Here was a neat conundrum. Meigs would not allow wagons until the regiments had crossed the river into Virginia, ready to advance. But Mansfield would not let troops go across to McDowell until they had transportation! Exasperated, McDowell told Meigs that "between you two I get nothing."[1]

Even if he was forced to be satisfied with driblets, still McDowell saw his army slowly grow and take shape. Besides the three brigades formed when he first took the command, he formed another on June 3 from the 8th and 25th New York, and the 1st Connecticut. Brigadier General Daniel Tyler took command. On June 12, Brigadier General Robert C. Schenck took over another new brigade formed of the 1st and 2d Ohio Infantries. Later in the month the 5th Massachusetts and the 4th Pennsylvania were brigaded under Colonel William B. Franklin, and the 1st Michigan and 11th New York were given to Colonel Orlando B. Willcox. And so it went, slowly and painstakingly. But despite all the obstacles, McDowell built his army. His own persistence accounted for much. Equally important, however, if not more so, were the unbounded ardor and enthusiasm of the young men of the North who enlisted in legions to put down the rebellion.[2]

They came from everywhere. Michigan raised four good regiments, the 1st, 2d, 3d, and 4th, formed of the hardiest of the state's youth. Some of the boys paid their own rail fares in order to reach the training camps, so anxious were they to enlist for "three years or the war." "If it is my destiny to fall on the Battlefield," wrote Private John Gregg, "I shall do it willingly and without a murmur."

These rowdy Michiganders would earn a reputation as being among the most ferocious fighters of the war, perhaps because of their rugged frontier background. One company of lumberjacks in the 3d Michigan had no one under six feet in height. When they traveled to their training camps, a company of the 2d Michigan from Battle Creek cleaned out every grocery store at their stops along the way. The word was telegraphed ahead that they "stole every thing movable at some of the first stations," and at the end of their trip the Battle Creek boys found all stores closed to them.[3]

Across the continent in New England, the situation seemed far more in hand. There the sons of Boston's Brahmins and Newport's nabobs had far more consciousness of their station, more a sense of responsibility not just to defend the Union but to show that soldiers could be upper-class gentlemen at the same time.

They were sure to settle all their accounts before going off to war, unlike some of the crude Westerners who found in enlistment an easy avenue to avoid creditors.

Men of the 1st Massachusetts were quartered in historic Faneuil Hall in Boston during their first days of service. Even here there arose aspects of soldier life which offended the fastidious tastes of some. Meat had to be eaten with the fingers at their first dinner, and their bread buttered with the handle of a spoon. Some, of course, did go into a local bar, but Charles Perkins and a friend "decided neither to take, touch or handle intoxicating liquors while on military campaigns."[4]

New York would send, in all, some eighteen regiments to Washington, and the men trained all over the state. Some were fortunate enough to be quartered in and around New York City, and for them an evening or weekend pass could mean fun and frolic. Even during regular duty hours, when the men were marched to the rivers to bathe, it was still a lark. "It is a splendid place to bathe," wrote a private of the 38th New York, made the more agreeable because oysters and clams could be gotten. These New Yorkers were a playful, cocky, lot, often a nuisance to their officers. What they did not like they ridiculed. When the 27th New York thought their supper ration of beef was "a little too fresh and lively," they put it all in a box, securely fastened, formed a procession, and to the tune of "The Rogues' March" solemnly proceeded to an orchard. Here, in an improvised cemetery, a stirring funeral oration was delivered and the beef was buried "with all the honors of war." Their commander called the eulogist before him and scolded him for the affair, declaring it a breach of authority. The poor private could only reply that "I never knew that beef had any particular rank," however rank the beef might have been.[5]

From Connecticut, from Maine, from Minnesota, Ohio, Pennsylvania, Rhode Island, Vermont, and Wisconsin they came. Their stories all sound much the same. Like the hundreds of thousands who would follow them in the years ahead, they were common soldiers through and through, the essence of that stereotype soon to be known as "Billy Yank."

Many of the young recruits from the Northern states got their first taste of things to come in Maryland. While several of the regiments traveled to Washington by rail through Pennsylvania, a number had to embark aboard steamers at New York, proceed thence to Philadelphia or Wilmington, Delaware, and then go by rail to the capital. That meant that they had to pass through Baltimore, and however much Federal occupation may have subdued the Southern sentiment in the city, it could not obliterate it. Experiences in passing through the city varied from silent indifference to open violence. No one could ever predict what would happen. When the 38th New York marched across the city, they were met with a stony silence. "I saw a good many secessionsists [sic]," wrote one boy, "I know I did, they looked so sour while we were passing them."

More serious proceedings met the 2d Wisconsin on its march through Baltimore. "A howling mob of rebels and their sympathizers crowded the streets, uttering the wildest imprecations on the men. . . . It was with difficulty that our men were restrained from the opening fire." The worst would come when the 2d Michigan marched their gantlet.

The men were told not to cheer as they walked, or to respond to anything said by civilians except to answer polite questions. "We have two miles to march," Private Haydon writes in his diary. "The streets are densely crowded on both sides. The children & ladies cheer in great numbers for us & the union & several wave flags. The men are much more careful what they do. Cheers for Jeff Davis are heard occasionally from groups of 3 or 4. With very few exceptions we march in perfect silence & in excellent order." Some of the men standing on the sidewalks tried to trip those who walked by.

Finally the regiment reached the Washington depot, and here there was some vocal Union demonstration. But just as the men boarded the cars, a man stepped from the crowd and threw a large stone and some bricks at one of the companies. The stone hit the sergeant of Company E, "a tiger of a fellow," around the knee and injured him painfully. In an instant the sergeant took a rifle and shot his assailant dead. "They say that he bored him through on the spot," wrote a private. Then it was on to Washington.[6]

Once in the national capital, most of the regiments had their first taste of being brigaded with other regiments, often with men of two or three different states making up a brigade. When this happened, it was often up to the brigade commander, rather than the men in the ranks, to establish whatever personality or character the brigade would have. Relying as he must on his brigade leaders to give a sense of pride, loyalty, and belonging to the regiments in each of the brigades of his growing army, McDowell met with mixed success in his first appointments.

Next to Benjamin Butler, David Hunter was perhaps the ugliest of the Union's leading generals, and in time he would surpass Butler as the one most hated in the South. He was fifty-eight years old, a West Pointer with no battlefield experience but with almost forty years of continuous service. He managed to ingratiate himself with Lincoln before the President's inauguration, and this in large part led to his being commissioned a brigadier general of volunteers on May 17, 1861. It made him the fourth-highest-ranking volunteer general in the service. He enjoyed neither competence as a field commander nor many of the finer points of humanity which someone in his powerful position should possess.

Daniel Tyler, on the other hand, was an admirable figure, and one who still had some notoriety as a military figure. He was sixty-two years old, an 1819 graduate of the Military Academy and, though he saw no combat service in his fifteen years in the Army, he did become one of the very foremost authorities on ordnance. Leaving the service in 1834, he went into private business and in the next twenty-six years climbed ever higher as a successful canal and railroad builder, iron manufacturer, and entrepreneur. At the outbreak of war he assumed the colonelcy of the 1st Connecticut Infantry and shortly thereafter accepted an appointment as brigadier general of Connecticut volunteers. His bearing was markedly distinguished, his carriage erect despite his age, and his eyes deep set and piercing. One might expect much from him.

Samuel Peter Heintzelman filled a niche right between Hunter and Tyler. Physically he was anything but impressive. Slightly paunchy, with a scraggly graying beard and thinning hair, he looked more like a bemused farmer than a daring commander. Yet there was grit in the man. Younger than the two others, Heintzelman was born in 1805, and graduated from West Point in 1826. For twenty years he served in the dull garrison duty of a peacetime army, but when the war with Mexico erupted he fought with distinction, showing particular bravery in the action at Huamantla. Later he was equally gallant in some of the more remote Indian campaigns in the Southwest, and at the beginning of 1861 he was a lieutenant colonel. With the commencement of the war he was promoted first to colonel, and then brigadier on May 17. There was no sure way of telling if he had the stuff of a good commander, but he had at least displayed more than adequately that he knew how to fight.

Robert C. Schenck, unlike the three others, had no military training at all. He was a genuine political general. First a lawyer and then a state legislator, he served four terms in Congress and then went to Brazil as minister for the State Department. He campaigned extensively for Lincoln's election in 1860, and was suitably rewarded on June 5, 1861, with an appointment as brigadier general of volunteers. It was more than just a reward, however, for Schenck's popularity in the populous state of Ohio would make him, as a general, a valuable recruiting tool. But it was a most unfortunate way to get recruits in this war, for many of those raised would die needlessly in the service of these inexperienced politicos.

The most distinguished of the early brigade commanders was William B. Franklin. He alone of all McDowell's lieutenants had graduated first in his class at West Point. He took part in several noted exploration and mapping expeditions, and served gallantly in the Mexican War, winning a promotion at Buena Vista. Thereafter he stayed in Washington, where, as a leading engineer, he oversaw the construction of the new dome above the Capitol and one or two other major Federal building projects. Along with several others, he was commissioned brigadier on May 17, 1861, and soon thereafter took command of his brigade.

The youngest of the first brigade commanders was Orlando Bolivar Willcox, one of those rough and ready Michiganders. He left West Point just in time to go to Mexico but too late to win any glory in the fighting. For the next nine years he saw only outpost and garrison duty and in 1857 resigned his commission to go into private law practice. Then came 1861, and with it he accepted the colonelcy of the 1st Michigan. On July 1 his own regiment and the late Ellsworth's 11th New York were brigaded under his command.

There were more colonels and brigadiers to come in the weeks ahead. McDowell's army was growing despite his handicaps, until soon Washington looked more like an armed camp than a city. The men themselves were incorrigible tourists. For most it was the first visit to the capital; for many it would be the last. They crowded every street. "Washington is a *splendid* place, I tell you," one Maine youth wrote home. "The city is alive with troops," wrote another. Despite the intense heat and humidity of a Washington summer, the men left no public building unvisited. "I have seen an abundance of interesting things to day but they are too numerous to describe," wrote one boy after a trip to the Capitol, the Patent Office, the Post Office, and the White House. Many soldiers walked right into the Executive Mansion. Private Perkins of Massachusetts stepped into the main reception room, walked into the Green Room, sat down and wrote a letter. Occasionally the soldiers saw the President as they wandered through his house. "Saw Abe Lincoln," wrote one diarist. "Good looking man," he decided.

The Smithsonian, too, proved a popular spot, but the Patent Office outranked the other Washington sites in popularity. The men were fascinated by the array of models of patented inventions. For many of the men seeing the city for the first time, a sense of pride in their Union and its institutions seemed to emerge. "I could not help taking a stroll through the capital and gazing with reverence upon the place where our beloved Washington first took the reign of american independence in his own hand and where our immortal Jackson ruled with honor this republic," one Michigander wrote home. "All these things were forced upon my mind and I felt more like shedding tears than anything els[e]—with a quivering lip again I vowed to myself that while I had one drop of blood it should be devoted to my country." The fact that Washington never ruled here seems to have escaped the boy.

A more immediate presence than the memory of Washington was the almost spectral visage of President Lincoln. Nearly every regiment that arrived in the city passed in review before the President and General Scott. Almost as regularly Scott pronounced each regiment in succession to be the best he had seen yet. It may not have done much for the general's credibility, but it did great things for the morale of the raw troops.

"You can go up into the dome of the capitol and see the tents of the federal army in every direction as far as you can see," a boy wrote home. In every camp the routine was the same. Arise at 4:30 A.M. to the beat of the drum. Roll call at 5, breakfast at 7, sick call and guard detail at 8. Two hours of drill at 10 o'clock was followed by lunch and then, in a much appreciated deviation from the first weeks of training, the rest of the day belonged to the soldiers until 6 P.M. After an hour of battalion drill came supper, and then more free time until 9:30, and lights out. It was a routine so comfortable amid the pleasant surroundings—barring the heat—that some found themselves almost lulled into forgetting that they had come for war, and that within a few miles of them an enemy army was also in training. Few on either side of the Potomac could entirely put from their minds the fear that inevitably these infant armies must meet and make war.[7]

Though the Federals in Washington were the most visible sign of Union mobilization, there was yet another army forming. When Patterson's department was broken up and his command redefined to include Pennsylvania and Delaware, the old general shifted his headquarters to Philadelphia and here commenced organizing and forwarding regiments to Mansfield in the capital and the Federal commander in Baltimore. But once the situation in those cities seemed secure, Scott ordered Patterson to turn his attention to Harpers Ferry. Any advance into Virginia—whether Scott like the idea of an invasion or not—would require a simultaneous movement by McDowell against the Alexandria line, and some sort of movement to pin down Johnston in the Shenandoah. Otherwise the Confederates in the valley would be free to proceed via the Manassas Gap Railroad to strike McDowell in the flank as he faced Bonham.

As a result, Patterson must start the accumulation of regiments in and around Frederick, Hagerstown, and Cumberland, Maryland, a suitable jumping off area for a movement into the Shenandoah. At once Patterson sent five regiments west to Chambersburg, Pennsylvania, and on June 2 he himself left to establish his new headquarters there. He had already settled on a plan of action. Upon his arrival he believed he would have six or seven regiments armed and ready, with another ten awaiting arms or en route to Chambersburg. With this force in hand, and once fully armed, he would advance beyond Hagerstown, set up a line of camps stretching from there the ten miles to the Potomac, threaten Harpers Ferry just twenty miles down the river, and then push a column on west to Cumberland.

When Scott learned that Patterson had his eye on Harpers Ferry, he wired the general to forget about Cumberland for the present, and concentrate instead upon driving Johnston out of the the arsenal town. It was then that Patterson, apparently for the first time, revealed to the general-in-chief his plans for the coming campaign. Cumberland and other such movements were largely feints. His principal object was to threaten Johnston out of his position, and if that did not work, then Patterson would send his troops around Harpers Ferry to cut off Johnston's line of retreat into the valley. "I wish to place such a force on the Virginia shore as can hold every inch of ground gained, and, however slowly, to advance securely, after Harper's Ferry falls, upon Winchester." Scott promised to have McDowell make a demonstration on the Alexandria line to cover Patterson's movement and keep Bonham from reinforcing Johnston. Scott also should have been on his guard about something in Patterson's telegram. In an age when all generals promised speedy movement, and delivered sloth instead, one who warned that he would advance "however slowly" was hardly deserving of great confidence. Yet Scott seemed to place more hope in this anticipated movement against Johnston than in McDowell's inevitable advance against the main Confederate army in and around Manassas.

Patterson started his campaign with a flurry of activity—all on paper. On reaching Chambersburg he immediately wrote Scott of his intentions for the beginning of the grand campaign, but already began to throw in words of caution. "The information I have received leads me to believe a desperate resistance will be offered at Harper's Ferry," he warned. Still, he promised to start on June 8. To the men gathering in and around Chambersburg, Patterson put up a bold front. "The restraint which has necessarily been imposed upon you, impatient to overcome those who have raised their parricidal hands against our country, is about to be removed. You will soon meet the insurgents."[8]

Just who would be meeting "the insurgents?" Within a few days Patterson's army would make up some five brigades, most of them stronger in numbers than McDowell's. His First Brigade

was led by an obscure colonel, George H. Thomas, whose loyalty
was not above suspicion. After distinguishing himself in battle in
the Mexican War, he went on to serve in the 2d United States
Cavalry, whose colonel and lieutenant colonel were, respectively,
Albert Sidney Johnston and Robert E. Lee, both now high-ranking Confederates. Indeed, Thomas was himself a Virginian, and
Governor Letcher had actually offered him a position as chief of
ordnance in the Virginia forces if he should resign his commission
and cast his lot with his native state. But Thomas remained loyal
to his oath and his Union.

Among the regiments in Thomas' brigade there was one whose
colonel never had his loyalty questioned. Ambrose E. Burnside
presented one of the most imposing military visages in the officer
corps of the Army. He simply had the look of a great soldier, his
leonine features accentuated by the contrast of a balding head
above, and great muttonchop whiskers curving into a mustache
below. The whiskers running from his hairline down in front of
his ears—though not unusual for his time—in his case appeared
so remarkable that the general style would come to be known as
"burnsides," a term whose anagram "sideburns" would enter the
language as a permanent fixture in the colonel's lifetime.

He was a West Pointer, class of 1847, who saw almost no action
in Mexico but later served in operations against the Apaches in the
Southwestern territories. He left the service in 1853 and went into
private enterprise, manufacturing a breech-loading rifle of his own
design which would see some service in this war. His personality
was smooth and easygoing. He ingratiated himself easily with people in power, and not surprisingly his adopted state of Rhode Island drew upon his military experience to make him major general of state militia just before the war. When secession became a
reality, he quickly raised and equipped the 1st Rhode Island Infantry, and it came as no surprise that he was awarded its
colonelcy. Here was a man to whom many would look for daring
and action.

There were a number of other officers, some good, some
indifferent, in Patterson's little army. The one with the most campaign and battle experience was Colonel Dixon S. Miles. He was
fifty-seven, unfortunately a heavy—or at least steady—drinker,
and had the dubious distinction of graduating from the Military

Academy very close to the bottom of his class. Yet he fought well in the Seminole campaign in Florida, won a brevet promotion in the war with Mexico, and served almost continuously thereafter in the Indian campaigns on the Western frontier. He rose to a full colonelcy, but no one really knew how competent he was to lead large numbers of troops in the field. A white haired, distinguished-looking man with a patriarchal white beard, he now commanded a brigade consisting in part of the only Regular Army infantry in Patterson's small army.[9]

Even while Patterson was organizing his brigades, Scott threw him the first delay. On June 4 the general-in-chief advised him not to advance until troops that would leave two days later should arrive. Even without them, Patterson's command numbered perhaps as many as 17,000 of all arms, a goodly force with which to advance on Johnston. Scott had confidence in Patterson's plan to force the Confederates out of Harpers Ferry, but he was absolutely unwilling to risk any engagement unless victory was assured. "There must be no reverse," he told his subordinate. "A check or a drawn battle would be a victory to the enemy, filling his heart with joy, his ranks with men, and his magazines with voluntary contributions." Patterson clearly received Scott's message. "Attempt nothing without a clear prospect of success," the old hero ordered, and Patterson, already of a hesitating, cautious nature, took the imperative to heart.[10]

He completed organizing his army by June 11, dividing his brigades into two divisions. On June 15, a week after he had originally promised to start offensive operations, Patterson's first brigades started their march toward the Potomac. It was a short-lived advance. Already made wary by Scott's injunction not to lose, now Patterson was also told that there might not be a diversion on the Alexandria line after all, but perhaps only a small expedition toward Leesburg. Now, like McDowell, Patterson also discovered that his transportation was inadequate. He would need more. Then, when Scott wired him that he hoped the army would cross the Potomac on June 17 or 18, Patterson suddenly felt threatened. All he had said he wanted to do was take Hagerstown and perhaps threaten Maryland Heights, overlooking the Potomac. Conveniently Patterson forgot the original plan which he outlined to Scott on June 1, just two weeks before. He had clearly stated

that he wanted to cross the Potomac at Williamsport and outflank
Harpers Ferry, cutting off Johnston's communications. The day
before his march commenced, Patterson outlined to one of his
officers the necessity that "when our forces cross the river" they
must not withdraw. Yet now Patterson feigned surprise at Scott's
expectation that he would cross on the seventeenth or the next
day. "I had said nothing about crossing the river," he would protest. "But knowing and appreciating the great experience, skill,
and sagacity of my commander, I promptly adopted measures to
carry it out." In other words, if anything went wrong after the
crossing, he, Patterson, had only been obeying orders. The responsibility lay with Scott.[11]

In fact, Patterson should have been glowingly confident. Repeatedly reports were coming into him from reliable sources which indicated that Johnston was either abandoning Harpers Ferry or else
had already done so. His engineer, Captain John Newton, reported on June 15 that "Harper's Ferry is abandoned and destroyed." Patterson thought it "designed for a decoy." His men
could see smoke rising into the horizon off in the distance where
Harpers Ferry stood, but still Patterson would not believe. Newton
must go to reconnoiter yet again, to make absolutely sure that the
Confederates had left. Just in case they had, Patterson, from the
safety of his headquarters in a young girls' seminary in Hagerstown, ordered that a part of one of his divisions cross the Potomac and, with great caution, occupy the place.

After crossing the river above Williamsport, Patterson's columns discovered that Johnston had evacuated those troops at
Martinsburg, and further, all along the road toward Harpers Ferry
there were signs of a hasty withdrawal. Finally the troops marched
into the town itself. "Harper's Ferry has been retaken without
firing a gun," Patterson would boast to Scott that night. But still
he would complain that no demonstration had been made by
McDowell, a demonstration to aid an unopposed walk into an
abandoned town.

Now Patterson decided to make his headquarters in the captured stronghold. From it he would slowly—he emphasized once
again how slowly he proposed to move—spread out toward
Winchester and Strasburg. "We will thus force the enemy to re-

tire, and recover, without a struggle, a conquered country." Just what made him think the Confederates would not put up a "struggle" is a mystery, but it was a nice way to win a war, if it worked.

Once again he trotted out the old transportation problems. Then Scott handed Patterson a perfect excuse for sloth. Upon hearing that Harpers Ferry was taken, he asked if the general expected to pursue the withdrawing Confederates. Scott recommended no pursuit for the time being, and ordered that, instead, the regular Army infantry and cavalry with Patterson, along with Burnside's 1st Rhode Island, be sent at once to Washington. The Confederates were starting to build up on the Alexandria line, and he felt that McDowell needed the experience—not to mention the moral effect of having professional troops at hand—of these units to bolster the untried volunteers in McDowell's army. Besides, with Johnston's retreat, the obvious emphasis for an imminent confrontation had shifted back east of the Blue Ridge.

Patterson protested repeatedly. If the Regulars were taken away, he would have no artillery whatsoever. He believed that Johnston, on the other hand, had some twenty cannon or more. With them, the Confederate could shell him from the commanding Loudoun Heights across the Shenandoah River from the ferry, and force the Federals out at will. Furthermore, he was certain that Johnston's army numbered at least 15,000, while his own would be reduced to less than 10,000. In fact, Patterson had his numbers a little reversed. Johnston actually numbered slightly less than 10,000, while the Federal's command at this time, even after detachment of the Regulars, would be 14,000 or more. True, Patterson did have no other artillery, and this was enough to dissuade him from any further pursuit of his rather unaudacious plans. He sent off the Regulars as ordered, but then immediately warned his brigade and division commanders to be ready to evacuate to the north side of the Potomac if danger arose. Sure enough, word was received on June 17 that Johnston, with an army which Patterson in one breath numbered at 12,000, and in another 15,000, was advancing to attack Williamsport and thereby cut off his line of retreat to Hagerstown. Then, too, transportation was still a problem for the general. He saw no option but to withdraw back across the Potomac. By June 18 the movement was completed, and before long the revelation would be forthcoming that the anticipated attack by Johnston was a false alarm. And so ended the first great invasion of Virginia, the movement that promised to retake Virginia "without a struggle."[12]

CHAPTER 4

THE YOUNG NAPOLEON

While Patterson's exploits in the western part of Virginia may not have been exactly Homeric, along the Alexandria line the first genuine hero of the war came to take charge. Pierre G. T. Beauregard had captured the heart and imagination of the South.

He looked splendid. Though not tall, he had a good physique, an erect, military carriage, and all the strut of a confident soldier. His facial features were well formed, his nose sharp, eyes bright, jaw square and lightly ornamented with a wisp of a beard. He wore an immaculate mustache, and kept his hair medium length, the sides brushed slightly forward in the style of the day.

He could boast as fine a record as most officers of the old Army. Born in 1818, a Creole from an important family in St. Bernard Parish, Louisiana, he grew as one accustomed to the privileges of money, and one used to the exercise of authority in a planter aristocracy. The military always seemed a natural vocation for such highborn sons of the South, and young Beauregard proved no exception. He finished at West Point in the class of 1838, graduating second out of forty-five cadets. Finishing twenty-third in the same class was young Irvin McDowell.

His first service, in the prestigious topographical engineers, took him to Rhode Island, then to Pensacola, Florida, and finally he spent five years working in and around his native Louisiana. When war with Mexico erupted, Beauregard's first months were spent in heartbreaking inactivity on obscure posts while the war and all chance for glory passed him by. Then he secured a position as an engineer officer on Scott's staff—there were rumors that while a cadet young Beauregard and Scott's daughter pursued a deep but unrequited romance. In this staff assignment he served with others of Scott's military family such as Captain Robert E. Lee and George B. McClellan. In two ensuing battles at Contreras and Churubusco the young engineer performed well and won a brevet promotion to captain. In the taking of Chapultepec, Beauregard forsook his staff duties for a time and picked up a rifle to fight with a regiment of skirmishers commanded by Colonel Joseph E. Johnston. When Mexico City fell, he was slightly wounded no less than three times in the same day, and was the officer who actually met the Mexican flag of surrender. He ended the war with the brevet rank of major and a bright career ahead of him.

The next thirteen years were dull ones for the headstrong officer. He ran surveys on the Mississippi, supervised construction of a New Orleans customhouse, unsuccessfully sought the mayorship of New Orleans, and in November 1860 received orders to assume the superintendency of the U. S. Military Academy. On January 23, 1861, he took over his new post. The next day, knowing Beauregard's secessionist sympathies, the War Department ordered him to vacate the office. After an incumbency of five days, he relinquished his post, and shortly afterward he resigned his commission. In a typically theatrical gesture, he enlisted in a Louisiana militia unit as a private. All the while he was using his influence to win an appointment as a brigadier general in the Confederate service. On March 1 he won it.

Everyone entertained great hopes for the new general, while he himself never doubted his pre-eminent capabilities. Assigned to Charleston and working closely with Governor Pickens, he speedily saw to the build-up of the batteries that ringed Sumter. Considering the situation of Major Anderson's small, undersupplied garrison in the fort out in the harbor, it seems certain that any commander could have eventually forced a surrender. But Beauregard would get lavish credit just the same, and on May 28, 1861, President Davis ordered him to come to the new capital of the Confederacy for a new and as yet unannounced assignment. It would be the first of many meetings for the two over the next

four years, and one of the few which saw them both leave on ami-
cable terms. Davis was cold, distant, terribly convinced of his own
military omniscience. So was Beauregard, with a good portion of
conceit and hauteur thrown in. Not everyone welcomed the new
Napoleon as a coming savior. Many decided to wait and see what
his trip to Virginia would bring, while others had mixed feelings
about what would happen wherever the general went. One of
those was Pickens himself, who had worked closely with Beauregard in the operations at Charleston. Beauregard was "a true pa-
triot," Pickens would write to his good friend Bonham, but then he
confided that he thought the general "too cautious, and his very
science makes him hesitate to make a dash. His knowledge of Batteries and cannon and engineering is great, but he relies nothing
upon the spirit and the energy of troops, and has not experience
in the management of Infantry. His Reputation is so high that he
fears to risk it, and yet he wants the confidence of perfect genius."
Obviously, even with some of those who knew him well, Beauregard had much to do to prove his worth.[1]

The general reached Richmond on May 30, and the following
day met with Davis and Lee. They discussed the military situation
in Virginia, and Lee expressed his conviction that when McDowell began his inevitable move south he would march for Manassas
Junction. Here, then, is where they wanted Beauregard. On that
same day, May 31, Lee formally appointed the Creole to supersede
Bonham in command of the Alexandria line. The next day he arrived at Camp Pickens, near Bull Run, and took charge.

At once Beauregard began an examination of the defenses built
thus far, and of the surrounding countryside. This was the engineer in him, and he knew his business. The ground around Camp
Pickens was too open, offering too few advantages for defense.
The best place to stop a Federal advance was along Bull Run itself. At its several fords there were abundant natural defensive positions which, suitably strengthened and manned, offered a bright
prospect for success. However, it would take twice the 6,000
troops he had at hand. Thus, he must either be reinforced or else
withdraw. He did offer a third option. He could take his small
army, such as it was, and advance to meet McDowell and "sell
our lives as dearly as practicable." Already he was using his flair
for the melodramatic on his superiors. There would be more.

With relatively little show, the new general began to get acquainted with his command. Still wearing an old United States Army uniform coat, he rode here and there throughout the command, eying places for batteries, looking to positions for earthworks, testing the morale and condition of his troops. Indeed, he moved so unobtrusively in the first few days in command that his presence was regarded as only a rumor by many. "Then the troops began to take notice of a quiet-looking individual in an old blue uniform coat of the United States Army, almost undecorated, who . . . moved about quite unattended." Often they saw him, standing motionless on the plains about Manassas, looking off toward Bull Run and its fords, perhaps already imagining the glorious fight soon to come.[2]

He issued an exhortative address to the troops, calling on their bravery to save their country from the tyrant's heel, and to the citizenry of the Manassas area declared that "Abraham Lincoln, regardless of all moral, legal, and constitutional restraints, has thrown his abolition hosts among you, who are murdering and imprisoning your citizens, confiscating and destroying your property, and committing other acts of violence and outrage too shocking and revolting to humanity to be enumerated." He called on them to do all in their power to assist his army, and in particular asked their vigilance. Any and every movement of the enemy must be reported to him as soon as possible.

While he eloquently pleaded for the help of the citizens of the Confederacy, Beauregard was already getting all the assistance he could ask for from a select group of Union citizens. Captain Thomas Jordan, lately a quartermaster in the federal army, and now commanding some engineers on the Alexandria line, resigned his United States commission on May 21. Before doing so, however, he organized a crude spy network in the Federal capital with the view of obtaining important information on Scott's plans and relaying it to Confederate authorities. Jordan approached Mrs. Rose O'Neale Greenhow, an ardent secessionist and yet one much loved in the city. She had access through her friendships with most of the leading political and military figures to a great deal of information. Could she not send this to Virginia? Jordan gave her a crude code to encipher her messages, and they probably agreed upon a method of getting the dispatches across the lines. Besides

Mrs. Greenhow, Jordan arranged for others in the capital to keep their ears open to any news, and even managed to get the Washington and other leading Northern newspapers sent south. The information thus derived would prove valuable indeed. Attitudes toward security were terribly lax on both sides. Whereas the private soldiers often demurred from including military particulars in their letters home for fear of revealing something, the generals and politicos seemed incapable of holding their tongues at parties or before newsmen. Very valuable information was thus broadcast, to the point that both McDowell and Beauregard would have to warn their commanders formally against loose talk.[3]

It would be early July before really important information came from his spies in Washington, and meanwhile Beauregard had an army to build. Bonham, and Cocke before him, tried with some measure of success to accumulate a sufficient force at Manassas to defend the place. Beauregard enjoyed much more success, not because he tried harder or was more adept, but mainly because the Confederacy was maturing fast, and the regiments that had started to organize in April and May were ready for assignment by mid and late June. Though he would constantly complain of the need for more troops, Beauregard received a steady reinforcement throughout his first month of command.

What he did not receive was adequate supply. Colonel Lucius B. Northrop, newly appointed commissary general of the Army, would prove a headache to virtually every Confederate who commanded an army. He proved no less to Beauregard. When the Creole asked permission to purchase foodstuffs for his army locally in the Manassas area, Northrop declined and instead directed that supplies would have to come by way of Richmond. And their shipment to the army in the field was woefully inefficient. At every turn, he complained, Beauregard encountered obstacle, delay, and incompetence. He could not even get rope for well buckets, because bureaucratic procedure decreed that all rope belonged to the Navy. "If they would only send us less law and more rope," he complained. "To hang ourselves with, General?" asked one of his staff playfully. "It would be better than strangulation with red tape," replied the disgusted commander. The situation with the tools of war was not much better. Arms most of the men had or were soon issued. Ammunition proved another matter. A dis-

mayed clerk in the Confederate War Department moaned on June
18 that "We dare not make known the condition of the army."
There was not enough ammunition at Manassas to fight a battle.
"There are not percussion caps enough in our army for a serious
skirmish. It will be obviated in a few weeks; and until then I pray
there may be no battle. But if the enemy advance, our brave men
will give them the cold steel. We *must* win the first battle at all
hazards, and at any cost; and, after that,—how long after?—we
must win the last!"[4]

Somehow Beauregard kept the men fed, and clothed, and
armed. And as the regiments came into camp, his mood slowly
turned to optimism. By June 20 he felt he could finally organize
the Army of the Potomac into something more efficient than a
cluster of various regiments. He designated six brigades, among
which he divided the regiments. The South Carolina units, four
of them, he placed under their old leader Bonham. His Second
Brigade would be led by the newly commissioned Brigadier General
Richard S. Ewell, leading the 5th and 6th Alabama and the
6th Louisiana. Brigadier General David R. Jones of South Carolina
received command of the Third Brigade with the 17th and
18th Mississippi and the 5th South Carolina. Colonel George H.
Terrett headed the next brigade with its three Virginia regiments,
the 1st, 11th, and 17th, and Cocke retained command of his brigade
of three regiments, the 18th, 19th, and 28th Virginia, now
designated the Fifth Brigade. The Sixth Brigade went to Colonel
Jubal A. Early with the 7th and 24th Virginia and the 4th South
Carolina. It was a substantial army, nearly 15,000, more men than
even old General Scott had ever led in combat. To Johnston,
Beauregard would confide on June 22 that he now felt he could
actually attack McDowell if he wanted.[5]

As the regiments themselves came together in and around
Manassas, they too began to acquire the confidence of numbers,
training, and most of all leadership. They began to feel like an
army, and they began to feel like winning.

The matter of getting out to the Manassas camps presented no
small problem at times. When Colonel Joseph B. Kershaw's 2d
South Carolina took the train from Richmond, two Orange &
Alexandria trains collided, killing at least one soldier.
Significantly, the engineers of both trains disappeared at once,

leading to speculation that the collision was no accident. "The people about here are nearly all abolitionist," wrote one South Carolinian, and some suspected that either the engineers or those manning switches intentionally disrupted rail traffic. There would be more before this campaign was ended.[6]

Bonham's brigade, posted chiefly in advance of Bull Run, with regiments thrown as far forward as Falls Church, within a few miles of Washington and Alexandria, had been here longer than most units. Indeed, in early July the enlistments of the 1st South Carolina expired, and they marched off to return to their native state. For those regiments that remained, life was becoming routine, though daily the expectation of battle kept the men alert. When, late in June, most of the brigade advanced to Fairfax Court House, there was much speculation that an attack on Federals near Falls Church was in the offing. Faced with this, many of the South Carolinians were concerned lest Beauregard personally take command of them and lead the attack. "We would much prefer our own general to command," wrote one of Bonham's staff. He had done most of the work of organizing them and selecting their positions, and many would hate to see the credit for a victory go to Beauregard. Bonham was in fact fortunate to command such loyalty among his staff, for his excitable, sometimes dictatorial manner, and a generally offensive abruptness whenever something went wrong, hurt the feelings of many. Lieutenant Colonel A. P. Aldrich of Bonham's staff would confide to his wife that for the general's disagreeable behavior there was "no excuse, for a man capable to command others, should be able to command himself."

But the men in the ranks seldom if ever encountered Bonham's harshness. Indeed, were it not for the frequent marches to one point and another to shield the main force back at Manassas, Bonham's brigade would have enjoyed an almost tranquil summer. The artillerists of the Richmond Howitzers, unofficially attached to the brigade, lounged under the shade of their tents, lying on straw beds to read newspapers or novels, or letters from home. Cards were everywhere in evidence; euchre, seven-up, and poker were the favorite games. Some of the men actually brought Saratoga trunks to camp with them filled with fresh paper collars, white shirts and trousers, and even cuffs. Everyone seemed more than confident of success. "These Federalists," wrote one South

Carolinian, "are the poorest fighters I ever knew." Meanwhile, the chief concern of Colonel Kershaw of the 2d South Carolina seemed to be persuading Beauregard to change the name of the stream Bull Run. It was, he said, so "unrefined" a name for a place soon to be made immortal. Beauregard suggested that they might try to make it as gracious a name as South Carolina's Revolutionary War battlefield at Cowpens. Kershaw never asked again.[7]

If Bonham was confident of success, he being the ranking brigadier among the brigade commanders, the newest brigadier was anything but assured. Ewell was taken quite by surprise at his elevation. "I wonder if you were as much astonished as I was at my promotion," he asked Bonham. "I assure you it is a matter that gives me no rejoicing as the responsibility is painful." Having served until now under the South Carolinian's direction, Ewell would have been content to leave it at that. And he would just as much have preferred that Bonham still had over-all command of the Alexandria line.

Ewell was a unique personality. "He was a compound of anomalies," wrote an officer of his brigade, "the oddest, most eccentric genius in the Confederate army." Tender as a woman generally, he would become "rough as a polar bear" when provoked. At such times his verbal orders became incomprehensible. "His eyes would flash with a peculiar brilliancy, and his brain far outran his tongue. His thoughts would leap across great gaps which his words never touched." Speaking in a verbal shorthand, he expected those around him to understand intuitively what he was saying. Woe be to him who asked the general to repeat himself. An 1840 graduate of the Military Academy, the forty-four-year-old Ewell did good service in Mexico, winning a brevet and staying in the old Army right until secession. He was slender, bald, with an unbroken wreath of hair that encircled the back and sides of his head, ran down the sides of the face, and out his chin to end in a fluffy tuft of beard.

During most of June, Ewell was quite ill and as a result became worn, emaciated, and somewhat less than confident. But if illness had sapped some of his faith in himself and the forthcoming campaign, the ardor of his men was only increased as June moved toward July. "I think we can repel a force of ten thousand, with the aid of our intrenchments," wrote a man of the 6th Alabama, "and if we should retire to Manassas, all the 'Hessian Army' might assault us in vain." Indeed, some were impatient to learn "when the *fun* will come off." Almost all were caught up in the spirit of the times. "I am absent in a glorious cause," wrote one, "and glory in being in that cause." And if Ewell preferred that Bonham should command the army, his men found that "Every day convinces us more and more that Beauregard is *the General* of the age."[8]

David Jones was just as new a brigadier as Ewell, their appointments dating from the same day, but he was even less well known. A handsome, agreeable man, he was generally known as "Neighbor" Jones. Few knew if "keeping up" with this Jones would present a problem. By marriage he bore a distant relationship to President Davis. Like so many other officers, his gallantry in Mexico won him a brevet, and he performed well on Beauregard's staff in the siege of Sumter. He was a native South Carolinian, six feet tall, blue-eyed, with a tawny brown beard that reached nearly to his sword belt. He made his headquarters close to Bull Run in the farmhouse of Wilmer McLean in a bivouac dubbed Camp Walker. His command suffered particularly from the measles that raged through all the Confederate regiments, but still he drilled the men hard and steady. Yet not so hard that the boys of the 18th Mississippi could not play with and train their mascot, a pet rooster named Kilby. Here and there in the camp men were heard calling his name to see him come running. On occasion the officers were treated to the sight of Kilby, parrot-like, perched on a shoulder. Two years from now in this war, the agreeable Kilby would more likely have done service as a meal rather than a pet.[9]

Terrett would command the Fourth Brigade for less than two weeks. On July 2 came a new man, one who would make his mark in this war. James Longstreet was a South Carolinian, yet he waited until May 9, 1861, to resign his commission as a major in the United States Army. Once he did resign, however, he immediately set his personal affairs in order, then journeyed to Richmond to seek a place in the paymaster's department of the rebel army. He had no idea of taking a field command when, on June 29, he was told that he had been made a brigadier and was being given command of a brigade. "I had given up all aspirations of military honor, and thought to settle down into more peaceful pursuits," he would write. Longstreet was just forty, tall, hearty, a commanding presence behind an imposing dark beard. His battlefield talents were well proven in Mexico and against the Indians.

On July 6 he marched his regiments out into the field and put them through their first brigade drill. Thereafter the drill was steady. Regiments who had come to war armed with sweet cakes and pincushions soon saw their illusions of romantic camp life dissolve under Longstreet's grueling regimen. But with pride they would claim that before long "the whole line moved like a machine." Beauregard himself often watched their exercises. He and others also noticed Longstreet, "a most striking figure, about forty years of age, a soldier every inch, and very handsome, tall and well proportioned, strong and active, a superb horseman and with an unsurpassed soldierly bearing, his features and expression fairly matched." The men in the ranks were hardly so admiring at first, however. "It was the daily round of the galley slave," wrote one private. Amid the summer sickness and measles that almost daily sent young men to their inglorious deaths, along with the bad water so stagnant that many in the brigade could not drink it, there was the infernal heat. When they could, the men scurried for the shade of trees that rimmed their parade ground. The rest of the time they drilled. Eight hours a day. "Woe to weak legs," moaned a Virginian.[10]

Another Virginian, Cocke, was a well-known quantity by this time. There was little mystery about his Fifth Brigade and its camp routine. But the other Virginian leading a brigade, the Sixth, was a total stranger to most of the Army, though his reputation in the state was somewhat notorious. Even if Ewell was the greatest eccentric in the service, Colonel Jubal Anderson Early ran a close second. This war would not produce a more engaging or exasperating character.

He looked much older than he was. Enduring an almost life-long bout with rheumatism, he walked with the stooped shoulders of an old man. His prematurely graying hair and beard added to the picture, and his high-pitched, almost whining voice, with its country twang and slight lisp, completed the image. And it was an image which his personality fully justified. No more cranky, irritable, sarcastic man would command in either army in this war. And as events would show, not many were more talented leaders.

Born in 1816 in Franklin County, Virginia, Early had fond at-

1. "In Memory of the Patriots Who Fell at Bull Run." The dedication of the Bull Run monument on Henry Hill, June 10, 1865. The four officers to the right of the man in the top hat on the left side of the photo are Generals George Thomas, Orlando Willcox, Samuel Heintzelman, and Alexander Dyer. *Courtesy of the National Archives*

2. (LEFT) Lieutenant General Winfield Scott, general-in-chief of the Union Army. *Courtesy of the Kean Archives, Philadelphia* 3. (RIGHT) Brigadier General Irvin McDowell (shown as a major general), who led the Union troops to Manassas. *Courtesy of the National Archives*

4. (LEFT) Brigadier General David Hunter, Second Division commander, went into battle on his birthday. *Courtesy of the National Archives* 5. (RIGHT) Brigadier General Samuel P. Heintzelman, befuddled-looking Third Division leader. *Courtesy of the Kean Archives, Philadelphia*

6. (LEFT) Colonel Dixon S. Miles fought the bottle more than the enemy. *Courtesy of the National Archives* 7. (RIGHT) Brigadier General Daniel Tyler, McDowell's most troublesome division commander. *Courtesy of the Library of Congress*

8. (LEFT) Colonel Israel B. Richardson led the Union army's largest brigade, much of it demoralized at Blackburn's Ford. *Courtesy of the Library of Congress* 9. (ABOVE) Colonel William T. Sherman (shown as a major general) felt even before Bull Run that it would be a long war. *Courtesy of the Library of Congress*

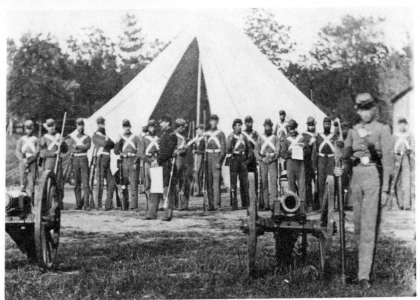

10. Men of the 7th New York State Militia in camp, May 1861, part of the early volunteers who formed the patchwork army gathered at Washington. *Courtesy of the Library of Congress*

11. (LEFT) Brigadier General Robert C. Schenk, who fought the first small action at Vienna on June 17. *Courtesy of the Library of Congress*
12. (RIGHT) Colonel Oliver O. Howard (shown as a major general), plucky leader of Heintzelman's Second Brigade. *Courtesy of the Library of Congress*

13. (LEFT) Captain Charles Griffin, who later became a major general, commanded one of McDowell's ill-fated batteries on Henry Hill. *Courtesy of the National Archives* 14. (RIGHT) Captain James B. Ricketts led the other decimated battery, was wounded, and spent months in a Southern prison. *Courtesy of the Library of Congress*

tachment for his mother. When she died seven years after his birth, however, he took the loss so hard that he never again formed an affectionate association with any woman. To give the boy a change from the Virginia hills, his father got him an appointment to West Point in 1833. "I was not a very exemplary soldier," Early wrote of his Academy years. He tried to leave in 1836 to join the revolution going on in Texas, but his father would not allow it, and Early finished his studies in 1837, graduating eighteenth in his class.

Immediately thereafter Early and many of his classmates went off to Florida to fight the Seminoles. The excitement of military life did not last long. In 1838, Early resigned his commission and returned home to become a lawyer. He dabbled in politics, served without seeing action in the Mexican War, and was an ardent opponent of secession in 1860–61. He served as a member of Virginia's convention which decided the issue, and bravely voted against leaving the Union. But once secession was passed, he saw it as his duty to throw his fortunes with the state "and to defend her soil against invasion." Shortly afterward Governor Letcher commissioned him a colonel in the state forces and sent him to Lynchburg to raise the 24th Virginia.

For the sake of organizational manageability, Beauregard would have done well to break down his command further into divisions of three brigades each. But he did not; the inherent weakness is obvious. With two divisions, the likelihood of orders from Beauregard to either of the division commanders being lost was slim. As it was now, he must get a copy of each order sent to six different brigade commanders. Chances of one or more copies miscarrying were considerable. And in battle, should a brigade not be where Beauregard needed it, the game might be lost.

If his organization could have been better, his energies in erecting his army's defenses could not. As Pickens had said to Bonham, Beauregard was an excellent engineer. He put virtually every man to work, first around Manassas, and then along the approaches to the junction. Bonham he placed at Fairfax Court House, his most advanced position and the focal point at which three main roads from Washington and Alexandria came together. When McDowell advanced, he would have to come through here. Here the first obstructions must be built. Large parties of the South

Carolinians went out armed with axes in order to fell trees across
the roads for distances of at least one hundred yards. "For miles
out, in all directions, wherever the road led through wooded
lands, large trees, chestnut, hickory, oak, and pine, were cut pell
mell, creating a perfect abattis across the road." They fully expected that it would take the Federals days to clear away the obstructions for men and guns to move forward. No defensive works
were erected here at Fairfax. Beauregard wanted only to delay the
enemy there, not fight him. To cover yet another route of advance
from Alexandria, Ewell's brigade was placed at Fairfax Station,
some five miles south of the courthouse.

At Centreville, the next place where the main roads through
Fairfax Court House and Fairfax Junction converged, the Creole
assigned Cocke and his regiments. For them it was a great relief.
Cocke's Virginians had found the camp around Manassas Junction
to be uncomfortable, disease-ridden, overcrowded. At Centreville
they had cool clear water and a friendlier civil population who
showered them with milk and eggs and butter. Here, again,
Beauregard did not intend to make a stand, and instead the men
felled more trees, picketed all roads leading toward Washington,
and practiced their vigilance, even when it meant arresting their
own colonels if they did not give a proper countersign.

While these three brigades were out in advance of Bull Run,
Beauregard kept the other three behind it. Jones's brigade he stationed at Camp Walker, along the Orange & Alexandria, between
Manassas Junction and Bull Run. Here, too, the Confederates
found a happy camping place, though they could always hear the
sounds of enemy cannon practicing along the Potomac. Yet it did
not worry them. "I am more & more convinced every day that the
contest which is to deliver us from that political pandemonium,
black republican rule and oppression, will be a brief one," wrote
one of Jones's Mississippians. Colonel Micah Jenkins, commanding the 5th South Carolina, felt much the same. "I feel confidant
in our cause and trust in God, and when the moment of battle
comes, the country shall not be ashamed of us."

Early was placed in several positions northeast and northwest of
Manassas Junction, covering the several crossings of Bull Run
available to an army marching by way of Centreville. Acting as
sort of a mobile reconnaissance force along the entire Bull Run

front, Early was ordered as far east as the crossings of the
Occoquan River, into which Bull Run emptied. He rode along his
line on an old plug, with an older saddle and still older saddle-
bags. Inside one of the bags was what an observer called "the inevitable canteen," filled with whiskey. Lieutenant Charles W.
Squires of the recently arrived Washington Artillery first met
Early as the colonel was riding down the road. His graying hair,
scraggly beard, stooped shoulders, and general demeanor were
unimpressive. "He was dressed as a farmer in ordinary circumstances," recalled Squires.

"Are you M-Mister S-S-Squires?" stuttered Early.

"Yes."

"Well I am C-Col. Er-Er-Early." And with that he rode on.

Beauregard was mistaken in not erecting earthworks at the several fords across Bull Run. Here, already under the disadvantage
of crossing a stream under fire, the Federals would be extremely
hard put to have to advance against fortifications as well. But instead, Beauregard concentrated his building in and around
Manassas, and the bulk of the work fell to Longstreet's brigade.
His Virginians were urban folk, "more familiar with the amenities
of city life than with the axe, pick, spade, or shovel," wrote Longstreet. Beauregard first had them spend two days felling trees at
Blackburn's Ford on Bull Run, but then decided that this was not
the best position and pulled him back. When some of the men
objected to the strenuous work, and that they, as gentlemen, had
not enlisted to work like Negroes, Beauregard got Negroes. He
persuaded local planters to lend him their slaves for much of the
work.[11]

While the work went on unrelentingly, Beauregard continued to
roam the ground, riding from ford to ford. His aide, Colonel
James Chesnut, would write to his wife that "I have been in the
saddle for two days, all day, with the General; to become familiar
with the topography of the country, the posts he intends to assume, and the communications between them." There was much
to study, much to learn. If he were to meet the enemy here and
defeat him, Beauregard must know every detail of this future bat-
tleground. Its peculiarities made it unique, and if he did not know
and master them all, it could mean disaster.[12]

Bull Run flowed from northwest to southeast on its crooked

route to the Occoquan. The country it divided was alternately rolling hill and gentle plain, but along almost all of the run itself the banks were steep and the waters too deep for wading. Thus it was only crossable at a number of fords and one bridge. Four miles above the mouth of Bull Run at the Occoquan, the road from Fairfax Station and Sangster's Station came down to Union Mills Ford. This was the far right of the line Beauregard had to protect. It was also the longest route to Manassas for a Federal column from Washington, but it still had to be protected.

The next crossing was another mile and a half above Union Mills, McLean's Ford, near the Wilmer McLean home. No road led directly to or from it, at least not a major road suitable for large numbers of troops. But this did not really matter to an attacking column, since less than a mile farther up the run sat Blackburn's Ford and, three quarters of a mile beyond, Mitchell's Ford. Both of these were served by branches of the main road from Centreville to Manassas, and both would probably be attacked. All three of these fords did share an advantage. They were located along a convex bend on Bull Run with the McLean house roughly the focal point. A strong force of two or three brigades could defend the banks of the run and the plain above with the advantage of interior lines. Thus, if Mitchell's were threatened, a Confederate force at McLean's could come to its rescue by a straight march of a mile, whereas attacking Federals, to go from McLean's to Mitchell's, would have to march around the bend of the run a mile and three quarters.

From Mitchell's, the next crossing was at Island Ford, like McLean's a minor point not served by a principal access road. But then another mile up the run came a succession of good crossings. Ball's Ford was fed by two roads leading out from Centreville. They converged just above the ford, and then crossed to run immediately into a steep ascent commanded on the right by a hill on which sat Portici, the home of Francis W. Lewis. Immediately above Ball's was Lewis's Ford, which crossed on the opposite side of the Lewis hill.

Above Lewis's Ford the turnpike from Centreville to Warrenton crossed at a stone bridge, the only structural crossing of Bull Run suitable for large numbers of troops with the exception of the Orange & Alexandria's trestle near Union Mills Ford. A good wide road led over relatively level ground right up to the bridge, crossed over at a downward incline, skirted the south slopes of a hill, crossed Young's Branch, and then passed the Robinson house on the slopes of Henry Hill before continuing straight toward Warrenton. Here lay one of the best potential Confederate defensive positions, thanks to the height of Henry Hill. It commanded the bridge and all of the road leading past with an almost unobstructed view. At the same time it controlled the road which crossed the Warrenton Turnpike, just below it, connecting Manassas with Sudley Springs. A mile and a half north of Henry Hill, Sudley Springs was the last and northernmost major ford across Bull Run. Any enemy force crossing there would have to pass Henry Hill to get to Manassas.

Thus Beauregard had much in his favor. Thanks to the spread of the land and the bends of the river, he needed only to make major concentrations of his forces in the Henry Hill and McLean house areas to command and defend all of the major crossings and avenues to Manassas except for Union Mills Ford. The ground around all of the fords was favorable for defense. In every case the enemy would have to cross under fire and then advance uphill into Confederate guns. If any of the crossings above Island Ford should fall, there were excellent natural positions to which he might fall back to continue the defense. However, on the northern part of the line it was vital that Henry Hill be held. Should it fall, he would lose control of four crossing points and the Warrenton road, down which McDowell could advance around the Confederate left flank and cut the Manassas Gap Railroad, separating Beauregard from Johnston. On the southern part of the line, the Federals had to be stopped at the fords. If they forced a crossing, there was relatively clear level ground all the way back to Manassas. With few good defensive positions, weight of numbers would count heavily on this ground. Should this part of the line fall, Beauregard's brigades to the north would be in danger of being cut off from any reinforcements that might be sent from Richmond to the junction. All in all, it was a good defensive line along Bull Run, but one not without its pitfalls.

It took Beauregard and the Confederate high command some time to evolve their plan of defense. In a contradictory—but characteristic—fashion, Beauregard, after expending great care in examining all of the ground, proceeded on June 13 to send to Jefferson Davis a hastily prepared and poorly thought-out plan of action. At this time Patterson was threatening Johnston, and it looked as though Harpers Ferry might have to be abandoned. Beauregard proposed that Johnston be ordered to do so, and that he come east to combine forces. Then they would advance "by a bold and rapid movement" to retake Alexandria and clear northern Virginia of the invaders' presence. If Johnston could not join Beauregard, however, then he suggested that Johnston retreat to Richmond, where Beauregard would join him. Then, allowing McDowell to invade Virginia at will, they would concentrate around Richmond and "crush, in rapid succession and in detail, the several columns of the enemy."

Davis had the good sense to reject the plan. No one knew for sure yet if Johnston would have to give up Harpers Ferry. The Confederates were not well enough armed to attack McDowell in his home lair, and if they did, Patterson could move through the then unprotected Shenandoah to strike Richmond or Beauregard's rear. And, interestingly, Beauregard proposed all this as though it would be up to him to command any combined movement with Johnston. Yet Johnston was his superior officer. Davis had informed Johnston that all brigadier generals in the Confederate Regular Army would automatically be elevated to the rank of full general. Beauregard's commission as brigadier was in the Provisional Army, and those brigadiers were not being so promoted. Beauregard knew this as well as Johnston.

Undaunted, Beauregard had moved Bonham, Cocke, and Ewell out to their advance positions after receiving Davis' rejection. By early July he felt he had divined the enemy's intentions sufficiently to call together all of his brigade commanders for a conference at Fairfax Court House. Spreading a series of maps before them, Beauregard declared his belief that McDowell would advance on Mitchell's Ford. Consequently, Bonham was to fall back to that place when the enemy advanced, while Cocke and Ewell would withdraw to the stone bridge and Union Mills Ford respectively. This would protect Beauregard's flanks while McDowell assailed Bonham. Then the rest of the Confederate brigades would recross Bull Run, striking McDowell's unsuspecting flanks. It was a nice plan, but it did suffer the one handicap of being entirely dependent upon McDowell's doing exactly as he was expected.[13]

With the three brigades moved forward to their advanced positions, Beauregard published his plans in a general order on July 8. But that same day he confided grave doubts about the situation to a friend in Richmond. He was heavily outnumbered, he complained, and undersupplied. He was determined to fight but feared the waste of life in meeting an enemy so much superior in numbers and equipment. His men were ready for a fight just the same, he said. "They seem to have the most unbounded confidence in me." So did Beauregard. "Oh, that I had the genius of a Napoleon, to be more worthy of our cause and of their confidence!" he closed. If there was one person in the Confederacy who did not doubt that Beauregard had the "genius of a Napoleon," then surely it was Beauregard himself. But his brilliance could not win without men and supplies. The letter, thoughtfully sent to a close confidant of the President, was for Davis' benefit, though the general had almost given up on making Davis see the situation as he saw it. In Beauregard's headquarters, officers sometimes referred to the President as that "stupid fool." Secretary of War Leroy P. Walker, when mentioned at all, was spoken of with contempt.

Then two days later, on July 10, Bettie Duval rode into Bonham's headquarters with her message that McDowell was expected to move on the sixteenth. Matters were now coming to a head. The next day Beauregard advised the President that he expected the Federals to move within two days, and that, although almost powerless to stop him, he would try. Should McDowell offer battle along Bull Run, "I shall accept it for my command, against whatsoever odds he may array in my front." It was a typically grandiose declaration. Defeat was almost inevitable, but Beauregard would meet the threat heroically. He would defend to the last drop of blood if necessary.

But then the very next day, or the day after at the latest, he was infused with enthusiasm for a complete turnabout, another offensive movement against McDowell! On July 13 he wrote a private letter to Johnston proposing that the Virginian leave four or five thousand men behind to hold the passes of the Blue Ridge, and then bring the balance of his force east to join with the Army of the Potomac. Thus, pitting Beauregard's 18,000 with what he supposed to be 22,000 under Johnston would give them a combined strength of 40,000 or more. "This force would enable us to destroy the forces of Generals Scott and McDowell, in my front." Then they would turn their attention to Patterson, who would presumably do nothing while Johnston was absent. They would go farther out into western Virginia to defeat the small Federal army commanded by Major General George B. McClellan, and, having finished with him, cross over into Maryland and threaten the rear of Washington. The entire campaign could be conducted in less than a month, thought Beauregard, and there was no question of success. "Oh, that we had but one good head to conduct all our operations!" he lamented. The "one good head," of course, meant P. G. T. Beauregard.

But his plan showed that the Creole's head was not as good as he thought it was. These attempts to devise offensive strategy simply ignored the facts of the situation. His army was unskilled in battle, his commanders untested. He was undersupplied and underequipped. Yet he proposed to make movements of major armies over several hundred miles with lightning speed and precision, trusting in the enemy to do nothing to upset him. And his carelessness toward detail showed dramatically. Whereas he just assumed that Johnston had 22,000 or more at his disposal, the Virginian's small army numbered in fact barely 11,000.

The same day that he wrote to Johnston, Beauregard sent Colonel John S. Preston of his staff to Richmond to urge this same plan upon Davis and Lee. The next day, so anxious was he to promote his views, he sent Colonel James Chesnut to Richmond as well with further refinements of the design. Davis received Chesnut while lying sick in bed and made an appointment for them to meet later that evening. Lee and General Samuel Cooper, the ranking general in the Confederate Army and its adjutant and inspector general, joined them to hear Beauregard's plan. Chesnut carefully laid the whole story before them, roughly as the Creole had proposed it to Johnston, only making it clearer that, if possible, Washington itself would be attacked. Davis and the others listened attentively, charitably pronounced the plan brilliant, and then pointed out that Johnston had less than half what Beauregard thought he had. Further, McDowell was too close to his defenses in Washington to be defeated. Faced with superior numbers, he would simply retire to his entrenchments. Chesnut was compelled to admit that Lee's views were intelligent and soldierly. After leaving the meeting he wired Beauregard of the result, and then privately to his wife spoke in high terms of Lee's "military sagacity."[14]

Beauregard was greatly disappointed by Richmond's rejection of his proposal. Left with no choice now but to assume the defensive, he looked once more to his positions. One novel aspect of his defenses were four signal towers erected by Captain E. Porter Alexander of his staff. He had devised a system of signaling by waving flags—sometimes called "wigwag"—while in the United States Army, and Beauregard brought him to Manassas to install his system in order to speed communications all along the line. One tower Alexander located near the McLean house. Another he placed at Centreville. A third went up at Avon, the Van Pelt house on a small hill a half mile west of the stone bridge, and the fourth, main, tower was erected a mile east of Manassas. Poor Alexander was given very little to work with. "I have had so much of the little *detail* of my work to attend to personally, depending on quartermasters & commissaries, & borrowed horses," he complained to his wife, "that my progress in arranging the signals has not been commensurate with my labors." Beauregard gave him only private soldiers to work with, and he had to see to everything for them, even going from tower to tower to feed them. "Some of them are so stupid that I have to knock them down & jump on them & stamp & pound them before I can get an idea into their heads."

Materials for his operation came slowly, but by July 10, Alexander had most of his stations communicating with one another by daylight, and some of them by torches at night. While all four of the towers were not in sight of one another, signals from Centreville or the tower near the stone bridge could quickly be relayed via the McLean tower to the main station near Manassas. Guards were stationed to protect the towers, and as the days wore on into July, Alexander's men practiced relentlessly with their flags. Alexander himself borrowed a six-shot Colt repeating rifle from Longstreet "which in my hands will be the lives of six Yankees besides what my revolver can do," he boasted.[15]

While Alexander saw to communicating information locally, Beauregard and his adjutant, Colonel Thomas Jordan, continued their efforts to get reliable intelligence from Washington. The day after Bettie Duval presented her warning to Bonham, she sent him another note with some details on Federal troop movements, including the information that McDowell's advance elements would soon be advancing toward Fairfax Court House. Unfortunately, the advance of Federal pickets beyond Alexandria cut off further warnings from Miss Duval, but not before Jordan sent a man recommended by Chesnut into Washington. His name was G. Donellan, at one time a clerk at the Department of the Interior, and he was a man well known to Mrs. Greenhow. When he entered Washington, he came bearing a paper on which was written in cipher, "Trust the bearer."

At about noon on July 16, Mrs. Greenhow gave him an encoded message and sent Donellan off in a buggy. Somehow he got through McDowell's guards and, once across the Potomac and out of Federal sight, he switched to a swift horse. By eight o'clock that evening, Donellan or his message reached Beauregard's headquarters. Quickly Jordan decoded it. "McDowell has been ordered to advance to-night" it read. Beauregard, through Jordan, sent thanks and a request for further information back to Mrs. Greenhow, and then sat down to face the situation before him.[16]

McDowell now had the initiative. No more grandiose plans for a combined attack on Washington; no more grand strategy to end the war in a single bold stroke. Beauregard was about to be attacked by an army certainly superior to his own. Now he must muster every man. The battle that everyone expected to decide the outcome of the brief summer's war was on its way.

CHAPTER 5

McDowell Plans a Campaign

Beauregard was not the only general making plans that June and July. Just as the Creole and Richmond seemed to feel each other out to find a plan of action, so did McDowell and Washington, with almost equally frustrating results. Just as Beauregard's every grand intention was countered by an interfering Davis—as he saw it—so did McDowell have to deal with an increasingly difficult General Winfield Scott.

On June 3, Scott asked McDowell to submit to him a plan for an advance on Manassas Junction, and perhaps Manassas Gap as well, in a movement to be co-ordinated with a push against Harpers Ferry by Patterson. McDowell responded immediately. He readily recognized the potential for heavy reinforcement that the Manassas Gap Railroad offered to Manassas, and accordingly suggested that no less than 12,000 infantry, two batteries, and nearly a regiment of cavalry would be necessary to take the junction. At the same time, another 5,000 would be needed in reserve. With reports of 6,000 Confederates at Manassas under Beauregard and another 10,000 now with Johnston, this was a reasonable estimate of the Federals' needs in order to have a good chance of success. If more troops could be put into service quickly, however, then McDowell favored doing so. "In proportion to the numbers used," he said, "will be the lives saved." Why not make such a show of force against the enemy that common sense would force him back from Manassas rather than battle? "Might it not be well to overwhelm and conquer as much by the show of force as by the use of it?" he concluded.

The plan was reasonably sound, but events would require its modification over the next several days. By June 5 came a new report: Beauregard was supposed to have over 20,000 in and around Manassas and Fairfax Court House. No one expected this. Perhaps, it was suggested, the rebels at Fairfax Court House and Fairfax Station could be bypassed by marching northwest from Alexandria to Vienna, some fifteen miles, and then southwest another fifteen miles to strike the Confederates at Centreville. Heintzelman had reports that there were only 3,000 Confederates at Centreville, and if they reached it without alerting those at Fairfax, then the Federals could attack and destroy the place before Beauregard gathered his supposedly overwhelming numbers. McDowell, meanwhile, would retreat to strike another day. And Beauregard would have been tied down while Patterson was moving against Johnston.

This plan came apart when Patterson's anticipated advance was halted on June 15, and it did not revive when he eventually crossed the Potomac to take Harpers Ferry. At least Scott did not revive the plan. McDowell, however, held to it. He still thought the Vienna bypass offered possibilities, and on June 16 sent Tyler on a reconnaissance up the line of the Loudoun & Hampshire as far as Vienna to scout the roads and bridges. Tyler found everything in good order, though the rolling stock itself had been mostly destroyed. Still, McDowell could move this way if he wished.

The next day, June 17, McDowell sent General Schenck with 700 men of the 1st Ohio to explore the country further, aboard a train up the Loudoun & Hampshire. They were ordered to proceed to a wagon road which crossed the tracks just south of Falls Church, and here relieve the 69th New York. From this point, McDowell expected Schenck to patrol the surrounding region toward Falls Church and Vienna, leave guards at all the bridges, and carefully survey the condition of the track. Since Tyler experienced nothing more than a sniper shot from a secessionist citizen the day before, McDowell anticipated no trouble for Schenck.

The Federals' train moved slowly to the wagon road, where

Schenck dropped two companies as a guard, two more companies to watch a bridge ahead, and sent yet two more off toward Falls Church. With the remaining four companies, numbering 271 men and officers, he moved slowly on toward Vienna. Within a quarter mile of Vienna they came to a final curve in the road before it ran straight into town.

The day before, Colonel Maxcy Gregg of the 1st South Carolina received orders to make a reconnaissance toward the Potomac. Leaving Fairfax Court House with 575 of his regiment and another seventy cavalry, he picked up on the way another seventy cavalry and two field guns. He saw nothing alarming that day or early the next and proceeded to Vienna to be ready to meet another Federal reconnaissance should Tyler's move of the day before be repeated. By 6 P.M. nothing had happened, and Gregg had the column ready to march back to Fairfax, when he heard a locomotive whistle. Immediately he marched his men back into town and emplaced the two guns on a hill overlooking the final bend in the railroad. He spread out his men on the hill to the right of the guns to await the enemy.

"The train of cars came round the curve of the railroad into sight at the distance perhaps of four hundred yards," Gregg reported. At once his two field guns opened fire.

Schenck at this moment was riding in a passenger car with Colonel Alexander M. McCook, commanding the 1st Ohio. The men themselves were toward the front of the train on flatcars, while the engine was behind the whole, pushing. The firing of the Confederates took them completely by surprise. The men on the platform car in front of the train were not hurt, but the two cars behind them caught heavy fire from the Confederate guns. Company H on the second car back lost two men killed and at least one wounded. Company G on the car behind them had six killed and three wounded. Somehow the engine itself was briefly damaged and could not be reversed to draw the train back around the bend to safety, so the men and officers quickly abandoned their exposed positions on the cars and took cover in the brush on either side of the track. At once they began to retreat back down the track, soon to be followed by Gregg's skirmishers and a company of cavalry. The Federals made good their withdrawal, however, and eventually the engineer—named Gregg, coincidentally—deteached his engine and one car and raced down the track toward safety, ignoring Schenck's men in the process.[1]

McDowell's reaction was to send a stronger force back toward Vienna at once. It was as much for morale as anything. It would do the men good to go back over the scene of their retreat with rifles in their hands, ready to do battle once more.

But Scott refused to allow such a move. And now, in view of reports of Confederate build-ups at Fairfax Court House, McDowell seemed to agree with Scott and to feel that even Falls Church was too dangerously advanced a position. He ordered Tyler to fall back from there, despite Tyler's vigorous objections that such a move gave up the best point of observation available to the Federals. Events were moving quickly in Washington, and, if their expectations were realized, Falls Church would soon be far behind the Federal lines and virtually worthless.[2]

Old General Scott still did not like the notion of a campaign in Virginia. He wanted to take control of the Mississippi, split the Confederacy, and by denying it supplies from Europe force it into submission without the necessity of a costly and bloody overland campaign. Some called it the "Anaconda Plan," and eventually it would help win the war. But not in 1861. There was a rebel army in Virginia, almost within sight of the capital, and the moral effects of such a presence could not be ignored. The people and politicians of the Union wanted something done in Virginia, to drive the Confederates away and remove the insult to the national city. Lincoln was under terrible pressure, and he, in turn, exerted no little persuasion to convince Scott that Beauregard must be met and defeated. In short, he ordered that an offensive be undertaken, and Scott was powerless to refuse. Butler had lost an insignificant skirmish at Big Bethel, not far from Fort Monroe, Virginia, the press were much agitated by the minor repulse at Vienna on June 17, and the people were beginning to ask when the Federals would gain some victories.

On June 21, Scott asked McDowell to submit plans and estimates for a column to co-operate with Patterson in a movement against Leesburg. The general did not care for the idea. He still did not have the wagon transportation he felt he needed. Then, too, any march toward the west would leave the left flank of his marching column open to attack. Once past Vienna, his line of communications back to Alexandria would be open to constant threat of interruption by the Confederates. "I do not think, therefore," he replied to Scott, "it safe to risk anything from this position in the direction of Leesburg." Instead, McDowell still felt that Manassas was their object. He believed that, if the Confederates could be forced out of that position, their next line of defense would have to be forty miles south, behind the Rappahannock River at Fredericksburg. Thus all of northern Virginia would be open to the Federals. McDowell could not know that Lee himself had actually proposed such a withdrawal sometime past.

But this would not satisfy Lincoln and Scott. The old general called upon McDowell personally and ordered him now to prepare a plan of operations looking toward an advance of the army against Manassas. Almost the same day McDowell presented a formal proposal for the campaign.

First, he estimated that Beauregard had at Manassas 25,000 troops of all arms, a considerable exaggeration. To this he expected that an additional 10,000 would be added when the Confederates learned of his approach, and this was only if Patterson succeeded in holding Johnston in his front and if Butler did not let the Confederates facing him on the Virginia peninsula get away. Thus, he expected to confront 35,000 at least. He dismissed any idea of surprising them. Despite all efforts at secrecy, the movement of his army could hardly be concealed for long in a countryside filled with disloyal citizens.

He outlined five ways to approach Manassas. First, the flanking approach he proposed sometime past, through Falls Church and Vienna. Second, via the Little River Turnpike through Fairfax Court House. Third, straight down the Orange & Alexandria Railroad line. Fourth, by way of a road running immediately south of the railroad. And fifth, by river transport down the Potomac to Dumfries, and then across country to cut off Manassas from the south. McDowell dismissed this last out of hand as impractical. His army was barely well enough trained and supplied for an overland campaign, much less an amphibious assault behind enemy lines.

General McDowell proposed to take 30,000 men divided into three columns, and keep a reserve of 10,000. The first column was to embark from Falls Church or Vienna and cut between Centreville and Fairfax Court House to join with the second column, which would march via the Little River Turnpike. He hoped that this movement, if executed quickly, would cut off and force to surrender or disperse Bonham's brigade at Fairfax. The third column would move straight along the line of the Orange & Alexandria and join with the two others at an unspecified point north of Bull Run.

McDowell knew that Manassas and several of the crossings on Bull Run had been fortified and protected with well-emplaced batteries. Consequently, he did not propose to attack them. Rather, he suggested that he render Beauregard's defenses useless by pushing his way around the Confederate left flank and cutting off the enemy's rail connection with Richmond. This he could do at any place on the Orange & Alexandria south of Manassas, but nowhere better than at the bridge crossing Broad Run at Bristoe about five miles below Manassas. He believed that Manassas had neither magazines of ammunition nor large stores of food and other supplies, and that it was entirely dependent upon constant succor by rail from Richmond. Thus, such a threat to Beauregard's communications would force him to withdraw all the way back to the Rappahannock. At the same time, however, McDowell faced the real probability that Beauregard would not withdraw without a fight, "and that the consequences of that battle will be of the greatest importance to the country, as establishing the prestige in this contest on the one side or the other."[3]

McDowell's plan was an excellent one, far better than anyone might expect from one with his lack of experience. Scott accepted it without comment and scheduled a presentation of it before the Cabinet. On the afternoon of June 29, Scott, Mansfield, Meigs, McDowell, Tyler, and Major General John C. Frémont, met before Lincoln and the Cabinet. Tacking a map to the wall of the conference room—McDowell still suffered from not having a fully accurate map of the roads of northern Virginia—the general began to outline his plan of campaign. Tyler would lead the largest column, the one to advance by way of Vienna. Tyler, by virtue of his experience, was entitled to this command. Also, since this was the column closest to Patterson, it made sense for it to be the strongest. The center column, moving on the Little River Turnpike, would be led by David Hunter, and the left-flank column he gave to Heintzelman. McDowell actually read his plan to the men before him, and when he finished no one had any remarks except General Sandford, also in attendance. He expressed his fears about Patterson holding Johnston, and also made the ridiculous assertion that it was bad policy to march to fight the enemy. How else McDowell was to battle Beauregard, Sandford did not say.

McDowell, too, felt fretful over Patterson. Whether he spoke to Scott about it in the Cabinet meeting or outside it is uncertain, but at about this time he told the old general that "I felt tender on the subject of General Patterson and General Johnson [sic]." The troops were green and untried, he told Scott. He would be doing well to defeat Beauregard alone. He could hardly hope to handle both the Creole and Johnston. Scott only replied that the Confederates were green too, and that "if Johnson [sic] joins Beauregard he shall have Patterson on his heels." When Lincoln or someone else in the meeting asked Scott when the movement against Manassas would commence, he, without consulting McDowell, said it would begin in one week. That was July 8. This gave McDowell very little time.[4]

The evening of June 29, McDowell met with Hunter, Heintzelman, Franklin, and a newcomer, Colonel William T. Sherman, at Hunter's quarters. They discussed what had happened in the Cabinet meeting that afternoon, and McDowell revealed to them the details of his plan of campaign. There was no dissent among any of them. Indeed, the only substantive objection raised by anyone came from Captain Daniel P. Woodbury, Corps of Engineers. He suggested that McDowell try to turn Beauregard's position by moving around to the right instead of by the left. McDowell objected. The movement by the left, toward Bristoe, would be decisive. Going around the other side of the enemy threatened only the Manassas Gap line and invited Johnston to fall upon his flank and rear by the use of that line. McDowell had his way.[5]

At the time of his meeting with Scott and the Cabinet, McDowell's Army of Northeastern Virginia numbered a total of 13,666 present for duty, with another 3,000 either on leave or otherwise immediately unavailable. He had twelve pieces of artillery. Within the next several days more troops were added in a last-minute rush to bulk up McDowell's command as much as possible. Colonel Miles was transferred from Patterson's command to take a divisional position with McDowell; more regiments barely trained poured across the Potomac, followed by newly arrived colonels like Sherman and Erasmus D. Keyes, who would lead the freshly formed brigades.

When July 8 came, however, there was simply no way that McDowell could move. Only on this day could he finally give some formal organization to his army. The fault was not his. He had asked for these new regiments weeks before, but only in the last rush before the campaign did they finally come to him. Without time to organize the chain of command, it would be impossible even to be sure of getting the marching orders out to everyone on time, much less put the men on the road.

He organized five divisions. Tyler took the first, with brigades led by Keyes, Schenck, Sherman, and Colonel Israel B. Richardson. This was the column to march via Vienna. The Second Division, David Hunter in command, would be the center column, and therefore needed the fewest men. It consisted of only two brigades, led by Colonel Andrew Porter, and the bewhiskered Colonel Burnside. Heintzelman, of course, commanded the Third Division and its three brigades under Colonels Franklin, Willcox, and Oliver O. Howard. A Fourth Division, actually only a strong brigade, was made up entirely of three-month volunteers whose enlistments would expire at the end of the month, and new three-year regiments that had been in existence for only a month. All were from New Jersey. In view of the untrained and uncertain condition of these men, McDowell made this Fourth Division his reserve under New Jersey's Brigadier General Theodore Runyon. The Fifth, and last, Division belonged to Colonel Miles. It had only two brigades, one led by Colonel Louis Blenker, and the other by Colonel Thomas A. Davies. This last division represented a modification of McDowell's original plan. Instead of three marching columns, he would have four. Miles was to advance between, and parallel with, Heintzelman and Hunter. This would give added weight to the left of his line, the part that was to turn Beauregard's flank and cut him off at Bristoe.[6]

McDowell's organization represented something of a novelty. It was not based upon the most efficient mode of managing troops in general, but rather it was geared specifically for the coming campaign. Ordinarily, every division would have an equal number of brigades, but in this order of battle he beefed up those divisions from which he expected the most or which, in the case of Tyler, were most vulnerable to an attack from Johnston. It was a sound concept, and in conjunction with his plan of campaign displayed that McDowell was so far quite worthy of the trust placed in him by an anxious nation. That past week a spectacular comet was seen overhead, moving northwesterly through the Ursa Major constellation. Its trail covered fifty degrees of the sky, presenting "a magnificent spectacle," thought a Treasury Department clerk. Those in the North who saw it could only hope that it was an omen for victory.[7]

Two days passed after the proposed start of the campaign, and still McDowell did not move. On July 10 he told his commanders that he expected they would be ready to move out on July 13. Still he faced his problems with Mansfield and Meigs. July 13 came and went and McDowell sat in his camps. "I had no opportunity to test my machinery," he complained, "to move it around and see whether it would work smoothly or not." Indeed, when McDowell tried to review eight of his regiments together to test their drill and maneuverability, Scott rebuked him for "trying to make some show." No one in the Army had managed such a large number of men in one body, certainly no one with McDowell at any rate, and even Scott had never commanded such a large force in the field. "I wanted very much a little time," McDowell groused, "all of us wanted it. We did not have a bit of it. The answer was: 'You are green, it is true; but they are green, also; you are all green alike.'"

Even Scott was green to the kind of war they faced, with rapid communications, the opportunity of speedy rail movement, and numbers unheard of in warfare when he led troops in the field. If not green, he was at least a bit rusty, for he made the mistake of placing too great a faith in the expectations of a commander who had already displayed a predilection for hesitance. He counted on Patterson. On Saturday, July 13, Scott conferred with Tyler and informed him that it was now expected that the army would march on the morrow. There would be "no excuse for an unfortunate result" to the campaign, said Scott. McDowell had numbers and equipment in his favor. "Suppose General Jo. Johnson [sic] should reinforce Beauregard, what result should you expect then, General?" asked Tyler. Scott, obviously sick to death of having the chimera of Johnston raised to combat his plans, grew heated. "Patterson will take care of Jo. Johnson," he sternly replied. Tyler replied meekly that he knew both Patterson and Johnston and that, considering the abilities of the two, he would be much surprised if "we did not have to contend with Jo. Johnson's army in the approaching battle."[8]

Still there was no advance. As of Sunday, July 14, many of McDowell's promised troops were still just on their way across the Potomac to him. The general called a council of his commanders and announced that they would move out on the next day. July 15 came. Still the men of new regiments were coming into camp. By now, McDowell could delay no longer. Once more he called his generals to him. They were getting so accustomed to delays that they were somewhat relaxed. Heintzelman and his staff found time, when they should have been rushing in all directions with final preparations, to sit for Mr. Mathew Brady, the photographer.

This July 15 meeting was the last one, however. The orders were to march on the morrow. Heintzelman was to follow the line of the Orange & Alexandria, leave it to run south of Sangster's Station, three miles from Bull Run, and then head for Brentsville, below Manassas. Hunter would follow Miles, who was ordered to march on the Little River Turnpike as far as Annandale, then turn off to the left on the old Braddock Road, which took a parallel course into Centreville. Hunter would continue on the turnpike after Miles turned off. And Tyler was still to lead his division toward Vienna, where he would turn south to head for Germantown, immediately west of Fairfax Court House, on the Little River Turnpike. With Tyler behind and Hunter in front, Bonham would be surrounded.

With so much indecision in Washington, so many dates of departure set and missed, it is miraculous that the troops in the army themselves knew when to go, much less the spies Beauregard had in the Federal city. But on July 16, as the men in blue—and every other color of the rainbow—pulled on their knapsacks and began the march, the enemy was already waiting for them.[9]

And the story was much the same seventy miles to the west, except that Patterson was a far less capable general than McDowell, or at least appeared to be. After safely withdrawing all of his column north of the Potomac on June 18, Patterson sent to Washington all of the Regular troops with him in response to Scott's order. But it left him with little confidence in the capabilities of the untried volunteers that now made up the entirety of his army. Instead, he would start gathering to himself every available regiment from Pennsylvania, hoping to replace the security of experience with the safety of numbers.

Almost at once Scott asked Patterson to occupy Maryland Heights again, with its commanding overlook on Harpers Ferry. Patterson declined, but Scott asked him to do so again on June 20, this time also asking him to submit a plan of operations to drive the 8th Virginia out of Leesburg while McDowell moved out of Alexandria. Promptly the old general replied. His solution was to abandon his present line of operations, place a brigade and some artillery on Maryland Heights to threaten Harpers Ferry, and then cross the remainder of his army several miles east at Point of Rocks. Here he would unite with Charles P. Stone's small command and "operate as circumstances shall demand." There were substantial benefits to gain from this movement. The withdrawal from Harpers Ferry disgruntled his men. Inaugurating a new crossing on a different line would "keep alive the ardor of our men," he thought. Still, Patterson closed with a reminder that, if he had had his way, he would have met Johnston in the valley. After showing consummate timidity south of the Potomac, his bravado north of it was startling. "I regret we did not meet the enemy," he concluded, "so confident am I that, with this well-appointed force, the result would have been favorable to us, and that this portion of Virginia would now be peaceably occupied." Of course the fault was all Scott's for withdrawing those Regulars.[10]

Patterson sent his engineer to scout Maryland Heights for proper positions for placing his guns. The final recommendation was for the building of a semifortress, with loopholes and parapets, to enable 500 men to hold out against all comers. Patterson reported this to Scott and appended to it a far more telling paragraph. His latest reports from intelligence indicated that Johnston had nearly 25,000 between Williamsport, on the Potomac, and

Winchester, thirty-five miles south in the Shenandoah. Further, Jackson was leading 8,000 of them in an advance toward the Potomac, a few miles west of Williamsport. "I shall not avoid the contest they may invite," Patterson told Scott, "indeed, if it meet the approval of the General-in-Chief, I would march my whole force . . . and drive him step by step to Winchester." It would take him ten days to clear the northern Shenandoah of the enemy, he declared. Clearly, Patterson once again wanted Scott to tell him to advance. Thus, if an "unfortunate" reverse should occur, such as his withdrawal from Harpers Ferry, the responsibility would lie with Washington. Patterson was no coward, but he lacked courage in his own convictions.

Scott gave him what he wanted. On June 25 he wrote to Patterson and said that, since the main force of Johnston's army was still apparently in his front in strength, then that was where Patterson should stay. If his army were equal to or greater than the Confederates', then Scott hoped that he would "cross the river and offer him battle." However, if Johnston were to retire to Winchester rather than stand and fight, Patterson did not have to follow him unless he felt he could maintain his numerical superiority deep in the enemy's territory. This was precisely the kind of instruction that an officer like Patterson desired. It seemed definite enough that, should he be defeated, he could always point to Scott and say that he was only following orders. On the other hand, Scott left him a perfect out for not giving a rigorous pursuit if Johnston should withdraw. Scott had given him an excuse for every contingency.[11]

Now, once again, Patterson hesitated. He did not have enough artillery, he said, and in truth he had only six guns. Scott ordered Stone's command, with Rhode Island battery, to join him, and this Patterson found joyful news. He reconnoitered several crossings of the Potomac, discovering that there were heavy concentrations of Confederates at most of them, and therefore decided to cross his entire army at Williamsport. By June 30 he felt he was ready. To Scott that evening he sent the long-awaited news: "I cross at daylight tomorrow morning."[12]

Miles to the south of Patterson, General Joseph E. Johnston suffered from somewhat the same difficulties as Patterson. Namely, though he knew the right action to take, he felt some anxiety about taking it on his own responsibility.

When he had arrived in Richmond in May, on his way to take command in the Shenandoah, Johnston conferred with Lee, who reinforced what Davis had already told him in Montgomery. Both Davis and Lee regarded Harpers Ferry as a natural fortress, commanding all entry and exit to the valley. As a result, Johnston's command there was more a garrison than an army. They expected that the place could be held with ease by the force there assembled.

But when Johnston reached Harpers Ferry, he could not agree. "Harper's Ferry is untenable against an army by any force not strong enough to hold the neighboring heights north of the Potomac and east of the Shenandoah," he concluded. He was quite right. The same commanding elevations at Loudoun and Bolivar Heights that made it impossible for the Federals to hold the place at the outbreak of the war also made it indefensible from attack via Maryland Heights on the north. On May 28, shortly after taking command, Johnston sent a report by one of his engineers, and with it his own endorsement of his objections to an arbitrary policy of holding Harpers Ferry. The engineer's report was to demonstrate how easily Patterson could force them out of the river town.

Lee's reply was hardly what Johnston wanted. In substance he said that Harpers Ferry must be held, and that only if attacked by an overwhelming force was Johnston to abandon it. Johnston voiced his objections in several letters to Richmond, and again, on June 7, Lee replied. He and Davis had discussed the matter. Still they placed great value on holding the position. Abandoning it would harm Confederate communications with Maryland, now that access through and around Alexandria had been cut off. However, Lee concluded, if an advancing enemy could not be opposed successfully, then Johnston could retire. "You must exercise your discretion and judgment in this respect," said Lee. "Precise instructions cannot be given you, but, being informed of the object of the campaign, you will be able to regulate its conduct to the best advantage." In other words, Johnston himself might decide whether or not to retire. Adjutant and Inspector General Samuel Cooper made this even more plain in a long and somewhat biting letter on June 13. "You had been heretofore instructed to exercise your discretion as to retiring from your position at Harpers Ferry," wrote Cooper, but apparently "you have considered the authority given as not equal to the necessity of the case." It appeared that Johnston wanted the responsibility for his possible retirement to fall on Richmond. Cooper agreed to take that responsibility. Henceforward Johnston was to feel free to abandon Harpers Ferry whenever he felt that an enemy advance threatened to turn his position and cut him off. Two days later Johnston replied curtly to Cooper that he never intended to imply that he wanted Richmond to take the burden for him. It was a hollow protest, for his every word since taking command pointed to his desire to have Richmond's express permission to retire before he would undertake doing so.[13]

Johnston's problem was his reputation. Governor Pickens, in the same breath in which he condemned Lee and berated Beauregard, declared that "General Johnson [sic] has real active talent." Speaking of Johnston's subsequent withdrawal from Harpers Ferry, Pickens said that "he has boldly maneuvred in the face of an enemy far his superior in numbers. And his maneuvres have shewn real talent." "I like his game," said Pickens. The trouble was, no one in the Confederacy was more conscious of Johnston's reputation than the general himself. As a result, he feared to take risks that might turn into mistakes to blot his record. Instead, he would take inordinate amounts of time to reach a decision, frequently missing an opportunity that the more venturesome might take advantage of. Nothing illustrates this character trait better than a story told in Richmond. "Wade Hampton brought him here to hunt," said the narrator. "He was a capital shot, better than Wade or I; but with Colonel Johnston —I think he was Colonel then—the bird flew too high or too low, the dogs were too far or too near. Things never did suit exactly. He was too fussy, too hard to please, too cautious, too much afraid to miss and risk his fine reputation for a crack shot." Hampton and others shot away at will, "right and left, happy-go-lucky," and bagged a fine take of the birds. Johnston never shot at all. The right time and place just did not present itself. But if he did not shoot, then he did not miss either. While the others came back with the birds, Johnston came back with his much-talked-of skill at shooting unimpaired. There were those who feared that this would be the way with his generalship as well. If he did not fight, at least then he could not lose, and to get him to fight, or make a movement that might prove unpopular, it appeared that he had first to be absolved of responsibility for the consequences. It was a shame, for Johnston possessed as much tactical skill as any general in the Confederacy, if not more.[14]

Now that he had Richmond's express permission to evacuate Harpers Ferry, Johnston no longer needed it. In fact, by the time Cooper's letter reached him, he had already pulled out of the supposed fortress. His cavalry outposts had brought word of Patterson's advance from Chambersburg on June 10, and soon thereafter he learned that McClellan was moving in western Virginia. The combined total of those coming against him was reported to be 20,000 or more. Against this, Johnston had less than 10,000. Clearly in Johnston's mind, the issue was now forced upon him. He saw no choice but to withdraw. On June 13 and 14 he sent his baggage and supplies southwest to Winchester, and on June 15 began marching the troops out of Harpers Ferry. Three days later, after a brief detour to threaten Patterson's crossing of the Potomac, Johnston had his army safely in their camps at Winchester.

This is where he wanted to be from the beginning. Winchester, he felt, controlled all the main roads for invasion of the Shenandoah from the north, and at the same time controlled the access to Manassas Gap and the railroad that ran to Manassas. Here he set up his camps, and here Richmond promised to send him reinforcements. Johnston felt rather secure once he learned that Patterson had crossed back to the Maryland side of the Potomac, so he advised that the bulk of the reinforcements be sent to Beauregard. Still, he happily accepted what was sent him. By the end of June, his army numbered 10,654. New officers had been sent to him as well, and it was time to reorganize.[15]

He formed an army of four brigades. The First Brigade, Army of the Shenandoah, was commanded by the remarkable Colonel Jackson, now a brigadier since June 17. Johnston molded the Second Brigade with the 7th, 8th, 9th Georgia, the 1st Kentucky, and the battery of Captain Ephraim G. Alburtis. Richmond sent him Colonel Francis S. Bartow to lead it, the Georgian who helped raise one of the regiments in the brigade.

The Third Brigade went to another brigadier appointed on June 17, General Bernard E. Bee of South Carolina. Bee was a West Pointer, with a gallant record in the Mexican War, and a

good postwar record until he resigned his commission in March
1861. Immediately he took a colonelcy in the South Carolina service, and shortly thereafter was brought to Virginia by the War
Department. Johnston gave him the 2d and 11th Mississippi, the
4th Alabama, the 1st Tennessee Infantry, and Captain John D.
Imboden's Staunton Artillery.

To lead the Fourth Brigade, Johnston had yet another West
Pointer, Colonel Arnold Elzey. (His surname was actually Jones,
but he dropped it upon leaving the Military Academy in 1837 in
favor of his middle name). Like Bee, he won plaudits for his Mexican and Seminole Wars services, and when war broke out was in
command of a United States arsenal in Georgia. He resigned his
commission in April 1861 and shortly thereafter took command of
the 1st Maryland Infantry. Now, in addition to his own regiment,
he would lead the 10th and 13th Virginia Infantries, the 3d Tennessee, and a battery under Captain George A. Groves.

Johnston's four brigades were roughly equal in numbers. In addition, he had Stuart's 1st Virginia Cavalry, and the nucleus of
the future 33d Virginia Infantry led by Colonel Arthur C. Cummings. Johnston ordered local militia to organize itself into two
regiments, though progress was slow, and he would shortly have
several more regiments coming his way. Considering the advantages of terrain and communications which he enjoyed over an
enemy advancing against Winchester, there was every reason to
expect that he could mount a successful defense.[16]

In the days that followed, Johnston kept a constant watch on
the Potomac crossings, sending Jackson forward toward Martinsburg to help Stuart's cavalry. At the same time, some of the
Tennesseans went north to the line of the Baltimore & Ohio Railroad and seriously hampered Federal communications along that
line, earning the congratulations of President Davis. Along with
his compliments, Davis stressed that, if Patterson had withdrawn
from his front in order to move against Leesburg or Manassas
Gap, this might be an opportune time for Johnston to move east
and join Beauregard in attacking Patterson.

But Patterson did not go east. On July 2 confirmed reports
reached Johnston that the Federals had started crossing the Potomac again. Stuart fell back steadily before the enemy advance,
advising Jackson of enemy movements. At once Jackson sent one
regiment and a battery to resist Patterson. At Falling Waters, on

the Potomac, his skirmishers met the Federals and a sharp engagement ensued. After falling back initially, the Federals rallied and moved forward once again, turning Jackson's position and forcing him to retire gradually. Soon two more Virginia regiments came up to support Jackson, while Stuart rode around the enemy flank to try to cut them off. Jackson, facing overwhelming numbers, decided to fall back to Martinsburg. He called Stuart back and slowly withdrew. Patterson's army followed only so far as the outskirts of Martinsburg, and during the night Jackson pulled away farther and marched to Darkesville, several miles south on the road to Winchester. Here, shortly after dawn, July 3, Johnston met him with the rest of the army brought forward from their camps.[17]

Now Johnston hoped to meet Patterson and defeat him. He had a good position at Darkesville, and he expected the Federals to advance and attack. Instead, Patterson stayed in Martinsburg. For four days Johnston waited. Finally on July 7, convinced that Patterson would not move against him, and unwilling to move on the offensive himself, Johnston withdrew to Winchester once more, certain that the enemy would not follow. He believed that Patterson had over 18,000, and that reinforcements were crossing the Potomac to swell his numbers. Despite the fact that Johnston's own monthly report of June 30 showed that he had 10,654 present for duty, he would claim that he had less than 9,000 effectives, hardly enough to favor an attack on the enemy. Years later he would admit that both he and Patterson "overrated each other's strength greatly."

On July 9 intelligence from Stuart changed Johnston's mind. The build-up of Patterson's army and movements around Martinsburg convinced him that Patterson intended to march that night to attack Winchester. "We are not prepared beyond the readiness of our men to fight," he warned Richmond. Still, he told Cooper, "Fighting here against great odds seems to me more prudent than retreat." Johnston's withdrawal to Winchester had been bad enough, in the minds of the people. It saddened and in some degree demoralized his troops as well. Now the prospect of meeting an enemy reputed to be twice the size of Johnston was doubly depressing. It was, then, fortunate that Stuart's reports proved false. Patterson made no move to attack.[18]

The fighting came elsewhere, on July 11, at a place called Rich

Mountain, in western Virginia. McClellan attacked a small rebel command led by Lieutenant Colonel John Pegram, and defeated him with heavy loss. Nearby a larger Confederate army of 4,000 skirmished with other Federal troops, and the next day began to retreat before the enemy pursuit. On July 13, while retreating across Corrick's Ford on the Cheat River, one hundred miles southwest of Winchester, Brigadier General Robert S. Garnett, commanding the Confederate army, was killed and his command severely battered. His campaign in western Virginia ended in disaster, and he became the first Confederate general to die in combat. Worse, the Federals now controlled a sizable stretch of the north and central reaches of western Virginia. The effect of the reverse upon the Confederate Government and public was terrible. "Poor Garnett is killed," moaned Richmond. Before he left for the field he had complained that "They have not given me an adequate force. I can do nothing. They have sent me to my death."[19]

Garnett's fate only added to Johnston's anxiety. Now Patterson, buoyed up by McClellan's success, was sure to come.

Or was he?

Predictably, Patterson's promise to Scott that he would cross the Potomac on July 1 did not materialize. His columns did not get their feet wet until the next day at 4 A.M., when they marched down to the fording place at Williamsport and started across. Before the first Federals reached the other side, Confederate pickets on the Virginia shore opened fire. The advancing host quickly drove them away and secured the ford. For the next five miles or more Patterson's advance regiments moved without difficulty. And then they ran into Jackson and his Virginia regiment and battery. Three Federal regiments faced the Confederates in front, assisted by a battery and a company of cavalry, before George Thomas led his brigade around Jackson's flank to force him out of his position.

Patterson's men felt a brief surge of triumph. The stigma of retreat from Harpers Ferry was erased, and they wanted to pursue the supposedly beaten and fleeing enemy. But Patterson decided that they had done enough for one day. He placed the strength of Jackson's regiment and attendant cavalry and artillery at 3,500, almost twice the actual numbers of Jackson's entire brigade! This was sufficient accomplishment for this first day of the campaign. He would spend the night at Falling Waters and proceed south in the morning.

On July 3 the Federals marched into Martinsburg without opposition in what Patterson called "hot pursuit" of Jackson. Here he would halt for a time to await supplies from his base in Maryland. "As soon as provisions arrive," he told Scott, "I shall advance to Winchester to drive the enemy from that place, if any remain." Even with his campaign thus far successful, Patterson saw grave difficulties on the horizon. The terms of enlistment of his three-months volunteers were soon to expire, and he doubted that many would re-enlist for the new term of three years or the duration. Still he needed more men, as always. Consequently, appeals went out with startling rapidity for reinforcements, while at the same time Patterson sought Scott's guidance, and responsibility.

Scott sent regiment after regiment on its way to Martinsburg. Five of them were on their way within twenty-four hours of Patterson's first plea for troops. Scott now hoped that the general might be able to pursue the Confederates and then move by way of Leesburg toward Alexandria. This would lead Johnston to believe that Patterson was on his way to unite with McDowell against Beauregard, and consequently would keep the Virginian where Scott wanted him, away from the army at Manassas. But great care must be taken, warned Scott. The countryside was favorable for the enemy defenders. Also, there were other ways to deceive Johnston by stratagem. Stop briefly in Winchester, said the general-in-chief. This would confuse Johnston as to whether Patterson would then turn east toward McDowell or go on south. Still, as ever, Johnston must be kept away from Beauregard.[20]

One at a time the regiments came into Martinsburg, but they were not enough, for Patterson had information that Johnston, too, received constant additions. Reports indicated that the Confederates had 26,000 or more at Darkesville. "I hope in proper season to give you a good account of them," wrote the general to Scott. On July 7, perhaps to ensure that a "good account" did come out of the Shenandoah, Scott sent General Sandford with two regiments to assist. Sandford came "in the best possible spirit," Patterson was told. This meant that Sandford was not

coming to relieve him, though he almost did. Washington grew
increasingly fearful of Patterson's hesitance after the delays and
setbacks of June. On July 6, Secretary of State William H. Seward
called Sandford to his office and informed him that the subject of
removing Patterson from his command had come up in a Cabinet
meeting. No action was to be taken at that time, but Seward did
suggest that Sandford, senior to Patterson, might be sent to the
Shenandoah. Out of deference to Sandford's rank, Patterson, who
seemed hesitant to fight, would then be expected to allow Sandford to engage the enemy. Sandford agreed and was on his way.[21]

By July 8, Patterson felt it was time to move again, having
given Johnston nearly a week to prepare to meet him. He issued
marching orders for the following day. Scott had informed him
that McDowell would be moving against Beauregard soon, and it
was impossible to delay his own movement any further. Johnston
might otherwise slip away. But then, this same night, Patterson's
officers began to persuade him otherwise. The troops would not
fight, they said. They were untrained, unskilled, untrustworthy.
Enlistments would soon be up, and few would risk death on the
battlefield with the prospect of going home in a few days before
them. Patterson postponed decision on the march until the morning of July 9, when there would be a council of war.

The meeting took place in the afternoon, and it was a disaster.
First the quartermaster and commissary reported that there were
not enough transportation and not enough food. His engineers
harped on their exposed position. "We have no business here except for the purpose of making a demonstration," said one officer.
Patterson himself seems to have missed the point that a demonstration was precisely why he was in the valley in the first place.
The main theater of operations had shifted to McDowell and
Beauregard sometime ago. All of the field commanders were unanimous in their opposition to any forward movement. The most
they would countenance was a flank move to Harpers Ferry or
nearby Charlestown, where their supply line could be more firmly
established with Maryland.

Sometime before these opinions were expressed, Patterson
addressed the officers on the reasons for their being in the valley.
His fears and apprehensions obviously ruled him, making him all
the more receptive to their caution. Why did Johnston retire be-

fore him? Weakness? Or a stratagem to lure the Federals into a trap? Soon the volunteers would muster out. Any defeat by Johnston would be disastrous for the cause, freeing him to join Beauregard. Yet if they withdrew, then Johnston could go east anyhow. More regiments under Sandford and others were coming within a few days. Soon Patterson would be stronger. "What shall be done?" he asked. His officers told him, and he gave in to them. There would be no movement after all. He would wait a few days.[22]

To be exact, he waited until July 15. McClellan's victory in western Virginia greatly buoyed Federal morale. Now, with as many reinforcements as he would ever get, and with Sandford commanding a division, Patterson had to move. They marched at dawn, almost immediately coming upon the signs of Johnston's withdrawal before them. Dead animals, abandoned equipment, stripped fields, all spoke of an army quickly falling back. By that afternoon the column reached Bunker Hill, little more than five miles from Winchester. Yet immediately Patterson went into camp. "I will make a reconnaissance tomorrow," he told Sandford, "and we will arrange to move at a very early period." Patterson had said that before, and to just about everyone. But now he was on the move once more, and the enemy lay only an hour or so away. There had been scattered picket firing all day, and no sign that Johnston had continued to fall back once reaching Winchester. This looked like the place the Confederates would make a stand. Much was expected by Sandford and the others who looked forward to meeting and beating the enemy. The morrow's reconnaissance would probably be decisive. Patterson may also have told his officers of something else that would happen the next day, Tuesday, July 16. By a prearranged code, Scott had informed him that McDowell would advance on Manassas. At last, for the rebellious Confederacy, a time of reckoning seemed near at hand.[23]

CHAPTER 6

THE MARCH TO BULL RUN

"On to Richmond!" was the rallying call of the war that would be ended before the summer. In the lines at the supply wagons, soldiers stood waiting for their three days' rations with a collective look more suited to a circus in Vienna than to an army in Virginia. A wide array of sizes, shapes, and variegated uniforms made up this motley army of the North. Their silken banners, "unsoiled and untorn," strove to catch what they could of the tepid Potomac breezes. In their buoyant expectations, their boundless confidence, and their naïveté, these men seemed to be engaged in a children's crusade rather than in a nineteenth-century war.

Irvin McDowell was the exception. Seemingly alone of the Union high command, he knew what to expect despite his own lack of combat experience. As a result, his final marching order issued on the morning of July 16 was as explicit as any this war would see. Everyone must know his place and when to be there. Tyler's line of march would take him to Vienna, where he would pass the night. Hunter was to advance on the Columbia Turnpike until it ended at the Little River Turnpike. There, just outside Annandale, he was to bivouac for the night. Heintzelman would take the old Fairfax road running south of and parallel to the Orange & Alexandria. At the most he was not to go beyond the crossing at Pohick Creek, where the road and railroad came together a few miles short of Fairfax Station. Miles and his division were to move straight out the Little River pike to bivouac at Annandale.

There must be no carelessness, no lack of vigilance, no relaxation, McDowell told his commanders. There were, he said, three things that would "not be pardonable in any commander." Coming unexpectedly upon an enemy masked battery or breastwork was the first, and well-positioned advance guards and vedettes would prevent this. The second commandment was not to be surprised. The same vedettes would prevent this as well. And the third law was not to fall back. The size of the marching divisions should be an ample deterrent to this. All of the baggage, mess equipment, and so forth would be brought along for them by wagon trains to follow the divisions. A train of wagons loaded with rations would follow one day behind, and a second supply train would follow that one by a day. A herd of cattle for beef would accompany each wagon train.

Finally, reminding the army that it was carrying the authority of the Union back into the erring soil of the South, McDowell enjoined his men to carry the national colors prominently at all times, and to display miniature flags from the cannon. Aware that some of the regiments in the army were clothed in gray, and that some of the enemy units wore blue, McDowell urged everyone to take great care whom they should shoot at.[1]

At 2 P.M., July 16, the march began. Before they left, hundreds if not thousands of the soldiers wrote what some feared might be their last letters home. "Least I should not be able to write again," began a private in Burnside's brigade, "I feel impelled to write a few lines that may fall under your eye when I shall be no more." The coming campaign might be a short one, he told his wife, "and full of pleasure." It might also be "one of some conflict and death to me." No matter, he said. "If it is necessary that I should fall on the battlefield for my country, I am ready. I have no misgivings about or lack of confidence in the cause in which I am engaged, and my courage does not halt or falter. I know how strongly American civilization now leans on the triumph of the Government, and how great a debt we owe to those who went before us through the blood and sufferings of the Revolution. And I am willing—perfectly willing—to lay down all my joys in this life, to help maintain this government, and to pay that debt." Never again in this war—or perhaps in any American war—would an army take the field so assured of its holy mission, so convinced that God's work was surely its own.[2]

McDowell made his headquarters for the first day of the march with Hunter's column, and for them it was an uneventful day. By McDowell's order, Burnside's brigade led the march out of the camps in Washington and across the Long Bridge onto the sacred soil of Virginia. No one wanted to be left behind. "Men who had been under the surgeon's care for weeks," wrote a soldier of the 2d New Hampshire, "buckled on their armor and obstinately refused to be left behind while the death blow was given the rebellion." The men were cheered as they marched across the bridge. When they set foot on the other side, the band of the 2d New Hampshire struck up "Dixie," and the soldiers broke into cheers and more marching songs.

They marched through the fortifications at Arlington, passed a tollgate on the Columbia Turnpike, where, presumably, they paid no toll, and on down the pike, across the Loudoun & Hampshire, to Bailey's Crossroads. Here Hunter's division stopped for supper, two loaves of bread and a pound of salt pork per man. Then the march resumed toward Annandale, until 10 P.M., when the division reached its assigned bivouac. There, for the first time, these men of war slept in the field. "Beneath the clear sky, studded with the sentinel stars, that paced their ceaseless round, we slept the sleep of soldiers." The scene was inspiring. The various drum corps of the regiments beat the tattoo in succession, each one beginning as the one before it ceased, "and, as the notes rose upon the air, now near, now distant, now full, and now subdued, we almost forgot that we were soldiers."[3]

The march went much the same for the other divisions as well on July 16. The Confederate rear pickets put up an almost constant brush firing on the Federal vedettes, but no actual resistance was met anywhere. Nothing but the trees felled across the roads retarded the march. To offset the boredom of the day's advance, some of the Connecticut men in Keyes's brigade of Tyler's division speculated upon just how they should chastise the Confederacy. After beating Beauregard at Manassas, they would take the train to Richmond, capture the city, and hang Jefferson Davis from a "sour apple tree," the hangmen being rewarded by a lock of Davis' hair. This was not to be taken as something of value so much as a reminder that "they had then and there done something for the elevation of at least one fellow being." Meanwhile, it was decided that McDowell should, from his seat in Richmond, start receiving the surrender of all nearby Confederates, and that those rebel commanders too far from the city to come personally might instead send their swords to McDowell by express trains. Then all were to go back home, the Federals to return to their towns covered with garlands and laurel wreaths, there to be carried on the arms of their admiring countrymen back to their homes. One of the Nutmeg men wryly confessed that "this plan was never fully carried out."

On this, the first real march for the army, some officers anticipated that the men would fall out at every opportunity for fresh water. It was hot, humid, and the road was long and dusty. A Wisconsin officer in Sherman's brigade had the foresight to fill all the canteens in his company with strong, cold tea, which quenched thirsts better than water and seemed to discourage the men from falling out of line at each passing creek. But not so with most of the other regiments. The need for water was too strong. McDowell complained bitterly of it. "They would not keep in the ranks, order as much as you pleased. When they came where water was fresh they would pour the old water out of their canteens and fill them with fresh water; they were not used to denying themselves much."[4]

Heintzelman's march south of the Orange & Alexandria passed as planned, and without incident. The enemy was seen on occasion, generally out of rifle range. Thanks to the indirect route planned by McDowell, the Confederates seem not to have expected a Federal column on this road. The civilians soon spread the word, however. The rebel axmen did their work well as a result. Wherever the road ran through woods, the Federals found tree after tree felled across the path. Often they had to detour through corn and wheat fields. The chief obstacle met, however, proved to be a natural one. Early in the evening soldiers down the line began to experience a series of inexplicable halts, until the patience of many was exhausted. Finally, around 10 P.M., the reason was discovered. At one place, the line of march ran through a

steep ravine crossed by narrow Accotink Creek. The only means
of crossing was a single log bridging the banks. Thousands of soldiers had to pass over this single trunk, and every now and then
the sound of a splash revealed that one of the saviors of the
Union had fallen off. "An axe, a little muscle and common sense,
might have erected a passable bridge in a few moments," complained a Maine soldier of Howard's brigade. When Howard himself rode up, he found scores of men sitting and removing their
shoes and stockings for fear of wetting them in crossing. "Each
brigade before mine had taken full two hours to pass a stream
not more than twenty yards wide and the water nowhere above
their knees. Howard could not take this. He formed the brigade,
shoes, stockings, and all, and marched them straight across
through the water. It dampened their spirits—and feet—but it got
them into bivouac and their blankets three hours earlier than if
they single-filed across the log. "My men were somewhat in-
censed," wrote Howard later. Indeed, two of them accidentally
shot themselves on the march, though presumably not out of de-
spair over wet socks. That night, when finally in bivouac, Howard
found that "The one hour's sleep of god was very refreshing."[5]

By nightfall on July 16, despite enemy harassment and obstacles
man-made and natural, all of McDowell's divisions lay bivouacked
in their assigned places. He could well take satisfaction in this first
days march, for the army followed his instructions to the letter.
The only tardy units were a few of Heintzelman's troops held up
by a slow, heavy cannon and, of course, the crossing of the Accotink. But the morrow, July 17, would reveal far more of the
weaknesses of a new army and untried officers.

McDowell's plan of campaign called for the divisions to resume
their march at dawn on July 17. Tyler was to move south from
Vienna and cut between Centreville and Fairfax Court House,
sending one brigade in each direction and holding the remainder
of his division for discretionary use. Miles was to move out of Annandale on the old Braddock Road, which ran parallel to the Little River Turnpike, and then turn north, striking Fairfax Court
House from the south. Hunter, once Miles was out of the way,
would advance straight down the Little River pike to Fairfax.
Thus, the Confederates in the small courthouse town would be
struck from three sides, all retreat cut off. Meanwhile, the real

meat of McDowell's plan was Heintzelman. All of the moves on Fairfax Court House, besides serving the useful purpose of cutting off and capturing a Confederate brigade, would alert Beauregard to a certain frontal move on Centreville and Manassas. But Heintzelman was to continue on his road south of the Orange & Alexandria to Sangster's Station. If all went well at Fairfax, he might expect to have a fairly easy road across Union Mills Ford to get behind Beauregard, cut the railroad, and isolate him from Richmond. This last was not explicitly stated in McDowell's campaign plan, but it took little intuition to see the intention between the lines.[6]

On July 17, Heintzelman marched at daylight, and by 5 P.M. his division had reached Sangster's Station. It was not an uneventful day for the grim-visaged old soldier. Troubles with the baggage train beset him immediately, the slow heavy cannon caused constant delay, and the men themselves, tired from the five miles they had marched the day before, moved with less than spring-like step. After only a few hours on the road, Heintzelman received word that the enemy had placed entrenchments on the road, and he rode to the head of the column in person to inspect the situation. Enemy pickets had been surprised and driven back. Heintzelman's orders gave him discretion as to whether he should send part of his force north toward Fairfax Court House to aid in the general attack there. He decided at a fork in the road called Elzy's to send Franklin's brigade north toward the courthouse, while he hurried Willcox's command on to Fairfax Station and, eventually, to Sangster's. Howard, bringing up the rear, would halt at Elzy's as a reserve.[7]

Heintzelman was now ready to cut off Confederate retreat from Fairfax Court House by the south, or else move to attack the place himself. With his position he was in the perfect setting for executing McDowell's hopes to the full, if everyone else had played their roles properly. But they had not.

Tyler's march from Vienna proved uneventful. He found the road straight and good, the marching easy until Keyes's brigade, in the advance, came upon an enemy battery. He called Tyler forward, and that officer decided that the emplacement was either abandoned or was in the process of being abandoned. As they moved forward cautiously, Tyler found that his assessment was accurate. The only other obstacles were the ever-present felled trees, but even this gave little trouble to the axmen. Occasionally the rebels fired out of ambush in the woods, and at one point several of them sniped at the column from the cover of a log cabin beside the road. A few well-directed solid shots from a fieldpiece soon discouraged them, and Keyes's men were treated to the sight of Confederates pouring out of doors and windows, falling over one another in their haste to get out before the building collapsed.

It was back down the line of the marching division that the real problems occurred. Despite their fine advance of the day before, the men this day were tired, having been on the road since sunup. And they already displayed the volunteer soldier's disinclination to pay attention to orders and restrictions. Sherman's brigade proved particularly troublesome in this regard. He told them there would be no straggling, no harassing of the citizens or their property, no foraging for food in Virginia barn lots. It did him little good. He personally caught one strapping six-foot four-inch Wisconsin man walking along with a quarter of fresh mutton over his shoulder. "Didn't you know the orders against foraging?" he was asked. "Yes, but I was hungry, and it was rebel mutton, anyhow." Sherman promptly placed the man under arrest and then, rather than see the mutton wasted, told one of his orderlies to have it cooked for the staff's supper. Combatting the stragglers, Sherman and his officers were constantly riding up and down the column. "You must close up," they yelled; "you must not chase the pigs and chickens." And so on. Often as not the replies were not the least bit respectful. "Who are you, anyway?" hooted the privates. "Tell Colonel Sherman we will get all the water, pigs and chickens we want." When the officers rode off, they did so to a chorus of hoots and jeers. The height of folly was reached when a captain of the 79th New York, the "Highlanders," insisted on wearing his ceremonial kilts on the march. When he saw a loose pig, he drew his trusty saber and gave chase. The spectacle of a grown man in a skirt chasing a pig with a sword completely stopped the regiment, and presumably those regiments behind it in the column. For several minutes the captain chased the porker, his skirts flying in the air while the men called for him to "put on your drawers!" and "take off that petticoat!" Finally the hard-pressed pig raced for a rail fence and just managed to squeeze under the bottom rail. The enterprising captain, seeing his quarry about to escape, made a last desperate flying leap over the top rail, "and in the act made such an exhibition of his attenuated anatomy as to call forth a roar of laughter." It was the last time he wore the kilts.[8]

It is no wonder that Tyler's progress was slow, made the worse by the heat and dust. Once again the men fell out at every creek or well to fill their canteens. It did not help that when they did stop for rations the men had to eat hardtack—a hard cracker seasoned with salt—and salt pork. Nothing could have been worse. "Went blackberrying after eating [a] piece of salt meat," wrote a Massachusetts man of Richardson's brigade in his diary. So did thousands of others. "They stopped every moment to pick blackberries," complained McDowell. Others simply looted. As they passed out of Vienna, men of the 1st Massachusetts literally destroyed a grocery store, carrying off everything, even to the grindstones and hogsheads of molasses. All during the morning's march these and other circumstances caused needless halt after halt. Hundreds of letters were written as the men lay in the grass by the roadside, waiting for the march to resume. Despite their early start, by noon Tyler's brigades had barely covered the seven miles from Vienna to Germantown. During one of those halts, George D. Wells, lieutenant colonel of the 1st Massachusetts, wrote home that "We are now halting within five miles of Fairfax Court House, where is a large secession force. The rumor is they are *evacuating*. We are anxious to be at them but are halted here in accordance with the policy of this very *civil* war." For once, rumor was right.[9]

The advance of Miles and Hunter had been just as slow as Tyler's. Miles did not start out until well after eight o'clock, and the felled trees and Confederate pickets further slowed his progress. Hunter, meanwhile, had to wait for Miles to get out of the way before he could start his march. For Hunter, it was a straight march toward Fairfax Court House, Burnside in the lead. Once under way, Burnside moved with more speed than the rest of the army, clearing easily the obstacles left behind by the enemy. Fortunately, little or no enemy fire harassed them, and by around noon Burnside's were the first troops to come within striking distance of the courthouse. He drew his brigade into line, spoke a few words of encouragement, and then moved them forward. They found an empty town and abandoned earthworks. Fairfax Court House, where McDowell had anticipated the first substantial resistance from the enemy, fell into his hands without the loss of a life. The enemy had simply left it.[10]

On July 8, Beauregard had issued orders for Bonham, at Fairfax, to retire by way of Centreville to Bull Run if he was met by a superior force in his front. All through the night of July 16–17, Bonham heard rumors that McDowell was advancing in force on his position. Then that morning his scouts brought confirmation that the enemy was advancing on at least three roads. The intelligence was admirably correct. Bonham knew that he could not possibly hold out against an entire army. He had only his own four South Carolina regiments, a Virginia unit temporarily assigned to him, two batteries of artillery, and several companies of cavalry. But still he had to stay in place long enough to ascertain the full strength of the enemy, information Beauregard would have to have. Consequently, he sent his baggage and supply wagons to the rear, sent the men to their places, and awaited the coming of the Yankee horde.

Between 8 and 9 A.M. he heard the report of cannon a few miles to the north, toward Vienna. Surely it was Keyes's advance driving Bonham's skirmishers out of the log cabin. Bonham's men did not yet know that they were supposed to fall back rather than fight, and as a result were anticipating a serious engagement. Then messengers brought word that no enemy could be seen marching on the Little River Turnpike. Probably they simply did not go far enough to encounter the late-starting Hunter. As a result, Bonham pulled in his scouts on that road, just in time to see Tyler make his appearance in the vicinity of Flint Hill, two miles north of Fairfax where the road forked to Germantown.

Bonham was much impressed by the size of Tyler's column, but coolly stood in his entrenchments until part of the Federal advance was within less than a mile of him. He had to be certain that the enemy's numbers were as great as his scouts reported them to be. The men in the ranks felt the universal uneasiness of green troops before battle. "Excitement and consternation overwhelmed the camp," recalled a South Carolinian. "While all were expecting and anxiously awaiting it, still the idea of being now in the face of a real live enemy, on the eve of a great battle, where death and horrors of war, such as all had heard of but never realized, came upon them with no little feelings of dread and emotion."

Finally Bonham was satisfied. Shortly before the Federal advance pickets reached his outer lines, he gave his officers orders which until then had been sealed. They were to withdraw at once and follow the baggage and supply trains back through Centreville, where they halted for the night. Before leaving, it appears that some of the Confederates, with or without authorization, set fire to a few buildings in the town, perhaps those containing military stores which could not be evacuated.[11]

The destruction begun by the Confederates was completed with gusto by the occupying Federals. Without authorization, soldiers began to force their way into empty homes to loot them of "rebel" souvenirs. Meanwhile, when Tyler bypassed Fairfax and entered Germantown, he too found buildings ablaze, and his men behaved with little better demeanor than Hunter's. "We found several houses in flames," wrote a private of the 1st Massachusetts, "& the men of our brigade burned nearly all the rest before they left." A Lieutenant William Lusk of the 79th New York, while not condoning the damage done in Germantown, still remarked that "Germantown is but a poor place though and $200 would probably cover any damage done to it."[12]

For the men entering Fairfax Court House, the evidences of the hastiness of the Confederate departure were everywhere about them. "We found everything just as they left it," wrote a New Hampshire man of Burnside's brigade. "They even left meat cooking in their camps." When Miles's division got within a half mile of the town, his advance brigade, under Davies, ran into the abandoned camp of the 5th Alabama, one of Ewell's regiments that Bonham had warned of the enemy approach. They withdrew just as precipitately as the South Carolinians, but not before six of the Alabamians were taken as prisoners. Upon entering the Confederate camp, men of the 16th New York found "a good dinner, ready prepared." There were caddies of tea, barrels of sugar, "and many articles better suited for a picnic or a party in a summer house than to soldiers in the field." With no time lost in formality, "the boys discussed with relish" the meal so recently in-

herited. And they did so in the presence of the six Alabama prisoners, "who dined with less mirth."[13]

By this time Heintzelman, whose movements south of Fairfax
Court House had promised so much, was discovering that the
enemy had just escaped ahead of him. Franklin, proceeding toward Fairfax Court House, eventually came in contact with
Miles's bivouac immediately south of the town, and sent word
back to the general that Bonham had escaped. Willcox, meanwhile, moved to take Fairfax Station, finding there the evidence
of a hasty withdrawal by Ewell. Without resistance, Willcox was
able to push on to Sangster's Station, where Heintzelman joined
him with Howard's brigade that afternoon. Franklin, meanwhile,
turned back to the south toward Fairfax Station. As Heintzelman's division went into bivouac between three and five o'clock
that afternoon, they could see off to the southwest the smoke of
bridges being burned by the retreating Confederates. From here on
the advance would not be so easy.[14]

Undoubtedly McDowell was disappointed. He originally expected that his divisions would converge on Fairfax Court House
around 8 A.M., completely surprising Bonham's brigade. "I do not
suppose anything would have had a greater cheering effect upon
the troops, and perhaps upon the country, than the capture of
that brigade," he lamented. He blamed Tyler's slow march from
Vienna. Had he moved more quickly and reached Germantown
when he was supposed to, then Bonham would have been
trapped. Charitably, McDowell realized that the real fault lay
with the troops, their constant falling out for water and berries,
and their feet, unaccustomed to long marches. Then, too, there
was more than a reasonable quotient of caution among the high
command. Schenck's debacle at Vienna the month before had put
the fear of masked batteries into all of the Federal officers. To
make matters worse, the almost total lack of cavalry in the army
made reconnaissance a slow, difficult undertaking that further
hampered a steady march.[15]

All this was not to be helped, however. McDowell had to plan
his next move. Surprise was lost to him now; the enemy knew he
was coming and almost certainly they were rallying in Centreville
and behind the fords of Bull Run. Now three of McDowell's divisions were massed almost together in and around Fairfax Court

House, and Heintzelman's was somewhere off to the south, its position now not exactly known to the commanding general.

McDowell wanted to push on to Centreville that evening, or so he reported to Washington, but the men were simply too fatigued. Instead, they bivouacked where they had stopped in the afternoon, Tyler being closest to Centreville, about halfway between it and Germantown. What now seemed clear to him was that he would have to push on in the morning and take Centreville. Tyler should do this. It would maintain the impression that McDowell wanted to advance straight toward Manassas, while he still tried to feel his way around Beauregard's right, south of Manassas, to cut him off from Richmond.

At or around 9 P.M. that evening McDowell called Tyler to his headquarters and ordered him to attack Centreville at first light the next morning, July 18. Then, sometime after midnight, he set out to find and communicate with Heintzelman. He suspected that Heintzelman himself, with Franklin and Howard, was probably at Sangster's Station, though he could not know for sure. Willcox, he believed, was at Fairfax Station, having communicated with Miles earlier in the day. In fact, Willcox was at Sangster's now, and Franklin held the Fairfax Station. First McDowell sent a note to Heintzelman asking him to communicate his positions. But by the next morning McDowell still did not have definite word from his division commander. Shortly after 8 A.M. he set out to find Heintzelman. Together with the general, he wanted to reconnoiter the countryside ahead of Sangster's to find the proper route and river crossings for the anticipated turning movement which should be conducted while Tyler was threatening the Bull Run line. In order to have an expert opinion in choosing Heintzelman's course, McDowell asked Major G. Barnard of his staff to join him. Barnard, an engineer whose advice would be valuable, misunderstood McDowell's intentions and, not realizing that he was needed for the reconnaissance, declined, preferring to accompany Tyler's advance on Centreville. Inexplicably, McDowell did not order Barnard to accompany him, and thus he would make the examination of the ground before Heintzelman without the expert assistance so necessary for operating in unfamiliar country.

It was 11 A.M. when McDowell rode into Sangster's Station and found Heintzelman there. At once they looked over the country between Sangster's and Bull Run and the Occoquan. The result was disheartening. "The roads were too narrow and crooked for so large a body to move over," McDowell discovered, "and the distance around [Beauregard's flank] too great to admit of it with any safety. We would become entangled, and our carriages would block up the way." He was thus forced to abandon on the spot his hope of turning the enemy right. The only alternative, besides diving straight into the center of the Confederate line around Mitchell's or Blackburn's Fords, was now to try to move around by the right, as originally suggested back in Washington by Captain Woodbury. McDowell had seen some of the country through which he would have to move in such an operation, and it was more open and unbroken, more ready for maneuver.

Thus the plan was set. Back in his field headquarters at Fairfax Court House, McDowell issued new marching orders for the army. As soon as the supply wagons caught up with the bivouacs, the men were to draw two days' rations of beef and cook it. If the wagons did not arrive in time, then the division commanders were to purchase the beef from neighborhood farmers, giving money orders for fair market price. Once supplied, Heintzelman was to march to Little Rocky Run where it crossed the Warrenton Turnpike, just less than a mile short of Centreville. Miles was to go directly into Centreville, and Hunter as near to Centreville as he could get. Tyler, of course, was already under orders to take the town. In these new orders, he was further instructed to go beyond that place, staying on the Warrenton Turnpike. Just how far he was to go these general orders did not say. But in a message to Tyler sent just before McDowell went looking for Heintzelman, the commanding general told him that information indicated that he would meet no resistance in advancing on or taking Centreville. "Observe well the roads to Bull Run and to Warrenton," he said. Then he charged Tyler with an order that could not be misunderstood. "Do not bring on an engagement," he wrote, "but keep up the impression that we are moving on Manassas." Tyler was only to make a show of his force, not to commit it.[16]

At this moment, surely the only man in Virginia even less anxious than McDowell for a general engagement on July 18 was Pierre G. T. Beauregard. With Johnston apparently still in the

Shenandoah, with reinforcements still on the way from Richmond, Beauregard did not know how many men he would have to fight a battle when it came. For him, delay, any sort of delay, was a godsend.

Immediately upon receiving word from Mrs. Greenhow that McDowell was beginning his advance, Beauregard ordered Ewell to fall back to Union Mills Ford and burn the Orange & Alexandria bridge nearby. Bonham, of course, already had his orders to remain at Fairfax Court House until the enemy approached, and Cocke was to leave Centreville and retire to cover Island, Ball's, and Lewis's Fords.

Within a few hours, faced with the prospect of being attacked within a few days, Beauregard framed his battle plan. It looked more offensive than defensive. The general was still convinced that McDowell would attack at Mitchell's Ford, where he would face Bonham's South Carolinians. Consequently, he ordered Longstreet to be ready to take position at Blackburn's Ford, to the right of Mitchell's. Under the assumption that the Federals would not think even to reconnoiter Blackburn's, Longstreet was ordered to divide his brigade on the two banks. When he heard firing at Mitchell's, he was to cross his entire brigade to the northern bank and then attack the Federals' exposed left flank and rear as they faced Bonham. Jones, meanwhile, would move to McLean's Ford, cross, and strike for McDowell's flank and rear on the road to Centreville. Ewell was to attack Centreville as soon as he learned that McDowell had followed Bonham out of that place, and Cocke, too, was to attack Centreville. Bonham was expected to push forward once more when the flank attacks had demoralized the enemy, and Early was to act as a reserve. Like all of Beauregard's plans, it was a hastily concocted and ill-conceived notion that depended entirely upon McDowell doing exactly as the Confederate expected him to do.[17]

As day turned into night, Beauregard worked feverishly. To Richmond he wired for more and more reinforcements. He wanted the small brigade under Brigadier General Theophilus H. Holmes, now at Fredericksburg, ordered to him. This would add two regiments and a battery. Richmond also ordered forward the 5th North Carolina to Manassas. The infantry of the Hampton Legion would go by train to join the front, and its cavalry and artillery would follow on a march. The 13th Mississippi was sent on its way, and Beauregard was authorized to appropriate another North Carolina regiment, the 6th, then on its way to join Bee's brigade under Johnston.

Johnston, of course, was the major concern. Beauregard must have the Shenandoah army with him or else be forced to fall back or fight a losing battle. By the midmorning of July 17, as Bonham's outposts at Fairfax Court House were engaged with McDowell's forward elements, Beauregard wired Richmond that "The enemy has assailed my outposts in heavy force. I have fallen back on the line of Bull Run and will make a stand at Mitchell's Ford." Still he was convinced that McDowell would attack Mitchell's. Should the Federals prove overwhelming, then he would retire to the Rappahannock to save his army. He must be joined by Johnston. Finally, sometime on July 17, still with no word of whether or not the Virginian and his army would be coming to Manassas, Beauregard apparently accepted the fact that Johnston would not arrive in time. "I believe this proposed movement of General Johnston is too late," he complained bitterly to Cooper. "Enemy will attack me in force to-morrow morning."[18]

A general order had to be issued to stir the troops to fight their best. The Federals, he declared, "have advanced to subjugate a sovereign, and impose upon a free people an odious Government." McDowell outnumbered him, admittedly, but the enemy could be beaten, and Beauregard relied on his men to do so, and then drive the invaders back to their nests in Washington. "To achieve this, the highest order of coolness, individual intelligence and obedience on the part of each officer and man are essential." The "superior intelligence" of these sons of Dixie should make up for their lack of experience. Much reliance would be placed upon the bayonet, that much-feared implement which often struck terror into the heart of a foe yet which seldom actually touched flesh. Above all, however, the men must hold their fire until ordered to shoot. "Each man should take his aim and never discharge his piece without a distinct object in view."[19]

By evening, with Bonham now in Centreville and facing McDowell on nearly all sides, Beauregard was forced to face the situation and abandon his grandiose plans for an offensive. He ordered Ewell to stand fast at Union Mills Ford, and to com-

municate closely with Jones and Early on his flanks. Still, unwilling entirely to give up the hope of a bold movement, he gave
Ewell the option, "should you in the course of events find it practicable to make a sudden and successful attack on Centreville," of
crossing Bull Run and taking the town. That the idea was as
hasty and impractical as anything Beauregard ever proposed is
borne out by the lack of evidence that he ever informed any of his
other brigade commanders of the discretion given to Ewell.
Should the Virginian decide to move on Centreville, no one else
would be ready to move to his aid. He would be entirely on his
own. As for the Confederates then in Centreville, Bonham's
South Carolinians, this evening Beauregard sent orders for them
to withdraw to Mitchell's Ford during the night.[20]

The last two days had been anxious ones for Bonham and his
command. Bonham, in fact, would have preferred to stand and
fight the enemy at Fairfax Court House, and said so to Beauregard when he met with his brigade commanders there several days
ago. "I had some field works there," Bonham recalled, "& said I
thought we might successfully meet them on that plateau."
Beauregard, however, demurred, instead of outlining his plans for
an offensive which President Davis rejected. Faced with no choice
then but to wait for McDowell to bring the war to them,
Beauregard and Bonham agreed that the South Carolinian would
stand his ground only long enough to slow any enemy advance
and ascertain its strength.[21]

July 16 was, for Bonham's men, a day of constant rumor and
uncertainty, and the tension lasted well into the morning of the
next day. "I shall write to you this morning," a man of the 3d
South Carolina began in a letter to his wife, "wither you will receive it I can not say. . . . Excitement still prevails to such an extent that it amounts to suspense, and such intolerable suspense."
The day before it was rumored in camp that Bonham and his
regimental colonels had held council and selected positions for
every officer and company, even naming the surrounding hills so
there would be no confusion of orders for movements. "The natural impression and general conclusion was that a battle before
the dawn of day was beyond all kind of doubt." The impression
was enhanced late on the sixteenth when the baggage wagons were
brought into camp. Almost every sleeping private awakened to the

bustle, amid gossip that a night attack was expected momentarily. Yet no alarm was sounded, and the men went back to sleep not to be disturbed again until reveille the next morning.

The atmosphere in camp on July 17 was no less charged. "How long will this excitement continue?" Captain Thomas Pitts, an officer, wrote home. Even as he sat writing, events unfolded with alarming rapidity. "Orders have now just been received for each officer to have his trunk packed and be ready at once for any emergency. . . . What the object of this order is I can only surmise." He kept on writing as the baggage wagons were being packed, when a lieutenant walked past and told him that firing had just been heard on the picket line, and that there might be an engagement under way. "Another report has just reached my ears that the Yankees are encamped by the tens of thousands only a few miles away, and will pour down upon us like an earthquake in a few hours. I am satisfied we will have a fight in less than twenty-four hours." He hoped for a victory, and began writing of the need to consult God in the hours ahead, but interruptions continued, and he was forced to close his letter hastily. "Possibly and probably I shall never write you again," Pitts concluded. "God only knows. I must close without ceremony, as I have important business to look after before a battle."[22]

The men were awakened by the long roll and quickly put to packing the wagons, which soon left for Centreville. Breakfast was put on the fire, and then, as the sun's light began to bathe the countryside, the outposts saw a frightening sight. "At sunrise we could see the sun's rays reflected from thousands of Federal bayonets across the fields out on the road from Vienna," recalled one of Kershaw's men. Pitts wrote a few days later that "we could see from the bristling bayonets that there were thousands of them."

Kershaw's 2d South Carolina being out in advance of Fairfax Court House, two of his companies were at once sent forward to harass the Federal advance. Shortly afterward, another company went out to bring in the advance pickets. Meanwhile, Kershaw marched into Fairfax Court House and halted, awaiting the return of his companies once the pickets were safely retrieved. In order to slow the enemy advance, Kershaw had the first two companies draw up in line in front of a fence, with a broad expanse of open field before them. It was no position to receive an attack,

15. (LEFT) Rose Greenhow was imprisoned for her Confederate spy work in Washington, but not before she got valuable information to the South. *Courtesy of the Library of Congress*
16. (ABOVE) General Joseph E. Johnston, peppery leader of the Army of the Shenandoah, and over-all Confederate commander at Manassas. *From* Civil War Times Illustrated *collection*

17. (LEFT) Brigadier General Phillip St. George Cocke, first commander on the "Alexandria Line," and formulator of the basic scheme for the defense of the Confederacy. *Courtesy of the Valentine Museum, Richmond, Va.* 18. (RIGHT) Brigadier General P. G. T. Beauregard, the would-be Napoleon who commanded the Army of the Potomac in the battle. *Courtesy of the National Archives*

19. (ABOVE) Brigadier General Richard S. Ewell, whose brigade held the right flank of the Confederate army. *From* Civil War Times Illustrated *collection* 20. (RIGHT) Brigadier General David R. Jones, commander of one of several brigades that never got into the fight. *Courtesy of the Southern Historical Collection, University of North Carolina at Chapel Hill, North Carolina*

21. (LEFT) Brigadier General James Longstreet, who repulsed Tyler at Blackburn's Ford. *Courtesy of the Library of Congress* 22. (RIGHT) Colonel Jubal A. Early, who led his brigade to the right place at the right time. *From* Civil War Times Illustrated *collection*

23. (LEFT) Colonel Wade Hampton, leader of the remarkable
Hampton Legion, fought himself and his command to pieces early in
the battle. *University of South Carolina Library, Columbia, S. C.*
24. (RIGHT) Lieutenant Colonel J. E .B. Stuart led his cavalry
from the Shenandoah to hold a critical left flank as Johnston hurriedly
forwarded units to the front. *Courtesy of the Library of Congress*

25. (LEFT) Brigadier General Barnard E.
Bee fought with desperation, only to die after
giving life to Jackson's immortal sobriquet.
From Battles and Leaders of the Civil War
26. (ABOVE) Captain John D. Imboden used
his Staunton Artillery to hold the Federals at
bay for several hours until reinforcements
could arrive. *Courtesy of the Library of
Congress*

27. (LEFT) Brigadier General Thomas J. Jackson, the immortal Stonewall. *Courtesy of the Library of Congress* 28. (RIGHT) Brigadier General Edmund Kirby Smith rushed his brigade from their train straight into battle. *Courtesy of the Library of Congress*

29. (LEFT) Colonel Arnold Elzey succeeded the wounded Smith in brigade command, and led his men in the advance that put the Federals to rout. *Courtesy of the Library of Congress* 30. (RIGHT) Colonel Bradley Johnson, whose wife should have been a general, led the 1st Maryland as they turned McDowell's right flank. *From* Civil War Times Illustrated *collection*

but, as one of the South Carolinians on the line surmised, "the idea was that the sight of us would cause the enemy to lose time in forming line of battle for an attack, and time was what was wanted." Lieutenant Colonel J. B. Jones, commanding the two companies, asked a captain for a drink of whiskey, and then addressed the men with the encouraging thought that "we will all be cut to pieces in five minutes."

It was a fact that only the field and company officers had been informed by Bonham that Beauregard had no intention of fighting at Fairfax Court House. Consequently, when Hunter's and Tyler's Federal division came close enough, Bonham gave the order to retire, and Jones and his two companies withdrew, much relieved. "No one seemed at all excited," wrote a man of the 3d South Carolina, "although we could see their lines plainly extending for miles." Many of the soldiers in the ranks sensed that McDowell was trying to get around behind them and cut them off from Manassas.

The column started for Centreville at "common time," the standard march. First they had to pass over the extensive earthworks which they had labored for the past weeks to construct. In the process, the 2d South Carolina had to walk through a trench that faced the advancing Federals. To disguise their numbers, the Palmetto State men stooped low and scurried along the trench, dipping their flags in the hope that they would not be seen at all. Once out of the trench, they continued at common time until Colonel Samuel McGowan rode up in a great excitement. Bonham had ascertained that Tyler was moving toward Germantown to cut off his line of retreat. "Men General Bonham says double quick-double quick march." At once the pace was increased to the double quick, "a full trot," old Edmund Ruffin found, "& nearly as fast as I could run." Kershaw shortly met the regiment in the rear, his own 2d South Carolina. Self-important to a fault, he declared that "Gen. Bonham can give commands to this regiment only thro' me; common time march." And they common-timed once again. Soon afterward Kershaw saw the wisdom of the faster pace, and double-quicked his regiment until it passed Germantown. From here the infantry went back to common time, halting occasionally for rest while Captain Delaware Kempers' Alexandria Light Artillery lobbed shells back at the pursuing Federals. Finally, after a hot, grueling march that almost destroyed the regimental formations, they reached the outskirts of Centreville.

Here the brigade formed in line of battle, but Tyler did not press his pursuit further. "We stopped only a few hours, in order to let the enemy overtake us," wrote Captain Pitts, "the object of which was to deceive them and draw them on." But the Federals did not co-operate. Consequently, Bonham let the men rest at ease. By the score they sought the shade of the trees until nightfall. Then, once again, they formed line of battle. "The moon shined brightly early," wrote Ruffin. At first the men were allowed to lie down to sleep with their arms, but then shortly before midnight they had to rise once more and stand at the ready. Then they saw flare signals atop Captain Alexander's signal tower near Centreville. No one could see the replies, but surely the message received was Beauregard's authorization for Bonham to continue his retreat to Mitchell's Ford.

"Who in that retreat can forget the dark & chilly night at Centreville, where we remained wearied & unrefreshed by even a draught of water, in battle array until One O'clock at night?" wrote Major Emmet Seibels of the 7th South Carolina. Shortly Bonham rode up to the men in person and "with the greatest coolness & quickness" gave the order to resume the retreat. In almost absolute silence, so as not to alert Tyler of their departure, the brigade took the road once more at common time. So weary were they that it took four hours for them to cover the four miles to Mitchell's Ford. It was almost daylight when they marched into the rude earthworks covering the crossing of Bull Run.

"The retreat was managed with comsummate skill," wrote Major Samuel W. Melton of Bonham's staff two days later. It was, he said, "the most admirable thing I ever saw." He and the other officers had been prepared for such a movement for some time, but the men had not, "and took it hard." Some of them came up to their officers before leaving Fairfax Court House and said they would rather die than retreat. When they obeyed the order to withdraw, they did so reluctantly. What the men in the ranks could not know was the effect that their retreat would have on the Federals. A few like Ruffin and Pitts surmised it, though. "These retreats gave them (the enemy) great confidence, and they rushed on sure of victory." Beauregard was counting on taking advantage of just this confident rush.[23]

While Bonham's command bore the major role in offering token resistance to McDowell's advance, Cocke and Ewell played lesser parts. The former remained in position at Centreville until July 17. Then he called in all of his outposts, formed his brigade, and retreated without difficulty down the Warrenton Turnpike to the stone bridge over Bull Run. From this point, Cocke spread his brigade as previously specified by Beauregard, covering the bridge and the three fords immediately below it. Ewell, on the other hand, came much closer to encountering the advancing enemy. The bulk of his brigade had already been ordered back to Union Mills Ford on July 16, but the 5th Alabama remained at Sangster's Station, and at least a part of the 6th Alabama, under Major John B. Gordon, remained on the north side of Bull Run, along with a battalion of Virginia cavalry led by Lieutenant Colonel Walter H. Jenifer. Gordon and his battalion from the 6th Alabama only remained in the Fairfax Station-Sangster's Station area long enough to learn of Heintzelman's approach. Then he took his command back to Union Mills, telling the rest of his regiment there that he had "seen the enemy."

The 5th Alabama remained at Sangster's Station during most of the morning of July 17. At sunrise all but the sentries were asleep, when a shot was fired by one of the pickets. Colonel Robert E. Rodes, a handsome young officer in command of the 5th Alabama, had some sixty men out on picket, and before long they saw what they took to be 2,000 of Heintzelman's men approaching. They fell back to some breastworks and prepared to meet the advancing foe. In the skirmishing, one Alabamian had his ear shot away, while another was hit in the leg. As the fire grew hotter, the Confederates withdrew to a woods nearby and took cover behind the trees. In this position they held off the Federal advance for nearly an hour. "I got behind a large tree," wrote Private J. A. Gardner, "& every time I would stand up I would feel the wind of a ball in my face. The last ball that was fired at me by that Yankee missed my head about an inch & cut the rim of my hat almost entirely off. He happened to see me get behind that tree & tried his best to kill me." Fortunately for Gardner, the Yankee never succeeded.

Finally Rodes had to fall back, doing so without further loss, and shortly he had his regiment safely across Bull Run at Union

Mills Ford, "the strongest position you ever saw," thought Private Gardner. Here Ewell remained for the rest of the day, but in the afternoon his curiosity impelled him to send a reconnaissance back across Bull Run to deduce the enemy's progress and positions. He ordered Second Lieutenant Francis W. Chamberlayne to take twenty men and scout the enemy's advance. "I took the route of our retreat," wrote Chamberlayne, "and found the enemys baggage train . . . had left the main road to U. Mills." He found it on a side road instead. "This was my first realization of the panoply of war; with a field glass I could see distinctly waggon after waggon; occasionally a battery of artillery lined the road fully guarded by infantry on the flanks." He had found what he was sent for. His force being too small to attempt harassment of Heintzelman's supply trains, Chamberlayne returned to make his report to Ewell at nightfall.[24]

And so, by the morning of July 18, Beauregard had his entire army behind Bull Run except for some pickets in advance at the crossings. He now had a line stretching for some six miles, from Union Mills Ford on the right to the stone bridge on the left. Ewell held the right. Jones and his brigade stood above McLean's Ford. Longstreet guarded Blackburn's and Bonham held Mitchell's Ford. Cocke was spread over Island, Ball's, and Lewis's Fords. And a small "demibrigade" of just two regiments recently joined together, the 4th South Carolina and the 1st Louisiana, stood guard over the stone bridge. It had a small company of cavalry with it, and a battery. Its commander was Colonel Nathan G. "Shanks" Evans of South Carolina. Beauregard had placed artillery with each of his brigades. He knew more about the big guns, indeed, than he did about infantry, and his dispositions were sound. Ewell had a four-gun battery on the right, as did Evans on the left. Jones and Longstreet, holding less threatened crossings, had two guns each, while Cocke had a full battery to cover his three fords. But with Bonham at Mitchell's Ford, the Creole placed two full batteries. This was where he still believed McDowell would strike. Here, too, he massed half of his cavalry, ready to follow up a break-through in the enemy advance.[25]

With his dispositions completed, Beauregard faced the morning of July 18 confident that today or tomorrow the main attack would come. Certain, too, was he that he could not withstand the superior numbers arrayed against him. Thus it should have been good news when, that morning, a message came from Richmond informing him that, at last, Johnston had been ordered to make a junction with the army at Manassas. Instead, Beauregard threw the message on the table in his headquarters, disgusted that it had finally come only too late to save him. "It is too late," he told those present, Jordan and Colonel Alexander Chisolm. "McDowell will be on us early tomorrow when we must fight him and sell our lives as dearly as possible." He was certain there was no way he could get word to Johnston of his predicament.

Jordan disagreed. "Let us make the effort," he said. Chisolm volunteered to ride to find Johnston wherever he might be en route to Manassas. While his horse was readied, Beauregard wrote out a hasty message with some proposals for Johnston, and then sent Chisolm on what must have seemed a fool's errand. Johnston was last known to be some fifty miles distant at Winchester. Even if Chisolm should be lucky enough to find him, how could he possibly get his army to Manassas now in time to save Beauregard from disaster?[26]

CHAPTER 7

THE BATTLE OF BLACKBURN'S FORD

At 7 A.M., July 18, Daniel Tyler ordered his division forward toward Centreville, Richardson's brigade in the lead. The general did not expect the town to be occupied, but Richardson proceeded slowly nevertheless. He wanted to avoid any possibility of being surprised. He kept a light battalion of infantry a quarter mile in advance of the rest of the brigade, and in front of them threw out pickets even farther. Immediately behind these advance elements, Richardson moved two twenty-pounder rifled field guns. Then came the rest of the brigade. These West Point-trained artillery officers of the 2d United States Artillery were objects of some curiosity to the volunteers in Richardson's and other brigades. "If there was anything we volunteers early in the war had a great reverence for," wrote a man in Schenck's brigade, "It was a 'regular' officer. We looked on them as superior beings." Thus it came as a shock when these superhumans, as they passed by Colonel McCook of the 1st Ohio and took note of his "surplus of adipose tissue," called out derisively, "Hello, Guts" in rapid succession. "We stood appalled," wrote one disillusioned Ohioan. "If they had been stricken dead, as Uzzah was when he touched the Ark of the Covenant, we should not have been surprised."[1]

The march was a quiet one, and by 9 A.M. Richardson's brigade marched into Centreville virtually without opposition. On all sides the Federals saw evidence of the preparations for defense that Beauregard had built. Earthworks, trenches, even Captain

Alexander's now abandoned signal tower. And everywhere, too, they saw signs of the Confederates' hasty withdrawal of the night before. Tyler allowed the troops to halt and rest for an hour and a half, while he reported the occupation of the town to McDowell and awaited further instructions. At the same time he sent a squadron of cavalry to scour the countryside "to bring to my headquarters any respectable looking citizens" still in the vicinity. From them he hoped to obtain useful intelligence of the enemy's movements.

Within half an hour, six or seven local residents stood before Tyler and told him that Centreville had been evacuated the night before, part of the Confederates—Cocke—retreating to the stone bridge, and the rest—Bonham—toward Blackburn's Ford. Tyler believed what he heard. Since it was ten-thirty, and he still had not received further word from McDowell, he decided to reconnoiter the ground south of Centreville. He was certainly authorized to do this much by the message McDowell had sent at 8:15 A.M. that morning. "Observe well the roads to Bull Run and to Warrenton," it had read. "Do not bring on an engagement, but keep up the impression that we are moving on Manassas." Tyler mounted his horse at around noon, finally, and rode out of town to join Richardson.[2]

Upon entering Centreville and finding no one there, Richardson had marched his brigade through the little hamlet of fieldstone homes and on about a mile out the road leading to Blackburn's Ford. Water was scarce, and the air hot and dusty. Hearing that the Confederates had encamped somewhere on that road, Richardson reasoned that there must be water in or near the old enemy bivouac. He was right. Near a spring, he allowed his brigade to halt and rest. There they lay, "having a nooning," wrote one Michigander, when Tyler arrived. Richardson was just recently married to a strong-willed woman who accompanied his headquarters on the campaign. "Mrs. Richardson had gone up to the command of the brigade at the same time that the Colonel had," quipped one of his men. Even as they lay camped outside Centreville, Mrs. Richardson was seeing to it that the regimental quartermaster of the 2d Michigan was sent on his way back home for the inexcusable offense of tampering with the honey in the beehive she had brought as part of the headquarters baggage. One can only wonder if Richardson himself was not greatly relieved to get away when Tyler proposed that they reconnoiter the road leading to Bull Run.[8]

They took two companies of infantry and a squadron of cavalry led by Captain A. G. Brackett, and rode toward Blackburn's Ford. Tyler reasoned that it could not be more than a mile or so from them. In fact it was two miles, but, thanks to the heavily wooded terrain, their progress was slow and the distance seemed even greater, but eventually, after almost giving up and turning back, word came from an advance scout that he had sighted the ford. Riding ahead, Tyler and Richardson came out of the woods to see Blackburn's and Mitchell's Fords before them in full view. From the edge of the wood, a field stretched gently down to the water's edge. Along both banks, trees and underbrush grew in abundance, while off on the southern side Tyler could see the clear fields again. "We had a very good view of Manassas," said Tyler, though he must have been mistaken, for Manassas Junction was still a good three miles away. In particular, the general was amazed that Beauregard had not placed any substantial troops on this side of Bull Run. "I was perfectly astonished to find they had not occupied that position," he declared, for he believed that it completely controlled both sides of the run. Indeed, "The whole ground there, clear over almost into Manassas, was commanded by that position."

Tyler would tell different stories as to what he saw on the other side of the ford. In less than ten days he would report that all he saw were a Confederate battery, the usual pickets, "but no great body of troops." Years later, however, he claimed that "a rapid examination of the adjacent country convinced me that there was a considerable body of the enemy at Blackburn's Ford concealed by thick woods." The later estimate benefited considerably from hindsight. The former is the more honest. From his vantage point, Tyler could not see that all of Longstreet's brigade lay concealed behind the ford, though Bonham was plainly visible at Mitchell's. And Early's brigade lay behind them in reserve on that supposedly clear plain that allowed visions even of Manassas.

In fact, Tyler was having visions of Manassas, visions that had him crossing Bull Run virtually unopposed and, almost without resistance, moving to capture Manassas Junction before Beauregard could react. The withdrawal of Bonham and Cocke before

Tyler's advance of the previous two days had the desired effect. Tyler now believed that the enemy would only continue to fall back before him. Undeniably the knowledge of the acclaim that would accompany such a feat did not evade the general. He did not much care for McDowell. If he could take Manassas on his own initiative, he would eclipse the upstart.[4]

Tyler did harbor some fears that Beauregard might have a larger force concealed at Blackburn's, and decided to feel out the enemy position and force him to reveal his strength. At once the general ordered the remainder of Richardson's brigade to come forward. Meanwhile he placed the two companies with him out of sight in the woods, while ordering First Lieutenant Samuel N. Benjamin and his section of two twenty-pounders from Battery G, 1st United States Artillery, to place his guns on the crest of the slope overlooking Blackburn's Ford.

Despite Tyler's efforts to conceal his men, however, they were spotted by Longstreet's Confederates, who seemed to retire at the approach of Richardson's two companies. Other than this, however, and what Barnard thought was some movement of troops off in the distance toward Manassas, there was no visual evidence of an immediate enemy response to the Federals' presence. This impression was heightened when Benjamin had his guns in place on the right of the road about a half mile back from the stream, and opened fire. Two or three shots were aimed at the enemy battery across Bull Run, but no answering fire came back. Then Longstreet's two guns, a section of the Washington Artillery, replied. Being smoothbores with a limited range, they found that their projectiles could not reach Benjamin's effectively, and soon discontinued their firing.[5]

During the brief artillery duel, the remainder of Richardson's brigade, along with Battery E, 3d United States Artillery, led by Captain Romeyn B. Ayres and known to most men in both armies as "Sherman's Battery," came up. Until now, these men had enjoyed their "nooning" outside Centreville with nothing to upset their rest. Jerome Robbins of the 2d Michigan noted in his diary that no one really expected "how soon we were to engage in the work of human bloodshed." They watched the artillery under Benjamin and then Ayres go ahead of them toward Blackburn's Ford, and soon they found themselves on the march as well.[6]

Ayres reached the field before the rest of the infantry, and Tyler immediately directed the battery to take position with Benjamin and open fire. At the same time, Richardson took his first two companies and deployed them five hundred yards in advance of the cannon, and then started them forward, pushing aside the few enemy skirmishers encountered between him and Bull Run. Lieutenant Colonel George D. Wells led the skirmishers personally. Before them lay a half mile of ground, some of it wooded, and several small houses which apparently housed a few rebel skirmishers.

Wells promptly led forward his two companies, G and H of the 1st Massachusetts. Almost immediately they met fire from Confederate skirmishers, who nevertheless slowly gave way. Wells sent one company to take a house and barn on his left, which was done without difficulty, but then, when the company proceeded into a small wood, they ran into a company of Confederates dressed in uniforms the same gray color as their own. Lieutenant William H. B. Smith, seeing them, was unsure at first if it was the enemy. "Who *are* you?" he yelled. The rebels yelled back, equally uncertain, "Who are *you?*" Smith's reply, "Massachusetts men," brought an instant enemy volley. An instant later the lieutenant lay dead on the ground.

Wells led his companies onward, picking up a few additions to his command from men who, without orders, had run forward from Centreville to get into the fight. He was heading now for the enemy battery, but first, some distance into the woods, he came upon a dry ravine which ran down toward Bull Run. Once in the ravine, the gray uniforms of the Bay Staters caused some confusion with the 1st Michigan now coming on the field. The newcomers were on the point of firing a volley before the identity of the gray-clad soldiers was ascertained. This business of the multicolored uniforms in both armies was growing dangerous.

Once out of the ravine, Wells brought his companies up on an open slope immediately above the ford, to get an observation of the ground around them. Almost at once he found himself under a terrible fire from what appeared to be three directions. The men tried to take cover and return the enemy fire, but the hidden foe could not be seen. Volley after volley poured forth from across the ford. "We were in the thick of it full fifteen minutes," Wells wrote the next day, "the balls humming like a bee-hive. I am sure

I shall see nothing so close hereafter." It was, he said, "a hot one."[7]

All told, Wells's skirmishers met the enemy alone for nearly an hour before he finally pulled them back to the hill on which Richardson had his artillery. Earlier, Richardson had brought forward the balance of the 1st Massachusetts and the 12th New York. At this point, Tyler decided to send artillery to ferret out the still mostly unseen enemy. He called Captain Ayres to him and ordered two guns taken forward to the skirmish line and, if possible, to a clearing near the stream which would allow a good field of fire. At this moment Captain Fry of McDowell's staff arrived on the field. Either in council with each other or else independently, he and engineer Barnard arrived at the conclusion that Tyler was going beyond his orders. Up until now the Federals had "amused ourselves," said Barnard. Their demonstration had been harmless enough, yet it had revealed some strength in the enemy positions at Blackburn's and Mitchell's Fords, at the same time probably making a sufficient demonstration at the place to accomplish McDowell's goals. Barnard, at least, reminded Tyler of this. "I did all I could to get him to desist," said the engineer, but the general did not listen. Instead, he ordered Richardson to move his brigade forward toward the ford, and sent Ayres's two guns on their way.[8]

Fry, wanting to get a closer look at the enemy—and unable to dissuade Tyler from his attack—accompanied Ayres's guns, which were also escorted by Brackett's cavalry. Forward they swept, through the woods and down as close to the ford as they could get. Tyler thought that Ayres set his pieces just inside the edge of the woods, rather than in the open as ordered, but in either case the effect was the same. Loading his guns with canister—shotgun-like scatter loads of lead balls—Ayres sent several charges across the stream. At once his fire produced the desired result. Several volleys poured forth from the Confederates concealed there. Now Tyler knew the strength and dispositions of the enemy. As for Ayres, one of his guns lost almost all of its horses from the fire, and one officer and several enlisted men were killed or wounded. Without awaiting orders, he limbered the one gun that still had a team, and withdrew it to its original position, at the same time reporting to Tyler. Brackett's cavalry, which had been dismounted, got on their horses and withdrew as well. Ayres then ordered one of his lieutenants to take a fresh team and limber from the guns on the hill and return to the disabled cannon to retrieve it. The rebel fire was still stiff down there, though no longer in the form of volleys. "Just enough to make it interesting for my little detachment," wrote Lieutenant Harry Noyes. He got the gun back to safety.

While Ayres was skirmishing with the enemy, Richardson placed the 12th New York in line on the left of Benjamin's and Ayres's guns on the hill. At this time, Wells and his skirmishers were still advancing, and Richardson now ordered the 12th New York to charge in accordance with instructions received from Tyler. Obviously, the general had decided to go beyond his orders from McDowell.

Richardson then rode toward his right to place the 1st Massachusetts and the 2d and 3d Michigan on the right of the battery. Many of the men in the ranks did not like the way they were drawn up in line in the open. "We were taken out into an open field and formed in line of battle where we made excellent marks for the enemy who commenced firing at us," complained a Michigander. "The bullets whistled musically around us." Another man of the 2d Michigan found that the rebels were beginning to get their range as they stood exposed on the hillside. Cannon balls were just clearing the rim of the hill at about chest height, causing whole regiments to fall down on the ground to avoid being struck. "We did not like the sound of the things," one soldier wrote of the screeching cannon balls. The colonel of the 3d Michigan allowed his regiment to withdraw behind the crest of the hill until they should be ordered forward.[9]

When Ayres's guns were forced back from Bull Run, Tyler finally decided that it was time to halt the engagement. He had more than fulfilled his orders, while the obvious strength of the enemy made it impossible for him to exceed McDowell's instructions further with only one brigade. If he had his whole division in hand, he could still push his way through to Manassas, but all he could do now was to withdraw. Unfortunately, by the time he made this decision, it was too late to keep Richardson from starting the 12th New York forward. Thus, as they advanced, the New Yorkers would be alone without close artillery support, and without Brackett's cavalry out covering their left flank.

"We formed into Battle line by the side of the road," wrote a private of the 12th New York. "We staid there but a few minutes when we . . . was ordered on in advance of the Battery." The regiment passed down the open ground of the slope below the battery, and moved toward the ford. "There were pine under brush very thick, ahead of us and as we had marched into them about 1 or 2 rods, not thinking of danger quite so near, the bushes seemed to be alive with the rebels (judgeing from the firing for we never saw one of them at any time)." The effect was instantaneous. "Their first volley was the most murderous to us." At once the New Yorkers realized that they had run into a strongly placed foe and after the first volley they all fell on their backs in the brush and loaded their rifles. Then they rolled over and fired into the woods across the stream, promptly rolling onto their backs once more to reload. And so they continued for ten or twelve rounds. "After our 6th round our guns were so hot we could not lay a finger on the barrel any where," wrote one of the pinned-down soldiers. One poor man, on pouring the powder down the barrel for his twelfth shot, had it go off in his face from the heat and sparks still smoldering within.[10]

Others back on the hill watched with anxiety. The Michigan men watched as the New Yorkers "went within a very short distance of their battery without seeing it, when there was a heavy volley of grape fired into them without doing them much damage, however, as the range was too high." One Michigander ran down to join the 12th New York in its advance. He thought from the first enemy volley that the Confederates must have 20,000 concealed in the woods, "like so many 'ingins'." After the first fire, he like others, played the same game as the enemy, taking whatever cover was available and firing back at every opportunity. For half an hour or more, the fight along the line of woods on the stream became a bitter brush battle of unseen against unseen, shadow against shadow.[11]

The 1st Massachusetts readied itself to charge in support of the 12th New York, but then they saw the New Yorkers break and start to retreat, at first in some order, but then precipitately. The New Yorkers, as they lay on the ground firing, were told that their colonel, Ezra L. Walrath, had ordered them to retire. In fact, some of the men claimed that Walrath himself was nowhere to be seen along the fighting line. Regardless, as soon as his supposed order was passed along the front, the men began to fall back. "We retreated in order (what there was left of us) about 10 rods," wrote one New Yorker, but others who saw the movement likened it more to a rout. Richardson himself said the regiment fell back "in disorder," while a Bay Stater on the hill said that "without waiting for orders or permission, they broke, and fell back in complete confusion."[12]

This left the left flank of the 1st Massachusetts unprotected, even though two small companies of the 12th New York did valiantly hold out for a time. Soon the Confederates advanced across the stream from their concealed positions and pursued the fleeing New Yorkers. Within minutes they fell on the exposed flank of the 1st Massachusetts and poured in such a hot fire that seven companies had to lie down and let the bullets fly above them. For half an hour they remained in this position, unable to advance or retreat. Once again the rebels went undercover and poured out a heavy fire. "The enemy can't see us and we can't see them being covered by trees," wrote one Bay Stater. They received the enemy fire but could not return it. "Nothing but trees to fire at," complained one.[13]

Over on the right of Richardson's line, the Michigan regiments played the role of involved spectators. "Trees were thick & we could see nothing but could distinctly hear the whistling of the shot & shells," wrote one Michigander. While standing in formation in the heat, several of the men fell out with sunstroke. "The men generally behaved well," thought one, but he noted that they appeared careless, "& would slip out of the ranks to pick black berries when the cannon balls were plowing up the ground around them." Others noted the men off berrying "as though nothing was happening."

Before long, as the 12th New York fell back, the 2d and 3d Michigan came under heavier small-arms fire, and then the men had to take the affair more seriously. Like the Massachusetts regiment on their left, they lay down on the ground to avoid the fire. "The balls whistling around us like hail stones," wrote one; "I cannot compare them to anything else than a lot of Bumble Bees flying by only a great deal faster."

Men pondered their innermost thoughts when faced with this rain of death, and many were surprised at their findings. A few days afterward, John C. Gregg of the 2d Michigan wrote to a friend that "I have heard and read of the feeling of a person in a battle or just as they were going in but I can say that I was not half so excited as I have been before now standing on a runway waiting for a deer to come along when I expected him. I was not scared but what I took the opportunity of picking a few black berries that grew within arm reach of me while we were lying on the ground, the bullets flying in every direction."[14]

When the 12th New York first broke and began falling back, Richardson rushed to his left. "What are you running for?" he cried at them. "There is no enemy here; I cannot see anybody at all. Where is your colonel?"

As the men raced past him they shouted that the regiment was destroyed, and that the retreating forces were the only survivors. As for officers, no one knew where to find any of them, much less Colonel Walrath.

Richardson immediately sent word to Tyler of the 12th's withdrawal. Shortly afterward Tyler came over personally, and now Richardson proposed that he rally what was left of the New York regiment, use it as a support, and charge with his three other regiments to take the Confederates facing them. If Sherman's brigade should reach the field in time, then he could assist such a movement. Together they could "clear out those fellows from the bottom in two hours," said Richardson. Tyler liked his brigade commander. "'Fighting Dick' was one of those soldiers who whenever the enemy was in sight, always wanted to 'hit him,' irrespective of orders," the general would recall. But for now, Richardson had done all that Tyler could allow. He refused to allow the advance, and instead directed Richardson to pull his brigade back behind Benjamin's and Ayres's guns. As for the 12th New York, said Tyler, "let them go." They would eventually rally by themselves.

"Fighting Dick" was hardly pleased with his new orders. He believed that, with the assistance of Sherman, he could have forced the enemy out of Blackburn's Ford. As a result, his disposition turned somewhat ugly. Riding to the 2d Michigan, he spoke to its commander "in a scornful sort of manner," telling him to pull back before the enemy advanced on them. Similar orders went to the other regiments and, marching in perfect order, the line withdrew behind the artillery. Here, once again, the men had to lie on the ground for safety. "We had the pleasure of hearing something that sounded like mighty big bees in the shape of rifle cannon shot," from Benjamin's twenty-pounders. The enemy replied in kind, and for the next half hour the artillery of both sides monopolized the action, neither doing much damage. "The cannon shot whirred over our heads like a shower of bumble bees and struck in the ground a few feet beyond," wrote George Miller of the 3d Michigan. "I used to think it foolishness to dodge a cannon ball but I think the other way now, you can hear a cannon ball quite a while before it gets to you and sometimes you can see them. I saw several that were coming pretty strate for us in time to dodge them."[15]

Richardson's were not the only Federals dodging Confederate cannon balls. Around noon, back in Centreville, the men of Sherman's brigade could hear the firing of cannon off toward Blackburn's Ford. Soon the men were under orders to march to Richardson's assistance. First Tyler had ordered Ayres's battery forward, then he sent Sherman an order to bring up the whole brigade. The colonel put the men on the road at the double-quick and kept up the pace for three miles until they reached the rear of Richardson's position just after the Federals had been ordered back by Tyler. Sherman was appalled. "For the first time in my life I saw cannonballs strike men and crash through the trees and saplings above and around us, and realized the always sickening confusion as one approaches a fight from the rear."[16]

Sherman was forty-one years old this July, an Ohioan of distinguished parentage who was orphaned at an early age. Senator Thomas Ewing and his family brought the boy into their home, and years later Sherman married the senator's daughter. He grew into a handsome young man, and Ewing had no trouble getting him into West Point, where Sherman's roommate was a young Virginian, Thomas Jordan. He graduated sixth in his class, but hardly distinguished himself during his thirteen years of active service. Resigning his commission, he entered the business world in San Francisco, later becoming a lawyer in Kansas. Success eluded him in business, and he turned to the only other thing he knew, the military. He obtained the superintendency of the Louisiana State Seminary of Learning and Military Academy in 1859. Here he was in early 1861 when secession swept the South, and he

THE BATTLE OF BLACKBURN'S FORD   123

resigned rather than be forced to partake of the treason around
him. In May he accepted an appointment as a colonel in the Regular Army, to command the 13th United States Infantry. Then he
came to Washington to join Tyler. He was an unknown quantity.
Just what could be expected of him in this war no one knew, but
he had prophetic notions. On July 16, as the army was moving out
of Alexandria, he had written home that "I still regard this as but
the beginning of a long war."[17]

As soon as Sherman's forward elements came under the enemy
artillery fire, the men began ducking and dodging the shells that
flew through them. "The cannon balls whipped about us on all
sides," wrote a soldier of the 79th New York. The men began to
take cover behind trees and even saplings. "He who had a big, or
even a little tree, behind which to shelter himself, was looked
upon with envy." Sherman rode along his lines, disturbed at the
men leaving formation and ducking here and there. "Keep cool,"
he told them. There was no use ducking the shells that they could
hear, for, by the time the missile was audible, it had already
passed. Just then a large shell or ball crashed through the trees
directly over the colonel's head. Amid the terrible noise of the
passing projectile, Sherman instinctively ducked down close to his
horse's mane. When he raised his head again, it was to see a line
of grinning faces. He broke his usually stern face into a broad
smile. "Well, boys," he said, *you may dodge the big ones.*"[18]

When Sherman's brigade was entirely on the field, Tyler put it
on Richardson's left, and there both brigades sat, with nothing
now to do but dodge the enemy artillery fire. The big guns kept
up their duel until about 4 P.M. Sometime before this, McDowell
himself finally arrived on the field. Barnard and Fry may have
brought their complaints about Tyler's action to him immediately, but, if not, McDowell was already upset enough with Tyler.
As soon as the two met, Tyler proposed that his division could
beat Beauregard by sundown, but McDowell curtly told him that
he did not intend to fight the main battle this day. Tyler had
seriously disrupted his plans, and the commanding general would
not soon forgive him. For the time being, however, they must
combat the most immediate problem raised by Tyler's disregard
of his orders not to get involved in an engagement. Richardson's
brigade had been repulsed by the enemy, and the 12th New York

in particular was stampeded. The effect on army morale could be serious, and McDowell tried to counter it by ordering Tyler to reoccupy the crest of the hill where he began the fight. Placing a brigade here overnight would remove some of the sting of having been forced back earlier. Then McDowell left and rode to Centreville to establish a new headquarters.

Once the general was gone, Tyler apparently ignored his orders entirely, just as he had seemingly ignored McDowell's earlier directions before the fight. Instead of occupying the crest in front of him once more, Tyler put his two brigades on the march back to Centreville. "The men retired sullen & many of them sad from the field," wrote a Michigan private. "I know I felt mad & anxious to try it again." Sherman was plainly disgusted. Tyler's attack was unauthorized so far as he was concerned, and he felt the enemy had gotten the best of it. As for losses, he said, "I have not yet learned the full extent of damage, and as it was a blunder, don't care." In fact, Richardson lost nineteen killed, thirty-eight wounded, and twenty-six wounded and presumed killed or captured. Three-fourths of the loss occurred in the 1st Massachusetts and the 12th New York.[19]

The march back toward Centreville was a quiet one, marked by hundreds of men retrieving from the roadside overcoats, blankets, canteens, knapsacks, and thousands of other articles discarded on the hasty march to Blackburn's Ford. Here and there comrades were found still suffering from the sunstroke that earlier knocked them out of the column. When they finally went into camp just south of the town, it was with weary relief. Richardson was still angry at not being allowed to take the ford, and at the performance of the 12th New York. Worse yet, enemy fire had cut his bridle rein, making the management of his horst a difficult task. But once back in camp his anger cooled. Apparently in front of the men, "His pretty young wife embraced him in a most distracting manner when he returned," wrote one boy in his diary. It had a happy effect, for not long afterward he was sufficiently calmed to tell some of the men that he was quite satisfied with their performance in the fight.[20]

If Richardson was satisfied, how much more so was another brigade commander just a few years his junior. For Brigadier General James Longstreet as well as for Beauregard, the sight of Tyler's retirement brought no little sense of relief. This first test of the Creole's line had come where he expected it would, but it was not made in the strength which he feared. It bought him at least another day to hope for Johnston's arrival.

Inklings of what would happen that day reached the Confederate commander in what was almost a repeat of Bettie Duval's dime novel escapade of a few days before. Early that morning four howitzers of the Washington Artillery of New Orleans, under First Lieutenant Thomas Rosser, limbered and set out for Union Mills Ford. Once there Rosser reported to Ewell, who put him in position on a commanding height with a good view of the country occupied by Heintzelman's troops on the other side of the run. They could see Federal soldiers in the distance getting water from a tank beside the railroad, and Rosser wanted to shell them, but Ewell refused. There was little else to do, then, but let the men rest in the shade.

"While lounging under the trees," wrote one artilleryman, "we were surprised to see riding towards us a little lady." She had a small Confederate banner pinned to her dress. Immediately the Washington Artillerymen jumped to their feet, doffed their caps, and bowed low, startled by the incongruity of seeing so lovely a young lady amid the soldiers and frowning cannon.

"I'm from Fairfax Court-House," she said. "I came around the Yankees, and have information for your commander; who is he?" They told her that Ewell was the man, and Rosser promptly escorted her to the general. "What news she brought we never knew," mused an artilleryman. But Beauregard did, for eventually Rosser brought her to his headquarters near the McLean house, and here she told her story.

Her name was Miss Ford, she said, and she did live in Fairfax Court House. The day before, July 17, some Federal officers took up residence in the home of her parents, and she somehow learned from them that McDowell intended some sort of attack on the Mitchell's-Blackburn's Fords area in the morning. It is true that at about nine o'clock that night McDowell had ordered Tyler to take Centreville on the morrow, but nothing was actually said about going beyond the town until the following morning. Obviously, Miss Ford must have heard the speculation of officers who, knowing of the orders to take Centreville, merely presumed that

Tyler would go on to Bull Run and beyond if the enemy kept falling back.

Claiming that she wished to visit her grandmother, who lived six miles away, Miss Ford got permission to leave Fairfax Court House that night. She walked the distance to her grandmother's, and there got "an old and rough-going horse" which she rode to Union Mills Ford, and thence to Beauregard's headquarters. Once again a romantic heroine had come to save the day.[21]

How much credence Beauregard gave to the girl's story he never said. Indeed, he never even mentioned her intelligence, and why should he? He himself had already declared that the enemy would attack him on July 18, and that the attack would come at Mitchell's Ford. Consequently, on the morning of the appointed day he reinforced Bonham with the greater part of two regiments, later ordering Early to move his brigade into concealment in the woods behind McLean's house.[22]

Bonham's position at Mitchell's was much in the open and would be visible to any Federals on the heights across the run. Blackburn's Ford, however, was far more wooded, and here Longstreet was able to conceal his regiments. The 17th Virginia, Montgomery Corse's regiment, was placed immediately behind the ford. On his left stood the 11th Virginia, and on his right the 1st Virginia. Longstreet placed his section of two guns from the Washington Artillery in open ground some distance behind the ford.[23]

In the morning it was a scene of rest and repose. The men ate a breakfast of crackers and raw bacon (no fires were allowed), and then they sat about reading, playing cards, and napping. Longstreet stayed with the men, sitting on his horse at the ford and talking cheerfully with the men to keep them calm. Here, too, he would receive at once any word from his scouts on the other side about a Federal advance. The men, however, were apprehensive. Some confessed wishing that they were moles, that they might burrow into the ground to safety. "Our hands nervously toying with the hammers of our muskets, each one felt that his final departure was near at hand and busily repented him of his sins," wrote a boy of the 17th Virginia. Some prayed silently, others read their Bibles. One man said the Lord's Prayer to himself over and over seventy-five times, somehow thinking that the more he said it the holier he would become, and therefore that much safer. He threw away his deck of cards, promised to be a good, moral man, never to grumble about menial duties again, go to church, quit smoking, and, if he survived the war, to become a minister and preach the gospel. He even promised to forgive all his enemies, excepting only the scoundrel who, the night before, had stolen his canteen.

As noon approached, and the sun grew hotter, the anxiety of the men lessened somewhat as they began to shed their accouterments and spare clothing to relieve the heat. A few scouts came in with nothing to report. Men fell asleep. The whole line grew lazily silent, the stillness broken only by the buzzing of the beetles on the banks and the hum of the blueflies. Overhead a solitary crow cawed as it flew across the stream.[24]

Longstreet had picket companies from the 1st and 17th Virginia across Bull Run, and just before noon they came in with reports of Tyler's advance. At twelve o'clock all of the pickets crossed over the stream without firing, and shortly afterward the stillness was shattered by the discharge of Benjamin's two twenty-pounders. The first shot struck very close to one of the Washington Artillery's guns and, already under orders to withdraw if enemy artillery should have superior range, the gunners limbered their pieces and retired some distance.

The first Federal shell startled the lounging soldiers on the stream. The noise of that first projectile could not be described adequately. "It was more like the neigh of an excited or frightened horse than anything I can compare it to," wrote a boy of the 11th Virginia; "a kind of 'whicker, whicker, whicker' sound as it swapped ends in the air."[25]

For the next several minutes the Federals continued their artillery fire, and then Wells and his skirmishers moved forward. Confused, Longstreet believed that Tyler was sending three or four thousand against him, and so, apparently, did many of his troops. When Wells reached the bluff overlooking the ford and opened fire, part of the Confederate line broke and began to fall back. Longstreet, sword in hand, personally rode behind the frightened men, giving them the choice of the enemy in front or him in the rear. Since the general was a known quantity and the Federals were not, the frightened soldiers returned to their lines to take their chances with the enemy. Wells was repulsed with apparent ease by less than a regiment, leaving a much surprised Longstreet, who expected a far stiffer fight from the thousands sent against him.

A few minutes later Longstreet received another attack, this time the advance of the 12th New York. He called into line most of his reserve companies and managed to deliver such a galling fire that the New Yorkers were pinned down for some time before retiring. When, at last, the regiment did withdraw in confusion, Longstreet naturally expected that the next attack would be in even greater strength. At once he sent a message to Early at McLean's asking him to bring reinforcements as quickly as possible.[26]

Early and his men saw and heard much during the first hour of the conflict, for their vantage point gave them a good view of the ford. When Longstreet's entreaty came, Early began moving his whole brigade toward the fight, but just then an order came from Beauregard to take just two regiments and two guns. Early at once detached the 7th Louisiana and the 7th Virginia, along with Lieutenant Charles Squires's section of the Washington Artillery, and personally led them forward. As they double-quicked down toward the stream, they passed Beauregard. For some it was their first glimpse of the commanding general. "He was dressed in full Confederate uniform," wrote Squires, "save that he wore a straw hat." Men of the 7th Virginia, as they passed, noted that he was "calm, cool and collected." He spoke to them in low tones, betraying no excitement or anxiety. "Keep cool, men, and fire low," he told them, "shoot them in the legs."[27]

Sometime before he reached Longstreet's line, Early came under fire. His sarcastic vein always prominent, Early turned to one of his colonels and, recalling his own former days as a Unionist, shouted, "What do you think of secession now?" "Oh, the fun has just commenced," replied the colonel. "Well," said Early, "you will get enough of it before it is over."

Before long they began to encounter the wounded passing back from the front line. Longstreet had hoped to have Early join him before the Federals made a third advance, but he did not send for him in time. An attack, weaker than the first one of the 12th New York, was nevertheless repulsed. Then Early's reinforcements

approached. The 7th Louisiana reached the line first, and Longstreet immediately put it in line to relieve the 17th Virginia and
part of the 11th. At the same time, Longstreet called on the entire line to advance across the run and charge the enemy. Unfortunately, the regiments had not been well trained in maneuvers
for passing narrow places, and the actual crossing of the run at
Blackburn's was not more than a few yards wide. Consequently,
the crossing of Longstreet's regiments was slow and difficult.
While the operation was under way, Longstreet asked that the remainder of Early's command be brought up with Longstreet's to
make the crossing. Somehow Early misunderstood the order and
began placing the 7th Virginia in line some small distance behind
the ford. Then a volley from the enemy on the bluffs opposite
threw the 7th Virginia into confusion, and it began to fire without orders. Unfortunately, Longstreet's men were caught right in
the middle of the fire of the Federals and the 7th Virginia. "I
thought to stop the fire by riding in front of his [Early's] line,"
Longstreet recalled, "but found it necessary to dismount and lie
under it till the loads were discharged." Longstreet's horse got
away from him and ran riderless along the lines, causing some to
think that he had been killed.[28]

Early soon had the 7th Virginia under control, and then moved
it down to relieve the position of the 1st Virginia at the ford.
Meanwhile, Longstreet's men who had crossed Bull Run ran into
the left flank of the 1st Massachusetts and without much
difficulty succeeded in disrupting it before they heard the recall
sounded. The 1st Virginia and the 17th served with particular distinction in crossing the stream and routing the enemy. "The
storm of lead and iron passed through our ranks for the first
time," wrote one Virginian, "but the men stood it like they were
used to it all their lives." The 1st Virginia lost its colonel in the
fighting on the north bank, but through the smoke its battleflag
was seen constantly as it pressed Richardson's flank. Here a number of Federal prisoners were taken, and their smoke-blackened
faces gave testimony to the heated battle going on.

Longstreet had ordered the recall, fearing that another Federal
attack would come, and unsure that his men were ready for it
after the confusion caused by Early's misplaced fire. However,
Squires's guns, once in place, had opened a heavy fire on Richard-

son, who was even now being told by Tyler that he could not advance again. As the Federal infantry withdrew and Longstreet's tired troops recrossed the stream, the battle soon reverted once more to an artillery duel between Ayres and Benjamin, and Squires. Sometime later one of the missiles from an enemy gun passed far over its mark and landed in the house in which Beauregard and his staff were just sitting down to dinner. It came "very near destroying some of us," Beauregard's aide, John L. Manning, wrote later that day, "and our dinner spoiled." Beauregard, irritated, sent seven more guns down to Squires's position to return the enemy fire and avenge his lost dinner. After an hour or more, the fire slackened, and soon Longstreet could see Tyler leaving the field for Centreville.[29]

The Confederates were fully as relieved as the Federals that the fight was over. In terms of what battles would be like three years hence, the affair at Blackburn's Ford was not much. In later years it would rank only as a skirmish, hardly requiring a report to be made. But on July 18, 1861, it was a major battle, with numbers engaged only somewhat smaller than at the Battle of Rich Mountain a few days before. Longstreet's brigade numbered 2,500, and Early's 2,600, though not all of the latter were engaged. Richardson's brigade, the only Federals really in the fight, numbered about 3,000. They managed to inflict only minor losses on Longstreet—fifteen killed, fifty-three wounded, and two missing, probably captured. While some small demonstration took place at Mitchell's Ford, there were few, if any, casualties on either side, and no real fighting other than occasional shelling from artillery on both sides of Bull Run.

That evening, while Tyler's men were going into camp near Centreville, Longstreet's and Early's tired Confederates lay down in their positions behind Blackburn's Ford. Around their cookfires they told stories of their exploits earlier that day, showed the bullet holes in their clothing that told of narrow escapes, and bragged as soldiers will do to somehow make amends for the fear felt before the fight. Many thought that they had fought the big fight and that the enemy would come no more. Leveler heads knew better. But the whole Confederate army, from Sudley Springs to Union Mills Ford, took renewed heart from the victory of July 18. They had met and repulsed the enemy. If they could do it once, they could do it again. And if McDowell should advance once more on the morrow, or the day after, there was just the chance that the time bought by the repulse at Blackburn's Ford might be enough for Johnston to come from the Shenandoah. With him and his army at hand, then surely the Federals must be crushed and driven back to Washington. Virginia would be freed from the invaders' heel, and the Confederate States of America would not be just a current phase, but an enduring fact.

CHAPTER 8

SHADOWS IN THE SHENANDOAH

Colonel Alexander R. Chisolm rode like the wind itself. He did not know exactly where Johnston might be, but he knew the general direction to take. As soon as Beauregard had completed his message for Johnston, Chisolm mounted and sped off west along the line of the Manassas Gap Railroad. Taking such a course would, he hoped, lead him directly to Johnston if the Army of the Shenandoah was anywhere along the line on its way to Bull Run.

The first eighteen miles were easy ones for Chisolm, but hard on his horse. When he reached Thoroughfare Gap, where the railroad cut through the Bull Run Mountains, his mount was played out. It was growing dark, and along the road he spied an unattended horse in a farmer's pasture. There was no time for formalities. Chisolm promptly exchanged his horse for the fresh one, changed saddles, and swung back up to continue the ride. On he rode for another fifteen miles. It was getting close to midnight as he approached Manassas Gap itself. There, at the foot of the Blue Ridge, he drew rein at Piedmont Station and was at last rewarded for his grueling escapade. Soldiers were milling about the station. Locomotives stood on the tracks with long trains of cars behind them. And sitting calmly astride his horse was General Joseph E. Johnston.[1]

The last few days had been anxious ones for Johnston. After he fell back from Darkesville to Winchester, the general found that Patterson seemed indisposed to continue his advance. This gave Johnston time, time to organize a fifth brigade for his army, consisting of the 8th, 9th, 10th, and 11th Alabama, and the 19th Mississippi, with one battery. Measles, mumps, dysentery, and other camp diseases constantly sniped at his numbers so that the average effective strength of his regiments did not, he feared, exceed 500. Yet the army grew slowly just the same. The 33d Virginia was now fully organized and joined Jackson's First Brigade. Meanwhile, to command the new Fifth Brigade, Johnston assigned a newly commissioned brigadier, Edmund Kirby Smith of Florida.[2]

Before long, however, word came of Patterson's renewed advance, and Johnston and his army went on the alert. July 16 and 17 came and passed. Yet nothing happened. Reports indicated that, instead of moving toward Winchester, Patterson had turned his force eastward toward Berryville. Johnston's fear now was that the Federals planned to interpose themselves between the Shenandoah and Manassas. Without more definite information, however, Johnston could do nothing but remain in Winchester to await developments.

That afternoon or evening a telegram arrived from Beauregard. "War Department has ordered you to join me," it read; "do so immediately, if possible, and we will crush the enemy." This was fine. Johnston had all along approved of the plan of concentrating against McDowell. But he had no assurance that the War Department had really instructed him to join Beauregard. Certainly no such instructions had been received. He wired back to the Creole asking, "Is the enemy upon you in force?" It was about all he could do.

At about 1 A.M. on the morning of July 18, Johnston received a telegram from Richmond. He was probably expecting it. "General Beauregard is attacked," wrote General Samuel Cooper. "To strike the enemy a decisive blow a junction of all your effective force will be needed. If practicable, make the movement." Now Johnston had his orders.[3]

Half an hour later another telegram came from Beauregard, reiterating his urgent need for assistance. Johnston felt certain now that nothing he could do in the Shenandoah offered such promise for eventual benefit to the Confederacy as his moving to Manassas. The only problem confronting him was what to do about Patterson. He could either try to meet and quickly repulse him, or else try to escape the valley without the Federals knowing of his departure. The latter course seemed the most reasonable to Johnston, and this he adopted. He relied upon an early intelligence report from cavalryman "Jeb" Stuart's scouts after dawn to help with the final decision. When word came from Stuart that Patterson had not moved by 9 A.M., Johnston was ready to move.[4]

That morning, after reveille and breakfast, the Confederates had a brief drill and then lounged around their camps, lulled into laziness by Patterson's sluggish advance. Then, "In an instant a thrill pervaded everything," recalled Bradley Johnson, of the 1st Maryland. "Not a word had been said; not a trumpet sounded, not a drum beat, but every one felt that something had happened." The entire army was surcharged with silent expectation. Johnston called his brigade commanders to him not long after receiving the telegram from Cooper. Young Captain Imboden accompanied his commander, Bee, to the porch of Johnston's headquarters but waited outside while the meeting took place. For an hour or more the meeting went on. Then Bee came outside once more. "I saw he was excited," wrote Imboden. "What is up?" asked the artilleryman. Bee took his arm and as they walked back to their camp he revealed that on the morrow the army would march to join Beauregard.[5]

The men in the ranks, as well as their immediate officers, learned nothing of the import of the bugle calls that brought them to attention. The long roll was sounded, and orders given to prepare to march. Jackson's First Brigade was the first to take the road. Naturally, they expected that they would move north to strike Patterson. Jackson had them strike their tents, roll them up, and then leave them on the ground for the baggage wagons. At noon he put the regiments on the road—south. They marched through Winchester and then turned southeast toward the Blue Ridge. "We were all completely at a loss to comprehend the meaning of our retrograde movement," complained one Virginian.

Jackson marched them fast. "We footed it fast and furious," wrote one weary soldier. Only after they had been on the route for an hour and a half did Jackson stop them briefly. Johnston had anticipated that the seeming retrograde movement might sow dis-

couragement in the men, so he instructed Jackson and the other
brigade commanders, once out of Winchester and beyond all danger of word somehow getting to Patterson, to inform the men of
their mission. "General Beauregard is being attacked by overwhelming forces," read Johnston's announcement. "Every moment now is precious, and the general hopes that his soldiers will
step out and keep closed, for this march is a forced march to save
the country." The men responded with cheers and wild enthusiasm. After a brief rest, Jackson pushed them on until he reached
Millwood, near the Shenandoah River, and here again they rested
and ate a hasty lunch. All along the way ladies had lined the road
to hand the men little delicacies, thanks to Johnston's sending
staff officers ahead of the line of march to clear the way. By dark,
they were crossing the river itself, wading shoulder deep in the
swift waters. The men took off their trousers and carried them
and their rifles above their heads. Once across, they dressed and
began to ascend the road that led them up the slopes of the Blue
Ridge and into Ashby's Gap. Once through it, they trudged down
the other side and into the tiny hamlet of Paris at about 2 A.M.,
July 19. Here Jackson let the brigade halt to sleep for a few hours
while he personally stood the watch.[6]

For the other brigades of Johnston's army, the story was much
the same. One after another they marched out of Winchester,
chafing at their ignorance of what was going on. A few wrote
what they feared might be last letters home. "We have all
prepared for marching," wrote an Alabamian of Bee's brigade,
"and are now ready waiting orders. We are entirely ignorant of
the movement, whether in advance or in retreat." With some prescience, however, he confided to his wife that "I think we will
abandon Winchester and go to Manassas junction."[7]

There was some small rearranging to do with Elzey's and
Smith's brigades. The latter's command, either from incomplete
organization, or else due to slow movement, never really got
going. However, since Johnston had ridden well ahead of the
army to arrange for its transportation at Piedmont Station, and
since Jackson and Bee were on the march with their brigades, this
left Smith the only remaining brigadier in Winchester. Since his
own brigade was not ready to move quickly, Smith stepped in to
oversee and assist in the movement of Elzey's brigade, in effect su-

perseding Elzey in his command. Though no official evidence exists to corroborate the claim, Bradley Johnson believed that Smith had actually been given command of a division consisting of his own and Elzey's brigades.[8]

Elzey's Fourth Brigade marched out of Winchester last, but not before a final bit of drama with the darling of the 1st Maryland, Mrs. Bradley Johnson. She had remained with her husband throughout the past weeks, and now as the regiment marched through the streets of the town, she stood on a balcony of the Taylor House hotel waving her handkerchief as the men passed by. She might also have been taking a final look at the guns and ammunition she procured for them, as well as their somewhat peculiar uniforms. It seems that when she ordered the trousers for them the ladies who cut the cloth cut nothing but right legs, hardly the thing for a regiment of two-legged men. Other tailors righted the wrong. Now, as her husband rode by, posted at the left of his regiment, he could not resist a last farewell. He dismounted and ran up to the balcony for a parting kiss. Mrs. Johnson just happened to have a pint of champagne at hand, and the two of them drank to success in the coming campaign while the men below watched and cheered. That same day she and their son would take a train to Manassas in order to be on hand if needed. The compulsive urge for melodramatics just could not be denied.[9]

Johnston himself reached Piedmont Station well ahead of his troops, probably arriving before midnight. Here he would organize the transportation that would be needed to get his army to Manassas. Not long after he arrived, Colonel Chisolm was introduced to him. The breathless aide gave the general Beauregard's message, then stepped aside to eat a much needed meal and take a rest. Johnston opened the dispatch from Manassas, and read Beauregard's suggestion that he march the Army of the Shenandoah in two columns. One should join him at Manassas by way of the Manassas Gap road, while the other should march over the Bull Run Mountains, north of the railroad, to fall on McDowell's flank and rear at the same time that Beauregard assailed the Federal front. It was a foolish suggestion typical of the Creole's penchant for making plans without any realistic appreciation of the situation at hand. Johnston knew better. "I did not agree to the plan," he said, "because, ordinarily, it is impracticable to direct the movements of troops so distant from each other, by roads so far separated, in such a manner as to combine their action on a field of battle." Instead, Johnston would continue with the original plan to unite both armies entirely at Manassas.[10]

After Chisolm had eaten, Johnston asked him to remain with him to rest through the night, but the colonel insisted upon returning to Beauregard with the news that he had found Johnston and that he was on the way. It would make the Creole's spirits soar. Consequently, Johnston saw him off with the message that his army, or part of it, should begin arriving late on July 19 or early on July 20. Chisolm mounted his "borrowed" horse and rode out once more into the night. The way was torturous, the night black. "I could not see the reins in my hand," he would recall. Having been all day in the saddle without relief, he had to fight sleep every mile by spurring the horse into a gallop whenever he felt himself slipping into unconsciousness. Picking his path back through Thoroughfare Gap was dangerously difficult, but he made it, to have the satisfaction of finding his own horse still in the roadside field with no apparent sign that the farmer there had yet missed his own animal. Once again Chisolm switched his saddle from one mount to another, and was on his way once more. Silently, to himself, he wondered if that ignorant farmer would ever know the part he had played in bringing two great armies together. A few hours later, at 6 A.M., July 19, Chisolm rode into the camps along Bull Run, and up to Beauregard's headquarters. Beauregard was "much surprised to see me." Chisolm would recall, but how much more delighted he was with the news that his aide brought to him. Unless McDowell should attack today, there was every chance that Johnston would be with him tomorrow.[11]

First, however, Johnston had to get his men to Manassas. Jackson aroused his brigade before dawn and marched them the six miles or so to Piedmond Station, arriving at 6 A.M. Here he allowed them to break ranks and prepare their breakfasts, since the cars to take them to Manassas had not all arrived as yet. It was "a vexatious delay," but finally a train of freight and cattle cars pulled into the station and orders to board were given. There was one car better than the others, and a company of the 2d Virginia appropriated it for themselves. One of Jackson's staff ordered

them out, saying this car was for the officers, but the independent
Confederates, "saying they were as good as the officers," refused
to vacate, and nothing more was done about the matter As for
the rest of the brigade, "we packed ourselves like so many pins
and needles."

Before long the train was under way. It moved with painful
slowness, but for good reason. There was only one engine on this
part of the Manassas Gap Railroad. Thus, this locomotive would
have to take Jackson to Manassas, then come back and, brigade
by brigade, move each of the other commands by turn. Any break-
down to this engine could be disastrous for the movement over-all.
Consequently, the train moved at barely more than four miles an
hour. "We slowly jolted the entire day," wrote a Virginian. As
they passed each of the little country station towns along the way,
ladies lined the tracks waving their handkerchiefs and handing up
food and drink as the men slowly passed by. "All were excited to
the highest pitch," wrote a man aboard the train, "expecting, as
most of us did to come shortly in sight of the contending armies &
be just in time to turn the tide."

After almost eight hours on the rails, during which they covered
barely thirty miles, the men on the train could see smoke off in
the distance toward the junction. As they drew closer, they saw no
signs of fighting that day but, instead, began to spy the campfires
of a large army. "Instead of opposing lines we see groups of men
in earnest conversation, and still stranger, we see numbers of men
in Citizens clothes, and even women walking about in the most
quiet manner." When the train pulled to a stop in the station,
the crowd gathered around the cars. From these people Jackson's
Virginians learned that there had been a battle the day before,
and that the enemy had been repulsed. "As we stood and listened
to the glowing accounts of the victory, some little envy was mixed
with our gratification—all our excitement had been for nothing;
all our intended value lost, and they whom we thought to have
the honor of rescuing, have reaped all the glory." For all Jackson's
men knew, the first and last great fight of the war was over, and
they had missed it. Almost dejectedly, they fell out of the train,
formed ranks, and marched some four miles to camp in a pine
thicket. Thirsty, they took their first draught from Bull Run, and
found it "so gritty and muddy that it is as hard to take as a dose

of oil." There followed a collapse as the weary men, after covering almost sixty miles in twenty-eight hours, fell into their blankets for a much overdue sleep. Many wished that they were back in their beloved Shenandoah, for "we believe that the work here is done."[12]

Once it had delivered its human cargo, the train immediately reversed its course and steamed back to Piedmont Station. It arrived after a much faster run than the one to Manassas—this time it carried no load—and was ready for Bartow's Second Brigade men to start boarding the cars by sundown. He got the 7th and 8th Georgia Regiments aboard but did not have room to mount the rest of his brigade, which left the 9th Georgia and the 1st Kentucky stranded for the time being. The reason for the inadequacy of the transportation mystified Johnston, though many of the soldiers suspected that railroad officials were secretly Union sympathizers and were trying to hamper the movement to Manassas. This feeling was heightened when it took the train all night to reach Manassas, not arriving until about 8 A.M., July 20.[13]

This seemed to establish a pattern. Bee's brigade did not reach Piedmont Station until after sundown on July 19. Somehow Johnston got another train in service and had it at the station by midnight, but the conductors and engineers disappeared and were not seen again until the next morning. Consequently, it was well after sunup, July 20, before Bee loaded his men. He, too, could not get his entire brigade aboard. Only the 4th Alabama, the 2d Mississippi, and two companies of the 11th Mississippi found room. The 1st Tennessee and the remainder of the 11th Mississippi would have to wait. This train, however, made good time, perhaps because Johnston and Bee were aboard. They reached Manassas around noon, sending the train back for General Smith, who had been left with the task of getting his own and Elzey's brigades, along with Bee's and Bartow's remnants, on their way to the front. In all, nearly three fifths of Johnston's army was still awaiting transportation at Piedmont Station.[14]

By 10 P.M. Saturday, July 20, when the train returned to Piedmont, Smith's Fifth Brigade had not yet reached the station, but Elzey's had, parts of it arriving on the morning of that day. Thanks to some delays, Smith did not get Elzey's command, along with the 6th North Carolina, aboard until nearly 3 A.M.,

July 21. Obviously fearing that any further wait would make him miss the battle, Smith accompanied Elzey's brigade and, being senior to the Marylander in rank, he effectively took command of the brigade. All through the night they stopped and started as the cranky engine haltingly moved eastward. By dawn they were still miles from Manassas, and now when the engine stopped, a new delay sprang up to bedevil Smith. The men jumped off their cars and spread out on both sides of the track picking blackberries. Smith was curious. "If I had a sword I would cut you down where you stand," he screamed at them. The crowd of men streamed back to the cars, many of them seeing Smith for the first time and not knowing if he would back up his threat. After that they did not straggle away from the train again. As they slowly chugged toward Manassas, the sun rose ever higher in the sky. It was July 21, and few could hope that they would reach the field in time.[15]

One more train did leave Piedmont Station. Apparently it departed shortly before or after Smith's engine, and it carried the 1st Kentucky, the remainder of the 11th Mississippi, and probably the 1st Tennessee. They started out all right, but unexpectedly the engine suffered a collision—with what no one specified—and the cars could go no farther. Immediately the old suspicions of infidelity on the part of railroad officials rose up, and the poor conductor was placed on trial before a military court. He was charged with bribery and intentionally wrecking the train in order to delay the Confederate troops. Found guilty, the unfortunate man was shot summarily. Sometime thereafter the regiments flagged a freight train and started once again for Manassas, but they would arrive even later than Smith, and hope of being in time for the battle was slim.[16]

Johnston had ordered all of his artillery to mass at Piedmont Station under the direction of Colonel William N. Pendleton, his chief of artillery. He would march them overland the thirty miles to Manassas. Yet, by late July 19, he had only three batteries, his own, Jackson's Rockbridge Artillery, and the Wise County Artillery from Bartow's brigade. Rather than wait any longer, Johnston ordered Pendleton to proceed on to Manassas with the batteries at hand, and trust to the others to follow. He left immediately. "The darkness was intense, the road scarcely practicable for four-wheeled carriages, and the weather very bad," wrote Pendleton a

few days later. Everyone was tired. The colonel got guides, however, set out, and was met after midnight by more messages from
Manassas urging him not to lose a moment. He carefully rested
the men and horses every few hours, made a steady pace on the
road, and by 2 P.M., July 20, rolled into Manassas, having covered
thirty miles in about fifteen hours, half of it by darkness. He was
not a little self-satisfied. "This, I may say without vanity, was a
most important performance, requiring as much energy and judgment as any single service of the entire campaign." Lieutenant
Robert F. Beckham, commanding the Culpeper Battery, and Imboden, with his battery, made their own way to Manassas.
Beckham may possibly have accompanied Smith on the last train,
but Imboden went overland the entire way, arriving at 1 A.M. July
21.[17]

This left Stuart and the cavalry. The dashing colonel had felt
for some time that a great battle was coming. "Things are hastening to a crisis," he wrote his wife in June. The movement to join
Beauregard confirmed his feelings. When Johnston began his
movement on July 18, Stuart continued to keep his cavalry out in
advance, acting both as a screen to cloak the brigades marching to
Piedmont Station, and also to watch for any sign that Patterson
might suddenly turn to advance south once more. Once the infantry had gone, Stuart slowly withdrew across the Blue Ridge himself, riding over fields and through ditches to keep from congest-
ing the road. All along the way his horsemen had to keep a sharp
eye out to avoid riding over infantrymen who, exhausted from the
pace, had fallen out of line and collapsed. His own men and
horses suffered from the sleeplessness, bad food, and hurried pace
of the ride. His adjutant suffered a severe attack of dysentery and
had to ask to leave the column for a few hours to rest. Stuart eyed
him suspiciously, apparently thinking the man afraid. "Yes," the
colonel said in giving him permission, "but remember there is
going to be a battle tomorrow."

After a ride of thirty-six hours, Stuart's horsemen reached
Manassas in the evening of July 20, to find abundant rations and
a night's rest awaiting them. They also found "a busy scene of
martial preparation." The troop trains from Piedmont and Richmond were constantly coming and going. Wagons hauling supplies seemed always in motion. And there was a never-ending suc-

cession of self-important orderlies and other noncombatant staff officers "with the pompous gravity of those who believed the cares of the nation rested upon their sleek, well-greased heads."[18]

The armies were almost completely gathered. Holmes had arrived with the 2d Tennessee, and the 1st Arkansas reached the field after a forty-seven-mile march from Fredericksburg. One of the last major additions to the army was the Hampton Legion, whose own trip from Richmond was no mean feat. On July 19, while many of the legionnaires were sitting in their tents, word came that they had orders to leave for Manassas at 5 P.M. "There is a terrible battle being waged," one of the South Carolinians wrote home while waiting for the train. "You'll hear from me again after we've finished the affair at Manassas, or never see me again." They readied their flag, a blood-red field with a silver palmetto and crescent, and its color guard vowed to defend it to the death. "I have a position just under the flag," a boy wrote home, "and woe be to the Yankee who tries to take it from [me] for we've sworn to preserve it, or perish beneath its folds. What a glorious death!"

It was 8 P.M. before the infantry of the Legion was at the Virginia Central depot to board the boxcars that would take them to Manassas. But there was no engine. They had to wait for one to steam down to Richmond from Manassas. It arrived sometime after 10 P.M. and had to unload the wounded that it carried from the fight of July 18. Finally, around midnight, Hampton and his foot soldiers felt the tug of the engine as it slowly pulled them away from the station. The cavalry and artillery contingents of the Legion would have to go overland by road, much to their disappointment. "I cannot get there to take a hand in this fight," Lieutenant Colonel James Griffin, commanding the cavalry, wrote after Hampton steamed toward Manassas. "I doubt not this fight will be settled before we can get there."[19]

Hampton's train moved slowly, with a late night rain making its progress even more plodding. At Hanover Court House, less than fifteen miles from Richmond, the train had to stop while the engineer tinkered with his locomotive. Again they were under way, only to jolt haltingly along another ten miles before stopping at Hanover Junction. By now it was 7 A.M., once again the engineer tinkered, once again it rained. By 11 A.M. they reached

Trevilian's Station, and here the train sidetracked to wait for another train from Manassas to pass by. For hours it did not come,
and meanwhile the country people gathered around the cars. A
quartet sang patriotic songs to entertain the soldiers. It was 4 P.M.
before the train resumed its journey, and all the while Hampton's
men had been without rations. He wired ahead to Gordonsville to
have a dinner waiting for the men when they arrived. But all that
they found were a few women standing on the platform with pies
and cakes to sell to those who had money. This was not a wel-
come for conquering heroes.

At Gordonsville the train switched to the Orange & Alexandria line, and soon it was speeding, for a change, on its way to
Manassas. At half-past two in the morning, July 21, the engine
finally chugged into Manassas Junction. Here Hampton finally
succeeded in feeding his men as he arranged for quantities of
flour, bacon, ham, and coffee to be given out.[20]

Already the Confederate high command had achieved a
significant feat of arms. Making strategic use of railroads for the
first time in the annals of warfare, Beauregard and Johnston, each
outnumbered by the enemy forces in their respective fronts, had
managed to make a concentration to face one of their opponents.
Now the combined armies of the two Confederates numbered
roughly 35,000 to McDowell's 37,000. Essentially the odds were
even. And, with the exception of the late arrival of a few regiments on July 21, the entire operation had been effected within
two days over a distance of some sixty miles. It was a new chapter
in the rules of grand strategy, and one which almost everyone but
the original authors—Lee and Cocke—would claim to have written.

Once together, Johnston and Beauregard had important matters to settle, and almost from the time of their first meeting at
Manassas can be measured the decline of their personal and professional relationship. Two such colossal egos could not peacefully
coexist. The first item of business, predictably, was rank, and
Johnston came armed for this. Shortly after leaving Winchester,
Johnston had wired to Jefferson Davis to determine exactly the
relative position of himself to Beauregard. On the afternoon of his
arrival at Manassas, July 20, he received Davis' reply. Johnston
was a full general in the Confederate Army, said the President.

Beauregard was a brigadier. Johnston would command. Accordingly, that same afternoon Johnston promulgated the following order: "By direction of the President of the Confederate States Genl. Joseph E. Johnston assumes command of the Army of the Potomac."[21]

With that settled, the matter of what to do arose. Beauregard, true to his Napoleonic aspirations, had already planned an offensive based on his supposition that Johnston would follow his suggestion to march by way of the Bull Run Mountains to hit McDowell's flank and rear while the Army of the Potomac struck the enemy front. On the evening of July 19, Beauregard outlined this plan to his brigade commanders and told them, "Now, gentlemen, let to-morrow be their Waterloo." While he was detailing his intentions to them on the shaded lawn in front of McLean's house, an erect, bearded officer strode through the ring of pipe-smoking staff officers who lounged around the generals and colonels. It was Jackson, just arrived from the Shenandoah. Beauregard was much surprised to see Jackson. Was not Johnston marching his army so as to get on McDowell's flank, he asked? Jackson believed not, stating that he thought all of the Shenandoah army was coming to Manassas. Beauregard chose to ignore what Jackson told him, preferring to believe, as usual, that others would do as he expected them to. Johnston would come to strike the exposed Federal flank. Jackson was mistaken.[22]

The appearance of Johnston the next day forced the Creole to do some rethinking. Once the subject of command was out of the way, he took Johnston into his headquarters and described for him the situation of the two armies, as well as going into a detailed explanation of the terrain around Manassas and along Bull Run. This done, the generals turned to new strategic considerations. "I had come impressed with the opinion that it was necessary to attack the enemy next morning," wrote Johnston, fearful that any delay would allow Patterson to reach the field. Beauregard agreed, and then spread before them an inadequate map of the area which showed roads and watercourses but gave no idea of elevations. The positions of the Federal and Confederate brigades were approximately shown thereon, though not the dispositions of Johnston's newly arrived brigades. Beauregard pointed out the several roads crossing Bull Run which converged on Centreville, and proposed that at dawn all of his brigades should cross the stream and move against McDowell's camps. Bonham and Cocke were to march straight to the attack. Ewell would cross and wait in reserve. Jones and Early would do the same, being ready also to cut off Federal retreat via Fairfax Court House. Longstreet and Jackson would do likewise. Bee and Stuart would remain in reserve. Bartow and Elzey, who had not arrived as yet, did not figure in the battle. Without hesitation, Johnston approved the plan, then told Beauregard to promulgate the order of battle to the brigade commanders. Copies of the document should be prepared and brought to Johnston for signing, so that they could be put in the hands of the proper persons that evening. The battle would take place on the morrow, and now Johnston retired for a much needed rest.[23]

While Johnston slept, Beauregard set his adjutant, Jordan, to work making out copies of the battle order, while he personally saw to the placement of Johnston's brigades and the other reinforcements. He put Holmes's small brigade on the far right, immediately behind Ewell. Early was moved to the rear of Jones's position at McLean's Ford. Bee and Bartow were placed just behind and supporting Longstreet at Blackburn's Ford, while Jackson went into camp at the rear of Bonham's spot at Mitchell's Ford. In essence, all of Johnston's army then on the field was concentrated on the plateau around and behind the McLean house. Each brigade was in a good position to support any of the three fords in this bend of the stream. Meanwhile, Cocke stayed in position covering the three fords up Bull Run from Mitchell's, and Nathan Evans and his small brigade stayed in place at the stone bridge. Beauregard placed Stuart's cavalry, when it arrived, on the level ground well back of and in between Bonham's and Cocke's brigades.[24]

It was not a very good arrangement of the numbers at his command. The real might of Beauregard's army—or Johnston's, now—was on the right half of this six-mile-long line. Only one and a half brigades—of Cocke and Evans—took the task of holding three miles of the banks of Bull Run, including three fords and the best crossing on the entire stream, the stone bridge. The Run was shallower along their front, the banks less steep, and in all this was by far the most logical side on which to expect McDowell to attempt a crossing. Meanwhile, defending the lower three miles of the line, Beauregard placed nine brigades all told, seven of them to protect a mile-and-a-half stretch of Bull Run which had already proved itself highly defensible against the Federals on July 18. Yet Beauregard would not be swayed from his conviction that he knew as much about McDowell's intentions as McDowell. The enemy would attack Mitchell's Ford, and that was that. Beauregard would have two thirds of his army there to meet him.

But of course, Beauregard intended to attack first, yet here, too, his planning was faulty. The order for battle, laboriously being copied by Jordan, was ill conceived and abominably phrased. No more ambiguous or confusing battle plan would come forth from this war. At first he referred to the various combat groups as brigades. Later in the document he makes reference to two-brigade divisions, without saying who would command such divisions. There was no division organization within the army at this time, unless one considers the supposed division of Edmund Kirby Smith, neither of whose brigades was on the field. Later on, without actually using the word "corps," Beauregard implied that the army would ultimately move in two corps, consisting of several of these undesignated divisions, and that one of them would be commanded by Holmes. That general was never advised of his contemplated command, nor was a commander for the other corps specified.

The actual instructions for the army—brigades, divisions, or corps were couched in terrible language. A typical injunction to a brigade commander was for his command to "march via McLean's Ford to place itself in position of attack upon the enemy on or about the Union Mills and Centreville road. It will be held in readiness either to support the attack upon Centreville or to move in the direction of Fairfax Station, according to circumstances, with its right flank towards the left of Ewell's command, more or less distant, according to the nature of the country and attack." In essence, the brigade commander—in this case Jones—was to cross at McLean's Ford, then sit there and wait for the turn of events and decide at that time what to do. It was not exactly a Napoleonic battle directive. Worse yet, the orders for all but Cocke's and Bonham's brigades were virtually the same. And in every case, the directive stated that "The order to advance will be given by the commander-in-chief." Well, the general-in-chief on this field was Johnston, yet not everyone knew it as of sundown July 20. Furthermore, when the battle order was written, Beauregard signed it, which seemed to indicate that he would be giving the orders. But what about Johnston's brigades to whom he was the general-in-chief? Then, too, no time was set for the attack. Elzey's brigade was included in the order, though he had not yet arrived as of midnight July 20. And finally, the whole plan called for a sacrifice of all the advantages gained by Johnston's junction with the Army of the Potomac. By this move the Confederates had achieved a numerical equality with the enemy, and with their excellent defensive positions behind Bull Run and their superiority in cavalry and number of field guns, the advantage definitely lay with the South. Beauregard could let McDowell waste himself by attacking well-manned defenses. Now, however, Beauregard proposed to abandon those defenses and advance. That was bad enough. Yet he also proposed to attack McDowell's entire army gathered in and around Centreville with just two brigades of his own, Cocke and Bonham. The rest would act as supports, or reserves, or would simply cross Bull Run and wait to see what happened. From every point of view, the plan was simply impossible. Of course, this early in a war being fought mostly by men who had never led more than a company in battle before, it was unjust to expect fully mature battle orders before the generals gained experience in leading armies. But from one of Beauregard's education and experience—not to mention his pretensions—this battle order was a great disappointment.[25]

It was 4:30 A.M. on the morning of July 21 when Beauregard awoke Johnston to have him sign copies of the battle order. Johnston immediately noted that the order was already signed by Beauregard, making it appear that these orders were being promulgated at the Creole's direction rather than by Johnston, the commanding general. Regardless, Johnston signed the copies handed to him, noting that these were copies only for his own brigades, the explanation being that Beauregard wanted no confusion in the minds of Jackson, Bartow, Bee, and hopefully Elzey, about this being an authorized order. Rather than argue the point and waste precious time in the last hours before the attack was to commence, Johnston signed. Soon copies were dispatched via a motley group of ex officio couriers who attached themselves to Beauregard's headquarters. It was hoped that the brigade commanders would receive them. And then Johnston and Beauregard, Bee, Bartow, Jackson, and all the rest awaited the coming of the dawn.[26]

That same sunrise was important to many others of a different persuasion as well. There had been four armies in northern Virginia a few days ago. Now there were only three, thanks to the junction of Johnston and Beauregard. The two other armies would never be quite the same as a result of it.

Poor Patterson is easily dispensed with. On July 16, as he said he would, he made a reconnaissance from his new position at Bunker Hill. A small body of infantry and cavalry moved south a few miles toward Winchester, soon encountering Stuart's cavalry outposts. The Federals drove them back, and then met obstructions across the road. Here they halted, having made a demonstration as Patterson ordered. He knew that McDowell was marching on Manassas this day, and this demonstration was intended to make Johnston fear that an attack was coming on the morrow. Somehow Patterson expected that McDowell would reach the vicinity of Beauregard's army in one day's march and be ready to fight his battle on July 17. Thus, if Johnston, too, feared he would be attacked on July 17, he would be in no position to leave the Shenandoah and move to join Beauregard.

The demonstration, of course, did not work. Instead, it was Patterson who soon turned fearful. By now he was convinced that Johnston had 42,000 soldiers in Winchester and some sixty pieces of artillery! Patterson was losing his heart in the campaign the closer he came to actually closing with the enemy. All the brave talk of the preceding weeks dissolved in the face of his willing—almost joyful—acceptance of each new exaggerated account of the enemy strength. Still, he ordered an advance toward Winchester by the entire army to commence on July 17, when McDowell was supposedly battering Beauregard.

But then Patterson's weakness came to the forefront again, and he allowed members of his staff to persuade him not to move on Winchester. They preyed upon his fears of Johnston's superior numbers. And besides, they said, with McDowell trouncing Beauregard at Manassas on July 17—as Patterson expected—it was impossible for Johnston to get there in time now. Therefore, their object of keeping him in the Shenandoah was already accomplished. Why risk fighting? In addition, the officers raised once more the idea of advancing east to Charlestown instead. From this position, close to Harpers Ferry, they would be able to move to Washington or strike Johnston. Then, too, Patterson was continually worried by the expected expiration of the enlistments of some of his troops. All of his Pennsylvania regiments' term of service would expire within the next week. He did not feel he could depend upon them in a fight, and here, at least, he was probably right.

All of these factors easily persuaded this eminently persuadable man to abandon his advance on Winchester and to turn toward Charlestown instead. At midnight the orders were promulgated, and within hours the column was on its way. With the sunrise, Patterson's men could see thin columns of smoke rising in the distance over Winchester. Could it mean that Johnston was evacuating? If so, it did not matter. Patterson was going to Charlestown, and by late that afternoon his army had occupied the place without opposition.

That night a message arrived from General Scott, an impatient General Scott. He had heard nothing from Patterson for three days, but gathered from the press that the army had advanced. "Do not let the enemy amuse and delay you with a small force in front whilst he reinforces the junction with his main body," Scott warned. Patterson was perturbed. It was apparent from the telegram that Scott was still expecting Patterson to be moving on Winchester. It was also apparent that McDowell, who, Scott said, had just passed Fairfax Court House that day, could not possibly meet Beauregard for another day. Yet Patterson's move to Charlestown had effectively put his army seven miles farther from Johnston's than the day before. This could give the Confederate an extra advantage in slipping away from him. The memory of those columns of smoke over Winchester came back to haunt the general.

Patterson asked one of his staff for his interpretation of Scott's telegram. "I look upon that dispatch as a positive order from General Scott to attack Johnston wherever you can find him," was the reply; "and if you do not do it, I think, you will be a ruined man."

Furthermore, the officer continued, "in the event of a misfortune in front of Washington, the whole blame will be laid to your charge." Patterson thought intently for a few minutes, then declared that "I will advance to-morrow." His staff officer, aware of how such firm resolutions had dissolved in the past, urged that he hoped the general would not allow anyone to sway him in his decision.[27]

By 9 A.M., July 18, Patterson had orders distributed to his various brigades for the new march to meet Johnston, and at the same time he had informed Scott of his whereabouts. "The enemy has stolen no march upon me," Patterson declared to his chief. "I have kept him actively employed, and by threats and reconnaissance in force, caused him to be reinforced. I have accomplished more in this respect than the General-in-chief asked." At that moment Johnston's Army of the Shenandoah was under orders and readying itself for the march to Piedmont Station. Not long after midnight, after receiving Scott's telegram, Patterson had sent a quick dispatch off to Washington. Johnston was greatly his superior in numbers, he claimed. "Shall I attack?" Probably before receiving Patterson's interrogatory, Scott had further telegraphed that "I have certainly been expecting you to beat the enemy." It is difficult to comprehend what more specific indication of Scott's desires Patterson should require.

Shortly after 9 A.M., Patterson met with his officers to inform them that he had decided to make an advance. But later, fearing that his Pennsylvania troops would not stay with him, the general made a personal appeal to each of the Keystone regiments. He met with disappointing results. The men were tired, hungry, their uniforms in tatters, and their morale low. Their enthusiasm for a fight with the rebels had disappeared in the long series of promised advances and battles which never materialized. They would not serve an hour after their time expired, they told him. Faced with this, Patterson saw no choice but to abandon once more his intention of marching on Winchester. He could not hope for any success with a major portion of his army dissolving. Thus he informed Scott, but still he claimed more success than anyone could have hoped. At 1 P.M., July 18, as Jackson's brigade was marching east toward the Shenandoah, Patterson told Scott that "I have succeeded . . . in keeping General Johnston's force at Winchester." For now, he prepared his army to march back to Harpers Ferry, while sending one of his staff to Washington to explain in person to Scott the reasons for Patterson's actions. On July 20, Patterson finally ascertained that Johnston had, indeed, left Winchester bound for Manassas on July 18. He so informed Washington. It was one of his last telegrams to the War Department. A week later, Robert Patterson was relieved of his command and honorably discharged from the United States Army.

When Patterson's aide, Major William Russell, reached Washington on July 21, he went immediately to see Scott. He showed him a sketch from Patterson showing the formidable defenses believed to be at Winchester, and explained his general's reasons for not attacking the enemy. Scott's agitation was visible. "Why did not General Patterson advance?" he asked. Russell's reply that "General Patterson directed me to say to you that he understood your orders to him were to make demonstrations; to hold Johnston, not to drive him."

Scott was sitting in a swivel chair. He spun in it furiously and glared at the major. "I will sacrifice my commission if my dispatches will bear any such interpretation," he growled. At this point Major Russell had the good sense to excuse himself and ask to return later in the day when the old general had cooled his temper. As for Scott and Patterson, an old friendship of long standing was ended forever.[28]

Of course, Patterson's failure to attack Johnston was only half of the bad news for Scott. The other half was the constant fear, confirmed on July 20, that Johnston might slip away to join Beauregard. The two of them together posed a much feared threat to the third army now operating in northern Virginia, McDowell's.

It is fortunate for McDowell that he did not fully know what was happening west of the Blue Ridge with Patterson, for he faced problems enough of his own. Within the space of a few hours on July 18, his entire plan of action had crumbled. First the reconnaissance of the ground in front of Heintzelman, leading toward Union Mills Ford, revealed that it was unsuited for the turning movement on the left flank that he wanted. Then Tyler's unauthorized engagement at Blackburn's Ford mushroomed into something McDowell had not intended, with the result that the enemy had reinforced that portion of the Bull Run defenses and, presumably, the southern fords as well. A movement by the left flank was now impossible.

That night, after issuing to the army yet another warning against plundering and pillaging rebel property—referring indignantly to the destruction in Fairfax Court House and Germantown—McDowell met with Barnard of his staff to discuss ways to revise the army's movements. McDowell told him that he was now convinced that he would have to move by the right, around Beauregard's left. At last the wagon trains with the army's provisions were coming into their camps. It would take all of the morrow for the men to cook the rations they would need for another march, and so the earliest McDowell could move to cross Bull Run would be July 20. This gave him July 19 to reconnoiter for the best possible crossings. It was raining heavily that night, but the next day McDowell wanted Barnard to ride out personally to examine the roads and the fords, and the ground commanding both. By the evening of July 19, he must have his new plan of advance formulated and ready to execute the next day.[29]

While the men in the ranks began the task of cooking several days' rations the next morning, Barnard left with Captain Woodbury and an escort of cavalry to take a close look at the fords above Blackburn's. In particular they were interested in the stone bridge on the Warrenton Turnpike, and the ford at Sudley Springs. They had information that the bridge was, predictably, heavily guarded by as much as a brigade of infantry and one battery, or at least four guns. Also there were reports that it had been mined in some fashion that it might be destroyed if the Federals tried to cross. As for Sudley Ford, Barnard learned that it was a good crossing, unfortified, and guarded by only a few companies of Confederate infantry. Another good ford was said to exist between Sudley Ford and the stone bridge, while all of Bull Run above Sudley Ford was supposed to be fordable at almost any point. Unfortunately, Barnard did not know of any roads that connected with these fords from Centreville.

As he and his party rode out on July 19, Barnard first met an enemy patrol, but not before he tested out a rumor. He had heard that a short distance after the Warrenton road crossed Cub Run, a mile west of Centreville, a smaller road branched off to the right, and that by following this road and crossing some private grounds, one might eventually reach Sudley Ford and the other fords. Barnard believed he had found this to be so, and then encountered the Confederate patrol. At once, not wishing to attract attention, he retraced his steps to Centreville. Since Barnard did not actually follow the path all the way to the fords, McDowell tried to send out two more night reconnaissances just to make sure, but both encountered substantial numbers of Confederates on the east side of Bull Run and had to turn back.[30]

While this was going on, the men in the camps at Centreville rejoiced in their fresh rations from the supply trains. All day they cooked their corn meal and killed beef from the cattle herd. Once again there was coffee in abundance—drinking too much of it would keep Heintzelman awake much of the night—and the spirits of the hot, hungry men revived considerably, especially after the withdrawal from Blackburn's Ford. Pickets were engaged in desultory firing with Confederate sharpshooters all day and through the night; every now and then a stray shot tore through the air. "It was really dangerous to be about," wrote Heintzelman. He found the combination of long-range rifles and raw volunteers one not to be trusted too highly. To add to the confusion, there seemed to be a phenomenal number of private citizens from Washington in the camps without authorization. Congressmen and senators, businessmen, and even ladies from the capital were following in the wake of the army as it advanced, all wanting to be present to see the first and last battle of the war. By Saturday morning, July 20, the crowd of onlookers swelled to several hundred as they came out from Washington in their buggies, picnic hampers at the ready, many attended by their coachmen. Among them was Secretary of War Simon Cameron, whose brother James was colonel of the 79th New York, the Highlanders. Senator Henry Wilson of Massachusetts came on the field, as did a young congressman from Illinois, John A. Logan, who, unlike most of the others, had not come to watch. He sought out one of the Michigan regiments and determined to fight with it.[31]

Manassas was less than six miles in a direct line from Centreville, and on a quiet day it was not unusual for people in the latter to hear the whistles of trains pulling into the junction. Now the Federals could hear them, and it was only logical to assume that the engines arriving were bringing reinforcements and supplies. During the night of July 18, Sherman thought he heard trains at Manassas, and Israel Richardson would recall that "Friday and Saturday we heard the cars running all night." Franklin heard whistles all through one night, probably the nineteenth, and so did Barnard. Indeed, almost everyone in the army heard it at least once. McDowell, however, assumed an air of calm. Of course trains were coming into Manassas. "I expected that," he said. "I expected they would bring into Manassas every available man they could find." But McDowell did not expect these reinforcements to be coming from Johnston. Patterson was to take care of him. Even when a man came to him and said that "The news is that Johnston has joined Beauregard," McDowell did not believe it. The man heard it from someone else, who heard it from someone else, and so on. "But, great God!" he would say later. "I heard every rumor in the world." So did others. Heintzelman, too, heard a report that Patterson had fallen back and that Johnston was even now coming into Manassas. He began to fear that this delay of a day or two at Centreville would lead to serious consequences.[32]

A new problem arose on July 20. Along with the stifling heat there came the expiration of the enlistments of three of his units. One of them, the 1st Rhode Island, volunteered to remain with the army in active service until the campaign was concluded. Two other units, however, the 4th Pennsylvania and the artillery battery of the 8th New York, refused. Their enlistments expired on July 21, and they would not stay a moment longer. McDowell blamed their action on the repulse at Blackburn's Ford. If Tyler had not suffered a rebuff that injured the army's morale, the expiring units would have stayed to see the battle through. But now there was nothing he could do but allow the two units to prepare to return to Washington the next day.[33]

At noon on July 20, McDowell finally got a report from his engineers that they had found a way to the crossings above the stone bridge. Now that he knew how to direct his marching columns, McDowell gave the order to march at 6 P.M. that evening. He would move his army part of the distance that night, and then cover the remaining few miles in the morning when the men were fresh. The orders reached all of the division commanders, and

Heintzelman, at least, was preparing to obey them when, shortly before the appointed time, McDowell postponed the march until 2:30 A.M., July 21. Burnside and Sherman had objected to the plan of covering the marching distance in two days. Burnside said it would be less tiring on his men to do it all in the morning. "I yielded to it at once," McDowell said of Burnside's objection, "as it was only on account of the men that I wanted to stop." Indeed, Burnside would have preferred not to advance at all. The men were not ready for it, he argued. Even if the Union had to wait several months to train and equip a first-rate army, it would be better than going into a battle with what McDowell had at Centreville. The commanding general listened politely, then went ahead with plans for the advance.[34]

McDowell called a council of all his division and brigade commanders for 8 P.M. that evening. Sherman arrived early at the general's unpretentious headquarters in Centreville and sat down to write a last letter to his wife, using McDowell's table. Soon the commanders were all present, along with a number of the more prominent citizens with the army. The general's tent had no floor, so he spread his inadequate map of the surrounding country on the ground before them and began a careful explanation of the movements he wanted executed on the morrow. He did not ask for opinions, but rather told the officers what he expected them to do. "Tyler," he said, "you hold the lower fords of Bull Run and the Stone Bridge, making proper demonstrations; Miles's division will be behind you at Centreville for a reserve. Hunter, you go over Cub Run along the Warrenton Pike, then take the country road and move up to Sudley Church, or rather to the ford there, turn to the left, cross Bull Run, and move down; when the next ford is reached Heintzelman will cross there and follow you. I hope to seize Gainesville on the Manassas Gap Railroad before Johnston's men get there."

Heintzelman asked a few questions relative to his role in the movement, and then Tyler spoke up. "What force, General, do you think we have to contend with to-morrow?" McDowell's reply was sharp. "You know as well as I do," he said. He was not soon to be ready to forgive Tyler for July 18. Then, if Tyler can be believed, he told the general that "I am as sure as that there is a God in Heaven, you will have to fight Jo. Johnson's Army at

Manassas to-morrow." There were others in the room now convinced that Johnston had joined Beauregard, but McDowell did
not entertain any discussion of the matter. He had to advance on
Manassas. Lincoln, Scott, Washington, and the North would not
have it otherwise.[35]

Tyler was to leave his camps at 2 A.M. the next morning and
head straight for the stone bridge to make his demonstrations
and, if possible, secure the bridge before the reputed mines could
be detonated. Meanwhile, Hunter was to follow in Tyler's wake
until he crossed Cub Run. Then he was to turn off to the right,
follow the route discovered by Barnard, and cross at Sudley Ford.
Then he would turn south and strike the enemy flank probably in
the vicinity of the stone bridge. As for Heintzelman, he was to follow Hunter, after passing through Miles's camps at Centreville.
After turning north beyond Cub Run, Heintzelman was to stop
following Hunter at the point when a path led down to the ford
between the stone bridge and Sudley Ford. He would cross here.
Miles, meanwhile, was to remain at Centreville along with Richardson's brigade to act as a reserve.[36]

McDowell explained his plans while he suffered from a very uncomfortable stomach, probably the result of one of his herculean
performances at the supper table. Still, he devised an excellent
battle plan, certainly better than could be expected of a relative
amateur this early in the war. He had correctly surmised from the
affair at Blackburn's Ford that the enemy's strength was massed
in that sector of the line of Bull Run. Consequently, his flanking
movements by Hunter and Heintzelman bid fair to cross the
stream unopposed, with nothing between two divisions and
Beauregard's flank except Evans' half brigade. The only real flaw
in the proposal lay in the use to be made of Tyler's division. By
demonstrating at the stone bridge, it was to be expected that he
would draw numbers of the Confederates at Mitchell's and Blackburn's north. This would only bring them closer to the crossings
of the other two divisions, and thereby make their mission more
difficult. Better that Tyler should demonstrate at Blackburn's
once more, to hold Beauregard in place. But McDowell had had
his fill of that place on July 18.

McDowell did not invite comment, but some discussion did
take place regarding his orders to begin the movement at 2 A.M.

in order to start the action at daylight. "It is impossible, general, to move an army of regular troops under two hours, and you will take at least that time to move volunteers," Richardson said to Tyler in the hearing of the others. Reveille at midnight might get volunteers into action at dawn, he said, but he was skeptical. His objections were in vain. At 11 P.M. the meeting broke up and the officers retired to get what sleep they could before awaking on the morrow to end the war and march "on to Richmond."[37]

Sherman returned to his tent, perhaps to finish his letter to his wife. "I know tomorrow and next day we shall have hard work," he wrote, "and I will acquit myself as well as I can." Howard was equally serious in the last hours of July 20. "The Lord will take care of us," he wrote home, though he wished the army were not so wicked. Tyler's defeat had been a punishment for that wickedness, he was certain. Perhaps to erase as much wickedness as possible, he had assembled his regiments earlier that day in close order, ordered them to bare their heads, and then "the God of battles was entreated for guidance, for shielding in battle, and for care of those so precious in our far-away homes." He was pleased to note that every soldier in his command seemed thoughtful and reverent that night.[38]

While the council of war went on, the men of the army lay on the ground, resting as best they could. In the manner of all armies in all times, the grapevine intelligence system at Centreville seemed to have McDowell's information almost as soon as he told his generals. At 10 P.M., while the council of war was under way, the rumor swept through the camps that the army would march to battle at 2 A.M. Thus it was hard for many to sleep. Instead, they lay awake, looking up into the heavens. "This is one of the most beautiful nights that the imagination can conceive," wrote one Northerner. "The sky is perfectly clear, the moon is full and bright, and the air as still as if it were not within a few hours to be disturbed by the roar of cannon and the shouts of contending men." A newspaper correspondent rode his horse through the encampments that night and found it "a picture of enchantment." The moonlight cast shadows from the woods which encircled the field, while blazing campfires cast ghostly forms upon the ground and tents. On the far right, the New York Zouaves, the men of the gallant Ellsworth, who had died too soon for the next day's

glory, sang "The Star-Spangled Banner." To the left a regimental
band alternated patriotic songs with operatic airs. "Everything
here is quiet," wrote a correspondent, "save the sounds of the
music and the occasional shout of a soldier, or the lowing of the
cattle, whose dark forms spot the broad meadow in the rear."[39]

There was never again such a night north or south of Bull Run.
It was the twilight of America's innocence.

CHAPTER 9

McDowell's "Victory"

Of course, McDowell's neatly arranged plans went awry almost from the beginning. It was inherent in the inexperience of the army. Tyler sounded the reveille at 2 A.M., but getting the men ready to march took longer than he expected, giving Richardson some measure of satisfaction in his prediction of the night before. It was dark though moonlit, and confusion was easily begun and just as readily spread. Men could not find their places in the line, and the line could not find the road. As a result, it was 3 A.M. before Schenck's brigade, ordered to lead the march, was ready. Behind it, equally confused, formed Sherman, and then Keyes. Battery E, 2d United States Artillery, had been ready to move since 2 A.M., and not long after, Ayres's battery was ready too. There was also a massive thirty-pounder rifle that weighed three tons.[1]

Once under way, Schenck's progress was just as slow and tortuous as his formation for the march. He threw five companies of the 2d Ohio out in advance as skirmishers, a duty that should have been performed by cavalry, had McDowell a sufficient force of mounted men. "We scrambled along through the dense woods and thickets, the darkness so intense that, literally, you could not see your hand before your face," wrote one of the skirmishers. "We had to *feel* our way, keeping up our alignment at right angles with the road, as best we could, by the voice of the next man on the right. We never knew where a fence or a tree was located in front of us, until we ran slap against it." Well before the fight began, many of these Ohioans were bloodied and bruised from their bouts with unseen posts and bushes.

Schenck had barely a half mile to cover just to reach Cub Run, yet it took an hour or more at this pace. A further complication in addition to the darkness was the immense thirty-pounder, "a useless Medusa's head," which had to be hauled and dragged along with the column, its sloth delaying the whole division. Before reaching Cub Run, Schenck had reason to regret the gun, and there he found even more.

First the skirmishers stopped at the run. It was expected that the Confederates would have some earthworks here, or at least that they would have destroyed the flimsy wooden suspension bridge that arched the narrow, precipitously banked stream. The first streaks of gray dawn were already creeping out of the east when the first company of skirmishers crossed the bridge without incident. Just then Colonel McCook rode up and gruffly criticized the drill technique of the men until he was reminded that he was their teacher. He did not further impede their crossing, but here the thirty-pounder took its toll. The officer commanding the artillery, staring at the heavy field gun and the rickety bridge, feared greatly that the weight of the one would prove fatal to the other. The adjacent ford over Cub Run was obstructed, however, and there was no other avenue available. First the lumbering gun had to be gently taken down the steep ravine leading to the bridge. That done, with much breath-holding it was slowly rolled across the span. To everyone's surprise, the bridge did not collapse. Some might have hoped that it would, for now they had to manhandle the gun up the opposite slope. Meanwhile, as the gun usurped the whole road, the regiments behind slowed almost to a standstill.[2]

By now Tyler began fearing that the slowness of Schenck's march would dangerously delay Hunter and Heintzelman from

---

1. *The countryside between Centreville and Manassas Junction is shown in this map, giving the situation of the two armies at dawn, July 21. The Confederate units are still positioned for Beauregard's anticipated offensive, while McDowell's divisions are on the march toward the Bull Run Crossings.*

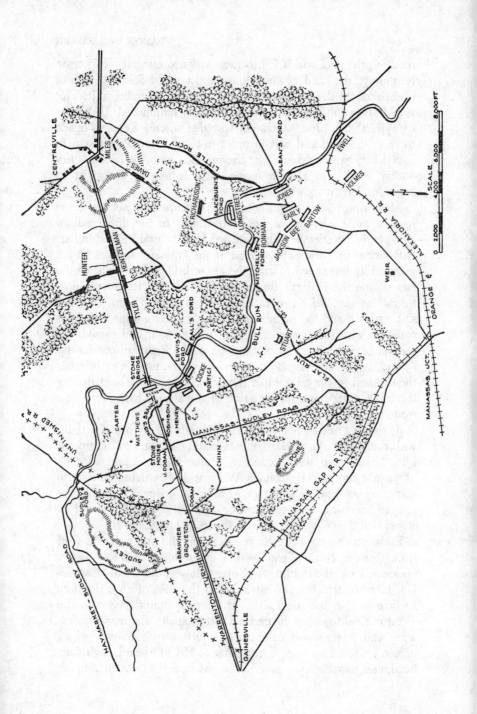

reaching the road which led to their assigned crossings. In person he rode to the head of his column and ordered Schenck to take his brigade off the road and march in the fields parallel to it. This would allow the brigades behind to march unimpeded. Unknown to Tyler at this time, McDowell had also ordered Keyes's brigade to leave the road and halt in order to allow Hunter's division to pass. Keyes turned off just past the junction with the back road to Sudley Ford, and Hunter immediately turned to the right to begin his flank march.[3]

Meanwhile, Schenck pushed on. His skirmishers shortly came upon a small schoolhouse beside the road. In the dim predawn glow, two Confederate pickets dashed from behind it, fired bullets that kicked up little puffs of dust at the Ohioans' feet, and then galloped at full speed toward the stone bridge, less than a mile away. Soon the Federals themselves reached the crest of the gentle incline that led down to the bridge over Bull Run. It was 5 A.M. or later, and the main elements of Schenck's brigade did not come up with the skirmishers until half an hour had passed. He formed his brigade south of the road while Sherman, coming up behind, turned his brigade to the right of the road. The brigades then moved to the crest while the skirmishers went about driving the few Confederates on that side of the stream back across the stone bridge.

Just then a red-haired officer rode rapidly off toward the right, with the enemy skirmishers' bullets kicking up the dirt all around him. "That man must be crazy," some Ohioans said to each other, not recognizing Colonel William T. Sherman. In days to come there would be those who genuinely believed him mad, or else an eccentric. But for now he was only looking for a ford across Bull Run somewhere above the stone bridge.[4]

There was an even greater eccentric on the other side of Bull Run. Colonel Nathan Evans—they called him "Shanks"—had a ferocious look about him. A thirty-seven-year-old South Carolinian, he graduated from West Point in the class of 1848, too late to take part in the Mexican War. He saw minor service in the West until 1861, when he cast his fortunes with the new Confederacy and was given a colonelcy. He was a rude brawler of an officer, insubordinate, gruff, roughhewn. His full beard, high forehead, and piercing eyes gave him a patriarchal aspect despite his grimness, but he was no saint. A Prussian orderly followed him everywhere with a wooden one-gallon drum on his back. Evans called it his "barrelita," and it was always filled with whiskey, of which he was much too fond. Indeed, Shanks was altogether too intemperate in many ways. "If Nathan is the bravest and best General [sic] in the C.S., if not in the world," wrote a man in his headquarters, "he is at the same time about the best drinker, the most eloquent swearer (I should say voluble) and the most magnificent bragger I ever saw." Still, there were those who knew him would rather serve in his command than in any other.[5]

Evans had his skirmishers out across Bull Run all night. With his small command—the 4th South Carolina, the 1st Louisiana, a small squadron of cavalry, and two guns—he could not afford to be surprised. He posted some South Carolinians on the heights north of the stream on the evening of July 20, and there they were the next morning when Schenck advanced. At the first sign of the enemy's approach, Evans' pickets pulled back to warn him, and within minutes he had his small brigade in line. The 4th South Carolina had spent the night on the hillside near the Van Pelt house, Avon, a half mile west of the bridge. Evans at once sent two companies down to the bridge, on either side of it, to act as skirmishers. He moved the remainder of the regiment down across the Warrenton Turnpike, behind the cover of the slope of the Van Pelt hill. The 1st Louisiana, meanwhile, remained behind and somewhat to the left. The effect was that all of Evans' command except his skirmishers was concealed from enemy view.

Around 6 A.M., Colonel J. B. E. Sloan, commanding the 4th South Carolina, thought he saw a Federal ride down toward Bull Run and approach within two hundred yards of the bridge, attempting to plant a flag of some kind. Probably it was Sherman, trying to mark a fording place if he found one. The Confederate riflemen fired briskly and soon drove the lone horseman back to cover. But then, a few minutes later, a thunderous report from the north side of the stream was heard. The battle was joined.[6]

The loud boom was the sound of Lieutenant Peter C. Hains firing his mammoth thirty-pounder rifle. It was in place behind Tyler's brigades before the rest of the artillery came up, and Hains was ordered to fire immediately three successive rounds. It was more than a bombardment. It was Tyler's agreed upon signal to

McDowell that he was in position and beginning his demonstration. Now, according to plan, Hunter and Heintzelman could begin their crossing at the fords above the bridge while Evans was kept occupied.[7]

But Evans did not play as expected. While Hains kept up his fire, and the other Federal artillery came into place and opened up, no reply was forthcoming from across the stream. The canny Confederate refused to reveal the positions either of his two fieldpieces or of his infantry. By so doing he very successfully kept from Tyler any inkling of just how small his miniature brigade was. Instead, he kept the two companies of the 4th South Carolina spread across his entire front, and allowed them to engage Tyler's skirmishers for almost an hour without anything decisive taking place. Eventually Evans allowed Major Clark Leftwich of Latham's battery to open fire in response to the enemy artillery, but still he kept his infantry concealed. He was surprised that Tyler did not make a more forceful move to cross the bridge and attack.[8]

If Sherman could have had his way, he would have attacked, for he had found a fording place where the stream could be crossed with much more safety than at the exposed and narrow bridge. The Confederates showed it to him. While the artillery was firing, and while he was still looking along the stream for a ford, two mounted Confederates rode down to the opposite bank and actually pushed their horses out into the stream and across to the other side. One of them had a gun in his hand. He waved it and yelled at Sherman, "You d—d black abolitionists, come on." Sherman allowed a few of his men to fire on them, to no effect, but he profited much from the incident. The ill-advised bit of Confederate braggadocio had shown him where horses could wade the stream, and where a horse could cross so could a man. Sherman had his ford, if only he could use it.[9]

By about 7:30 A.M., what Sherman and Schenck already knew, Evans had surmised. "I perceived that it was not the intention of

---

2. *The Confederate situation is still basically unchanged by 7:30 A.M., as Tyler approaches the stone bridge and firing begins. Beauregard commands Bee and Jackson to move toward his right to support the undermanned Evans.*

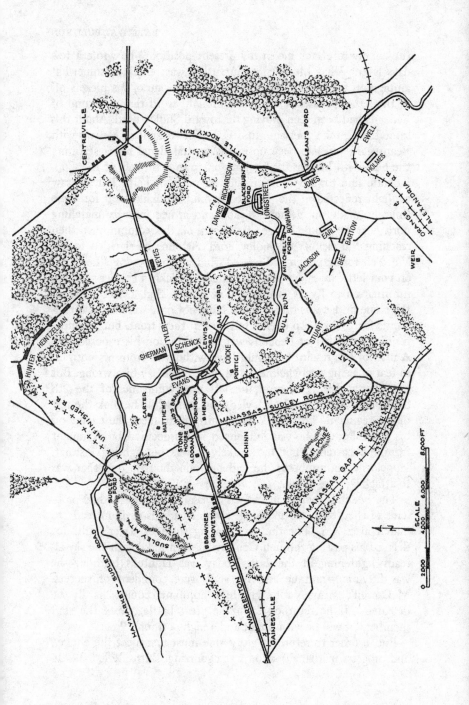

CENTREVILLE

LITTLE ROCKY RUN

ROCKY RUN

EWELL

HOLMES

DAVIES RICHARDSON

BLACKBURN'S FORD

MCLEAN'S FORD

JONES

LONGSTREET

ORANGE & ALEXANDRIA R.R.

KEYES

MITCHELL'S FORD

BONHAM

EARLY

BARTOW

WEIR

JACKSON

BEE

BULL RUN

HUNTER

HEINTZELMAN

SHERMAN

SCHENCK

LEWIS'S FORD

BALL'S FORD

STUART

FLAT RUN

TYLER

UNFINISHED R.R.

CARTER

COCKE

PORTICI

EVANS

MATTHEWS

LEWIS'S BRANCH

ROBINSON

HENRY

MANASSAS - SUDLEY ROAD

STONE HOUSE

J. DOGAN

CHINN

COGAN

MT. POHICK

SUDLEY FORD

SUDLEY MTN.

BRAWNER

GROVETON

MANASSAS GAP R.R.

HAYMARKET - SUDLEY ROAD

WARRENTON TURNPIKE

GAINESVILLE

SCALE

0   2,000   4,000   6,000   8,000 FT

the enemy to attack me in my present position," he wrote a few
days later. What the enemy's intention was remained somewhat
ambiguous for perhaps another hour. Then one of his pickets off
to the left with the 1st Louisiana brought word that a column of
Federals had been seen moving off toward Sudley Ford. About this
same time came a message from E. Porter Alexander. He was with
Beauregard and had been up in the central signal tower scanning
the field with his glasses. Looking off toward the left of the Confederate line toward the signal tower on Van Pelt's hill, he saw
sunlight reflected in the distance beyond. Looking hard for some
time, he made out a brass cannon and armed infantry marching
north of the stone bridge, the head of the column just then
reaching the vicinity of Sudley Ford. At once he signaled to the
Van Pelt tower, which had missed what was happening. "Look out
on your left," he said, "you are turned." Quickly a courier sped the
information to Evans, who was now certain that Tyler's move at
the stone bridge was only a feint. Now not only were his two regiments faced with two enemy brigades in their front, but an unde-
termined number of Federals were marching on his exposed left.
A man of less resolution would have withdrawn from his position
in fear of being overwhelmed, and none could say him wrong. But
not Shanks Evans. Instead, he left four companies of the 4th
South Carolina to hold off Tyler's division, while he took the rest
of the regiment, with the Louisianians, off to meet the enemy on
his flank. Perhaps he was influenced in his decision by a draught
from the barrelita, but more likely it was his fighting instinct.
Hopelessly outnumbered, he had but one thought, and that was
to attack.[10]

The Federals that Evans hoped to assault had already had problems of their own this morning. Hunter had his division ready to
march at 2 A.M., but the excruciating sloth of Tyler's advance
delayed his passing through Centreville until 4:30, with the sky already lightening in the east. Today was Hunter's birthday—he
was fifty-nine—and he and his staff were confident of success.
McDowell's army, wrote Hunter's adjutant, could "hardly be
defeated." If he returned from the great battle, wrote the staff
member, "it will be with honor and a high position."[11]

But in order to return to glory, one must first meet the enemy,
and progress in that direction was agonizing. Burnside led the di-

vision's advance, only to find the road clogged with backed-up regiments of Tyler's division. It was 5:30 or thereabouts when Tyler's last units cleared Cub Run and opened the way to the flanking road to those behind. Burnside advanced in three columns to save time. One marched on the road, while the others moved on either side. When they reached the suspension bridge over the run, some congestion ensued, made the more irksome by the necessity of having men work constantly to shore up the span to keep it from collapsing under the constant weight of men, animals, and heavy guns. Finally all were across and starting on their way to the right toward Sudley Ford. McDowell stood at the fork in the road, watching as Burnside passed. The general still felt ill, but he was up and directing traffic in the road in an effort to get his stalled advance back on schedule. And at about this same time, he could hear the skirmish firing between Tyler and Evans up ahead of him. There was a sense of urgency in his actions now. He must get Hunter and Heintzelman on their way quickly. If they did not strike soon, he feared that the Confederates might themselves launch an advance by way of Blackburn's Ford. Indeed, to be ready for such an eventuality, he halted Heintzelman's last brigade, Howard's, just as it was ready to follow those before it off to the right. This brigade would serve as a reserve in addition to Miles's division.[12]

For Burnside, leading the way toward Sudley Ford, the going was far more difficult than McDowell or Barnard had imagined. The so-called road was little more than a cart path, and often not even that. The 2d Rhode Island led the way, and with them they brought a wagon filled with shovels, axes, and picks, all of them used to fell trees and dense underbrush, as well as to remove trees dropped across the route by the enemy. Only here and there was a small clearing met to relieve the tedium of fighting their way through the woods. Making matters worse, the sun was up by now and, even though it was yet early in the morning, already the heat was intense, promising to become intolerable by afternoon.

In one of the small clearings Burnside's men came upon a little log house—a "hovel," thought some—with the dirtiest-looking woman some had ever seen occupying it. She told the soldiers that there were more than enough Confederates across the Bull Run to whip all that McDowell could send against them. Proudly she

boasted that her "old man" was one of them. Soon thereafter the
boom of a cannon off to the left told that Tyler was in place. But
Hunter was still three miles or more from Sudley Ford. He must
make all possible speed or the whole movement might fail.[13]

Here, at the worst possible moment, Hunter's guide made a
mistake. When Burnside's advance came to a fork in the road—or
path—to Sudley Ford, the guide chose the right-hand route, even
though that to the left also led to the ford. He ignored the latter
because, he claimed, it would bring the column so close to Bull
Run that it would be spotted some distance before reaching
Sudley Ford. Better to take the other route, which would conceal
their movement from the enemy. What the guide did not say—
and perhaps did not know—was that the route to the right was
three or four miles longer, taking a very roundabout way before it
reached Sudley Ford. Such a route would cause hours of delay to
an advance already much behind schedule, thanks to Tyler's slow
advance. But as no one seemed to know better, Hunter set off on
a long and needless march.

More and more fatigued by the marching, the dust, and the
heat, Hunter's brigades plodded onward. The men became hungry, many fell out for rest on the roadside, some even slept. But
they were soon forced to continue the march. When within about
a mile of Sudley Ford around 8:45, Burnside's advance finally
came out of the woods north of Sudley Ford and began the final
short march through a few cornfields and past some farmhouses
down to the ford itself. As Alexander was spying them through his
field glasses from several miles away, Burnside's dehydrated soldiers and horses drank deeply of Bull Run as they waded across to
the south side. They were the first Federals to set foot on the
Confederate side of the stream, and at this moment McDowell
rode past and shouted for them to hurry. "The enemy is moving
heavy columns from Manassas," he cried. Only a few minutes
later, as the skirmishers of the 1st Rhode Island passed Sudley
Church and moved toward the south, the sound of firing broke
out in the front. Here, at last, the battle was joined.[14]

This was not exactly where Beauregard had planned to be
fighting his battle. Indeed, almost nothing had gone as the young
Napoleon anticipated, except the very first news that morning.
Shortly after 5 A.M. a message arrived from Bonham stating that

the enemy had appeared in his left front at Mitchell's Ford. This is precisely where Beauregard had expected McDowell to attack. The trouble was, the Creole was not expecting the Federals to advance just then. He wanted to launch his own attack, and this news disconcerted him somewhat. There was worse to come.

Before long the firing of skirmishers in the vicinity of the stone bridge could be heard. The Federals were advancing there, too. Apparently McDowell was about to attack in force in at least two points on the left of the Confederate line. Consequently, all the elaborate plans laid the night before for an offensive against McDowell were now obsolete. Beauregard himself faced an imminent assault. What could he do?

Ever the grand strategist, he decided that he still might take the offensive. To Ewell he dispatched a message at 5:30. Ewell was to have his brigade ready to move on Centreville at a moment's notice, providing a diversion to relieve the expected heavy attack on Mitchell's Ford, and perhaps Evans as well. Holmes's small brigade would move to support Ewell, he said. "I intend to take the offensive throughout my front as soon as possible," Beauregard concluded. But he neglected to ensure that Holmes was advised of what he was to do, he apparently did not give Ewell's message to a reliable messenger, he failed to let Longstreet —under orders to cross Bull Run and advance on Centreville— know that Ewell would now make the movement, and all he told Evans and Cocke by messenger was that they were to hold their positions to the death.

Just what happened in the next hour or so is confused, thanks chiefly to the fact that Beauregard was apparently confused, or else someone on his staff was not following his orders properly. Even though McDowell's advance had negated any chance of carrying out the plan of battle that Beauregard had promulgated just a few hours before, no orders went out canceling the plan. Then, around 6 A.M., he sent Jones a directive that Ewell would take the offensive and that Jones was therefore to attack the enemy in his front (in fact, the message was so badly worded that, strictly speaking, it ordered Jones to attack Ewell!).

A later reconstruction of the situation that prevailed now in Beauregard's army pictures it thus: Longstreet, unaware that the earlier plan of attack was canceled, believed he was to cross Bull

Run and attack toward Centreville even though right now his left at Mitchell's Ford was threatened; Ewell was to wait for orders to cross and attack Centreville; Holmes was to assist Ewell, though no orders reached him; Jones was to cross and assist Ewell, having been told that the Virginian was definitely attacking; Cocke and Evans were to stay in place and fight; Early was now directed to move to Bull Run behind Jones and Longstreet to support them if needed.[15]

Imperceptibly, Beauregard was losing control of the battle to come. He tried now to regain it by speeding reinforcements to his endangered left. The enemy was attacking where he was weakest, Evans' flank, and now the general ordered Bee's brigade to hurry to the vicinity of the stone bridge along with as much of Bartow's command as had reached the field. At 7 A.M. he ordered Chisolm to find Jackson and conduct his brigade to the ground between Cocke and Bonham. As a result, though McDowell had not yet begun a major attack, Beauregard had committed his reserves to those points where he *expected* the main blows would fall. Meanwhile, Beauregard himself, accompanied by the now wakened Johnston, rode to the rear of Bonham's position at Mitchell's, expecting that this would put him close to the main action. Here he established his headquarters.

Almost immediately, Beauregard further amended his plans. Now he decided that, instead of merely making a diversion with his brigades on the right, he would launch an all-out attack on Centreville. All of his brigades from Bonham to Ewell would cross and attack. Johnston approved the plan, still reluctant to take over-all command of the battle. At once Beauregard had the new orders drafted and sent on their way, but then, just about 9 A.M., there came a message from Captain Alexander. He had seen the enemy in force crossing at Sudley Ford. The column was over a half mile in length, obviously a division or more. Now Beauregard had once again to abandon a plan. McDowell had stolen a march on him. The Federals were on his side of Bull Run in force, and they were starting to attack his weakest link, Evans' little brigade. An offensive of any sort was out of the question. The Confederates had to defend every piece of ground they could hold until Evans might be reinforced and the enemy advance checked. Forgetting entirely to cancel his attack orders to the brigades on the right half of his line, Beauregard now directed that Bee, Bartow, and Jackson go directly to Evans' aid.[16]

Evans could use all the help he could get. As soon as he decided to leave the stone bridge vicinity with the bulk of his command, he notified Cocke on his right of what he was doing, then double-quicked the men to the left. He intended to strike the enemy advance at the junction of the road from Sudley Ford with the Warrenton road. However, thanks to his speedy movement Evans found that he could go farther and meet Hunter before he reached that junction. Shanks moved his command up onto Matthews Hill, less than a mile south of Sudley Ford, placed the 4th South Carolina on the left, with one of his fieldpieces, and the 1st Louisiana on its right, with the other gun. They were well protected by a grove of trees, and they had a clear field of fire down the slope toward the open road down which Hunter would have to advance. By 9 A.M., or shortly afterward, he was ready, and at 9:15 the advance elements of Burnside's 1st Rhode Island moved out of the woods to the north. At once, Evans opened a heavy fire all along his line.[17]

Hunter had not exactly expected this. He first ordered the 2d Rhode Island and the Rhode Island battery accompanying it to advance to meet the enemy. With a shout, the men plunged through the woods along the road below the ford and out into the open. There the fire from Evans checked Burnside's advance, but Hunter did not authorize him to send up additional regiments. Instead, Hunter ordered the balance of Burnside's regiments placed in line behind the forming battle line to the right of the road. Porter was supposed to pass this line and go into the fray to join the 2d Rhode Island. But instead, Porter's brigade was deployed at first in the rear of Burnside's regiments, leaving the 2d Rhode Island and the battery momentarily on their own.

The Rhode Islanders found Evans' line drawn up between the Warrenton road, on its left, and a house on Matthews Hill, on its right. It seemed a long line, and it deceptively gave an impression of greater strength than it had. Porter believed that the Confederates had no fewer than four batteries on that line, when in fact it was two guns alone. Captain Charles Griffin at once advanced his guns of the 5th United States Artillery to within one thousand yards of the enemy guns and opened fire. Meanwhile, the Rhode

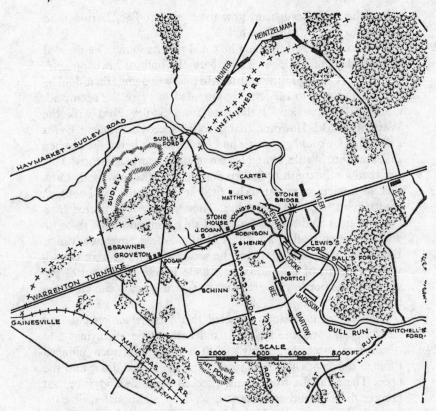

3. *At about* 8:45 A.M., *convinced that Tyler's move on the stone
bridge is a feint, Evans begins moving his men to the left, where reports indicate the enemy is starting to cross at Sudley Ford. Bartow
has joined Jackson and Bee in the race to support the Confederate left.*

Island battery became hotly pressed by enemy fire, and Burnside
had to send back to request assistance. Indeed, the fire had become so intense along the line that Hunter himself was struck,
the first general officer to be wounded in the battle. He received a
severe wound in the left cheek and neck while trying to get his
men to charge with the bayonet. As he was being carried off the
field, he met with Burnside. "I leave the matter in your hands,"
said Hunter, adding that the 2d Rhode Island "went in bravely,

and drove the scoundrels." Then, blood running freely down his neck and over his uniform, Hunter left the field. For him, the battle was over.[18]

In fact, it had not gone well for the Rhode Islanders in the first minutes of battle. Hunter had led the infantry and artillery up the slope of Matthews Hill, only to find the enemy outnumbering them. The infantry was quickly pinned down, the artillery forced to call for help, Hunter was wounded, and the colonel of the 2d Rhode Island, John Slocum, was hit twice and mortally wounded.

Burnside quickly brought the remainder of his brigade into the action. The 1st Rhode Island was the first to reach the front, sustaining several casualties before the 71st New York came on the field. As the fire grew hotter, Burnside's horse was shot from under him. Two guns with the New York regiment went into place on the right of the line and, in tandem with the fieldpieces of the 2d Rhode Island, they concentrated a heavy volume of fire on Latham's two guns in Evans' line. By this time Burnside believed that Evans had at least six regiments of infantry facing him, and certainly two or more full batteries.

While Burnside occupied Evans' right, Porter's brigade came into line to face the Confederate left, two full brigades now deploying to try to stop the attack of one small half brigade. Burnside had been sorely handled by the enemy up to this point, and Porter's arrival came none too soon. Porter, being senior to Burnside, at once assumed over-all command of the division and of this part of the developing battle.

No sooner did Porter take command than an urgent request arrived from Burnside, asking that the battalion of Regular troops of the 14th United States Infantry be sent to his aid. Porter at once sent them, and their commander, Major George Sykes, made a short address to the men before leading them into battle. "It was to the point," recalled one of the Regulars, "and gave us to understand that there would probably be some work for us to do." While Sykes led his men to Burnside, Porter oversaw the final positioning of his brigade on Burnside's right. He had just gotten the 27th New York into position and was sending two more regiments down the Warrenton road when one of Evans' attacks swarmed out of the woods on Matthews Hill and hit the center of the Federal line.[19]

This was the charge of the 1st Louisiana Battalion, led by Major Roberdeau Wheat. Evans had withheld the charge until he thought he detected Burnside's men falling back, probably at the time when Hunter's wounding brought about a momentary command lag. The Louisianians surged forward, the stout Wheat in the very front. Waving their terrifying bowie knives as they charged, some of the Confederates actually threw down their rifles and advanced with the blades only. They growled and yelled so in the charge that they fully justified their sobriquet "Wheat's Tigers." Sometime after the war, this would be altered to "Louisiana Tigers," the name by which Wheat's men would be known to posterity.

The charge hardly had the power to drive Burnside, especially with the reinforcements now coming into line. But it did delay any Federal advance, and that was all that Evans could hope. He was here to buy time. He bought it with the lives of many of the Tigers, and some thought with the life of Wheat himself for a while. In the charge, as he was urging his men forward, he took a wound that certainly looked fatal. A bullet entered his torso just under and forward of the armpit, and coursed through his chest to come out in roughly the corresponding spot on the opposite side. One lung was perforated, perhaps the other as well, and when he was carried back of the lines to the field surgeons, they told him that surely the wound would be fatal. "I don't feel like dying yet," he told them. "But, there is no instance on record of recovery from such a wound," the doctors protested. Their bedside manner was hardly encouraging.

"Well, then," the wounded major said, "I will put my case upon record."[20]

After Wheat's attack was spent and the Louisiana Tigers had returned to their line, the contending forces remained somewhat stationary for a few minutes, gathering their breath for the next act in the drama. Already, with two Federal brigades in line, the Union troops overreached both flanks of Evans' thinly spread position, though they showed no disposition to advance. Federal artillery had by now nearly silenced Latham's guns, however. It was obvious to Shanks Evans that he could not hold his line more than a few minutes longer, particularly since there was word of heavy Federal reinforcements on the way. But just now, around 10

A.M., or later, Evans learned that Bee's brigade was arriving in rear of his position. It could not have come at a more propitious moment. Bee moved forward at once, passed through Evans' line and into the engagement at once, allowing Evans' beleaguered troops a brief rest.

This movement of Bee's was a sign of great promise. Early that morning he had his orders to go to the vicinity of the stone bridge, and he left around 7 A.M., immediately after breakfasting his command. He took the 4th Alabama and the 2d Mississippi, along with the two companies of the 11th Mississippi that had reached the vicinity from the Shenandoah. The men shouldered their knapsacks and marched at the double-quick toward the sound of the firing at the stone bridge. They covered four miles, nearly reaching the bridge when Bee learned that Evans was being hotly pressed on the left. Without asking for or awaiting orders— Beauregard did send them at roughly this same moment—Bee changed his direction of march toward the left. Two more miles at double-quick brought the command up with Evans. The heat of the day and the scarcity of water along the road had already taken its toll in his column. "The men arrived on the battle-field much exhausted," complained a captain of the 4th Alabama.

Bee began the day in a furious mood. When he learned that Jackson and Bartow were to remain in reserve behind Blackburn's and Mitchell's crossings, while he was being sent to the stone bridge, he believed that they would see all the real action while he sat idle with Evans. "Bee was a fighter," wrote Captain John D. Imboden, commanding Bee's artillery. "His anger was due to chagrin at being sent away from where he thought the heavy fighting would take place." Bee ordered Imboden and his battery to accompany him. When the artillerist protested that his men had not eaten breakfast yet, Bee first angrily ordered him to obey, and then in a resigned tone added that there would be plenty of time to cook and eat while they sat out the battle listening to the sound of the guns elsewhere.

Imboden mounted and moved out toward the stone bridge, but after some distance he met a courier riding furiously and shouting that the whole Yankee army was attacking from the direction of Sudley Ford. Imboden halted his battery and personally rode ahead to the crest of a hill. From it he could see in the distance the Federal column to the north on the far side of Bull Run. Looking back, he could see Bee marching toward him. Imboden rode to the general and quickly reported what he had seen, only to discover that Bee had already divined the enemy's movements, probably from the sounds of firing. Together the two officers rode well ahead to the summit of Henry Hill just below the Warrenton Turnpike, and then beyond the road, across Young's Branch, and up Matthews Hill. In passing over Henry Hill, Bee surveyed the countryside briefly and told Imboden, "Here is the battlefield, and we are in for it! Bring up your guns as quickly as possible, and I'll look round for a good position." Then, while Imboden began emplacing his battery just in front of the Henry house, Bee led the upcoming regiments across Young's Branch to the scene of the action.[21]

He halted his two regiments in a skirt of woods about two hundred yards behind Evans and formed them in line of battle. Almost at once came the order to move forward, to Evans' right. "The enemy were right in front of us in overpowering numbers," wrote an Alabamian. When Bee got within a hundred yards of Porter's line, he ordered his men to halt and lie down. Instantly the firing along the line became brisk, Bee's men having to rise to fire, then lying down once again to load. Imboden was still back on Henry Hill, so the only artillery support they received came from one of Latham's guns still firing an occasional shot. Soon, however, the horses hitched to its caisson became frightened and bolted, carrying away all the gun's ammunition. When Imboden was ready to open fire, he sent an occasional shot into the Federals facing Bee, but now his chief attention had to be concentrated against an ever-lengthening blue line extending on Evans' front and on across the Sudley Springs road. Obviously the enemy was receiving heavy reinforcements and they were trying to turn the left flank of the hard-pressed Confederates.[22]

A little distance behind Bee in his advance to join Evans came Bartow with his two available regiments, the 7th and 8th Georgia. The night before, as these Georgians bedded down, Bartow spoke to some of them in a fatherly manner. He said that he had Beauregard's promise that they would get in on the opening of the battle the next day. "But remember, boys," he finished, "that battle and fighting mean death, and probably before sunrise some of us will be dead."

Bartow paced nervously the next morning when no battle developed in his front. Finally, desperate for news, he rode off into the woods, probably to find Beauregard or Johnston and learn what was going on. Shortly before 8 A.M. he came racing back. "Get ready, men! the battle has been raging for two hours on our extreme left, and we must go there at once." Within minutes the Georgians were in line and off at the double-quick. It appears that the colonel did not exactly know where the army's left was. As the column marched along, frequently passing clusters of troops of field guns standing by the road, he would ask, "Is this our extreme left?" For the men it was a "long, weary, woody, hilly, circuitous tramp" to reach the left. Finally, following largely in Bee's footsteps, they reached Evans and went into line on Bee's right, on the very summit of Matthews Hill. "We halted," wrote one weary Georgian, "breathless, foot sore, and exhausted, but eager for the fray."[23]

All told, the reinforcements under Bee and Bartow numbered about 2,800, less than a good brigade. Added to Evans' command, the Confederate line north of the Warrenton Turnpike counted less than 4,500 men-at-arms, not even half of the strength of the Federals arrayed against them. But gamely the Southerners prepared to attack. Bartow brought with him Ephraim Alburtis' battery, and his first action upon taking position was to have the guns open fire upon the principal enemy battery in their front, which everyone took to be the famed and dreaded "Sherman's Battery." The enemy battery, not "Sherman's" or Ayres's but, in fact, the batteries of Charles Griffin and J. B. Ricketts, returned the fire with vitality. Bartow, like Bee, ordered his men to lie down until the time came to charge. Some did not listen. Men of the 8th Georgia, seeing a nearby tree burdened heavily with apples, began throwing clods of dirt and rocks trying to knock down the fruit. Some even tried to climb the tree before their officers scolded them down. At the same instant, Griffin's and Ricketts' shots began to fall around them. "The boys dropped from the apple tree like shot bears," recalled a Georgian. On hands and knees they scrambled for their places in line.

The feelings of the Georgians lying there typified those that flowed through almost every mind in both armies, though many were too proud to admit it to themselves. "I felt that I was in the presence of death," wrote one. "My first thought was, 'This is unfair; somebody is to blame for getting us all killed. I didn't come out here to fight this way; I wish the earth would crack open and let me drop in.'" When an enemy shot sent a clump of dirt flying into the Georgian's back, he was sure he was killed. Just then Bartow rode up to the 8th Georgia's commander, Colonel W. M. Gardner, and exclaimed, "They have your range, Colonel, charge them!"[24]

The Confederate line at this time was fairly stabilized. Evans held the left, his own left resting on the Sudley Springs road. This was the 4th South Carolina. On its right was Wheat's 1st Louisiana. Evans' line ran up the west slope of Matthews Hill, and on its right, continuing up the slope toward the summit, was Bee's command, the 2d Mississippi on the left, the 4th Alabama on the right. Next to the Alabamians, Bartow placed the 8th Georgia, holding the 7th Georgia back somewhat in reserve. Alburtis' guns, along with the Georgians, occupied the very crest of the hill.

Now came the charge on the Federal batteries. The whole line advanced against Burnside's and Porter's brigades. Because of the angle of the Confederate line, its left being farther from the enemy than the right, and due to the right having to advance with no cover on its exposed right flank, Bartow's regiments suffered most heavily. "This bold and fearful movement," wrote one of the Georgians two days later, "was made through a perfect storm" of shot and shell. They ran forward a few steps, then halted briefly while Colonel Gardner made the obligatory speech to fire their ardor. Then it was off at a run for the enemy line.

The Georgians had to move down the face of Matthews Hill, across a small patch of open ground, and into a thicket or grove of trees that flanked the Federal guns. It was the advance over the open ground that was most fearful, though the 8th Georgia lost only one killed and one wounded in the move. Private Dunwoody Jones felt something strike at his feet, stopped, took off his shoe, and in the middle of a hot fight stood in the open prying a bullet out of the heel of his shoe before he put it on once again and resumed the advance.

Well before the grove was gained, the Confederates thought they could see the enemy posted behind breastworks. "I looked to-

31. A wartime view of Centreville, Virginia, springboard for McDowell's attempt to drive the enemy from Manassas. *MOLLUS-Mass. Collection, Carlisle Barracks, Pa.*

32. Confederates who fought at Bull Run. An unpublished photo of "Wheat's Tigers," the 1st Louisiana Battalion. *Courtesy of the Southern Historical Collection, Chapel Hill, N.C.*

33. Blackburn's Ford on Bull Run, where Tyler's reconnaissance backfired. *MOLLUS-Mass. Collection*

34. Ruins of the Cub Run bridge, which slowed McDowell's advance to Bull Run. *Courtesy of the Library of Congress*

35. The Sudley Church and crossing where McDowell's turning movement was to ford Bull Run. *Courtesy of the Library of Congress*

36. Mill and hotel at Sudley Springs where civilian refugees gathered as Hunter and Heintzelman marched past toward the battle. *MOLLUS-Mass. Collection*

37. The stone bridge over Bull Run on the Warrenton road. Here Tyler was supposed to cross. *Courtesy of the Library of Congress*

38. A Mathew Brady photograph of Bull Run taken on the morning of July 21, 1861. *Courtesy of the Library of Congress*

wards the enemy," wrote one boy that night, "and for the first
time since we left home, I saw the once Glorious Stars and Stripes,
floating over the enemy." There was little time for reflection, however, for "The balls just poured on us, struck our muskets and hats
and bodies." Finally they reached the thicket. One boy would call
it "the place of slaughter."

At once they opened on the enemy batteries and some companies of infantry stationed nearby. Almost at the same time, considerable bodies of the enemy moved forward against them,
overlapping their exposed right and part of their left as well. Then
the fire that poured into that thicket truly made it a place of
slaughter. "It was a whirlwind of bullets," wrote one who survived. "Our men fell constantly. The deadly missives rained like
hail among the boughs and trees."

The Georgians were there fifteen minutes. The adjutant of the
8th, Lieutenant J. Branch, was killed. Colonel Gardner's horse
was killed and he hit in the ankle. When asked if he could be
helped he said, "No, shoot on." In one company, five men were
killed, twenty-five wounded, and another five lost and probably
captured. Bartow's horse was killed as well, and he then sent his
aide, G. B. Lamar, to ride back to the rear to bring up the 7th
Georgia as well as to get him another horse. Lamar rode off and
delivered the orders to the other Georgia regiment but could not
find another horse for Bartow. Determined to give the colonel his
own mount, Lamar galloped once more through the heavy fire to
return to Bartow.[25]

Before reaching the thicket, however, Lamar detoured across
the bloody path of the 4th Alabama's advance. Evans, it appears,
did not get far in the charge, and the 2d Mississippi in Bee's brigade not much farther. The 4th Alabama, however, advanced vigorously. Their route of march took them through a cornfield and
up a slight incline to meet the Yankees. They fought without the
cover of a thicket like that protecting the Georgians on their
right. And they held their ground longer than any of the other
regiments in the charge. It cost them dearly.

"Our brave men fell in great numbers," wrote Captain Thomas
Goldsby, "but they died as the brave love to die—with faces to
the foe, fighting in the holy cause of liberty." In fact they died in
pain and blood and dirt. "Oh! how we boys did fight to gain a vic-

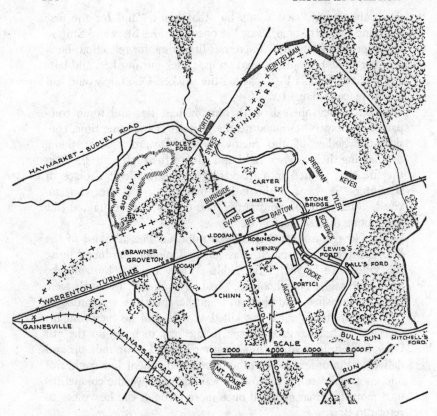

*4. Between 9:45 and 10:45 the action accelerates rapidly as Evans,
Bee, and Bartow face first Burnside, and then Porter, on Matthews
Hill. Meanwhile, Jackson is still on his way to the left, while Sherman
is beginning to cross upstream from the stone bridge.*

tory for the Sunny South," remembered one Alabamian of Company K. Most of the survivors believed that they stood their
ground for over an hour—as long as an hour and twenty minutes,
thought one. In one company alone as many as thirty men were
killed or wounded. One Federal took deliberate aim and shot the
captain of Company K dead instantly. Another company commander was put out of action when a cannon ball struck a fence
rail and sent it flying into his ankle, painfully dislocating the
joint. Another captain was killed elsewhere on the field, and all

around the private soldiers fell. The Alabamians believed that they repulsed three individual enemy attacks before they noticed that Evans and the Mississippians were no longer on their left. Instead, the Federals were advancing there, beginning to fire into their exposed flank. At the same time, a glance to the right showed that Bartow no longer held the embattled thicket where so many Georgians fell. There, too, the enemy was advancing.

Bee's men were facing an enemy on three sides, now advancing steadily, and the only outside support the Confederates received came from an occasional shot sent by Imboden's battery some distance in the rear. Obviously, the 4th Alabama could remain here no longer. Bee ordered the regiment to fall back with the rest of Confederates now spread along the south bank of Young's Branch. At once the men began complying with the other, but a retreat under heavy fire is almost as destructive as an advance. Men fell everywhere. One of them was Colonel Jones. Throughout the fight thus far, Goldsby would write a week later, "Our gallant Col. Jones . . . during the hottest of the engagement, sat conspicuously on his horse, as calm as a statue giving orders as they came." Just as the withdrawal began a cannon ball shattered Jones's leg, knocking him from his horse to the ground. There was no question of the wound being mortal. Private Joe Angell stayed with the colonel even after the rest of the regiment had gone. Jones himself told the boy to get away while he could. Angell, finding that he could not move the wounded officer by himself, went after the regiment to get help in bringing Jones to safety. But he got caught in a crossfire first and fell on his face. A cannon ball, just skimming the tops of the weeds and grass, struck Angell's knapsack, strewing its contents all over the cornfield and stunning the soldier for several minutes. Eventually the enemy would pass him by, thinking him dead. Someone robbed him of his pistol, knife, and cup.

Not long after Angell left the dying Jones, Bartow's aide, Lamar, rode across the ground lately covered by the 4th Alabama, and now covered by so many of its dead and bleeding. He found Jones and stopped briefly to talk with the colonel and comfort him. Then Lamar mounted once more and rode toward the thicket where he expected to find Bartow. He covered barely fifty yards before at least eight enemy bullets struck his horse and sent

both animal and rider reeling to the ground. Lamar tried to comfort the wounded horse as he had the dying colonel. As he patted
the animal's head, five more bullets struck the quivering animal
and killed it instantly. Now afoot, Lamar tried to rejoin Bartow in
the thicket, only to find that he was not there. Eventually he
made his way back to the Young's Branch line. The attack that
was to stop the Federal advance was over. The Confederates were
in retreat, and the enemy now held unquestioned dominion over
the northern part of the Bull Run line. Beauregard's left was
turned and the enemy was advancing.[26]

However much this turn of events may have dismayed the Confederates, it was seen in quite an opposite light by McDowell. His
turning movement from Sudley Ford had been stalled for at least
two precious hours. After the time already lost in the slothful advance to Bull Run, he could ill afford any more wasted minutes.
Unless Burnside and Porter advanced at least to the Warrenton
road, the stone bridge could not be cleared to allow Tyler to cross.
If Tyler did not get across, then little more than half of McDowell's
army would be on the Confederate side of Bull Run. Meanwhile,
with the time bought by Evans' stand, Beauregard and Johnston
could be rushing reinforcements to their left to be ready for the
Federals with a perhaps superior force. The stalled Federal advance
must get going again.

The initial encounters between Hunter's brigades and Evans
had left at least two of the Federal regiments, the 8th and 14th
New York, seriously demoralized. While Porter plugged other regiments into the line to replace them, other officers strove to reas-
semble and rally the broken units. It was at this point, with the
line starting to stabilize, that Porter saw the first of Heintzelman's
units coming up from Sudley Ford. It was about time.[27]

It had been no better for Heintzelman so far this morning than
for any of the other division commanders. Like everyone else, his
march started late, and when it got going, he was constantly
slowed by the hesitant advance of Hunter in front of him. Worse
yet, when Heintzelman's advance came to that point on the back
road to Sudley Ford where a side road was supposed to lead off to
another ford on Bull Run, he found that "the road for me to turn
off did not exist & I had to follow on to Sudley's." As a result,

Heintzelman could not get across Bull Run until after Hunter had completed his crossing. Worse yet, Heintzelman's troops would be tired from the extra marching, and at the same time the center of McDowell's three anticipated crossings was now eliminated. It was Heintzelman who would have cleared the stone bridge for Tyler to cross. Now Hunter's brigades, already tired from their long march and stiff engagement, would have to do it.

Patiently Heintzelman waited for Hunter to complete his crossing. As the hours wore on he heard Tyler's signal guns at the stone bridge. Sometime later he heard Hunter's advance come in contact with Evans. The general could see two clouds of smoke rising from different parts of the field, and the sparring gradually increased into a battle. Even more worrisome, he could see what appeared to be clouds of dust off toward Manassas. They could only mean that thousands of rapidly marching feet were hurrying toward the front. Confederate reinforcements were coming, and here Heintzelman sat on the other side of Bull Run.

Finally, about 11 A.M., orders came from McDowell to bring some men across to reinforce Porter's embattled line. At once Heintzelman hurried his 1st Brigade forward, William Franklin commanding. Leaving the brigade's artillery behind and giving orders for the rest of the division to follow, Heintzelman personally led the 1st Massachusetts across Bull Run and down the Sudley road toward Porter's right. The 5th Massachusetts went with him, while a staff officer led the 1st Minnesota over and toward the center of the engaged Federals.

When he reached the front, Heintzelman found no one present directing the battle. The Confederates had just been driven back from an assault, and the general stopped his men to find out what was happening. At that moment McDowell appeared once more and ordered Heintzelman to send one of his batteries close to the enemy while leading one of his regiments, the 5th Massachusetts, in an attack. Heintzelman sent Ricketts' battery forward and led the Bay Staters where he was ordered to take them, but quickly saw that he was doing no good there, and that the key position on this field was off to his right where he might turn Evans' exposed left flank. He quickly ordered two regiments forward to attempt to take the enemy flank. They attacked but were repulsed by

Evans. Meanwhile, Heintzelman sent back orders for the 11th New York, Ellsworth's Zouaves, to come forward. He would lead them in a charge on the enemy center.

The Zouaves rushed across Bull Run and toward the front. They dropped their knapsacks along the way, moving even faster when those they passed called out, "For God's sake, hurry up, boys. We're driving them, but they're killing all our officers." Without rest, without water in the stifling heat and dust, the New Yorkers rushed up to the line. Immediately they met orders to go forward. "The General has decided to put you right into it," yelled a colonel. "Come on boys and show them what New York can do!" cried the officers. "And with that," wrote a boy of the 11th New York, "the pet lambs were led to the slaughter."[28]

But, at this time on the field, the slaughter lay a few hours in the future. As the Zouaves were crossing Bull Run, the Confederates had already fallen back from Matthews Hill. The reasons were twofold; Heintzelman and Sherman. Bee and Bartow had gone forward in their charge to the cornfield and clump of trees. They battled Burnside and Porter almost to a standstill. Then Heintzelman could be seen coming into line on the right of Porter's brigade, threatening to completely envelop Evans' flank. That was bad enough. Then Bartow, on the right of the Confederate line, saw a considerable body of troops approaching on his far right, completely enfilading his position and threatening his rear as well. He had no idea who they were or where they came from, but their appearance decided the course of affairs on this part of the field. Even as Evans had withdrawn beyond Young's Branch before Heintzelman's advance, now Bartow retreated. Sherman was coming.

For several hours that morning, after Tyler fired the signal guns, things had been relatively quiet on his part of the field; only a constant skirmishing engaged the attention of the troops. Since intelligence was hard to come by, and Tyler was curious to know what was happening elsewhere on the field, he sent one of his staff climbing up a tall pine with a field glass. Training the glass in the direction of Sudley Ford, the officer sent down a continuous report of the action to the north. By eleven o'clock, with Hunter stopped in his tracks and Heintzelman just reaching Sudley Ford, Tyler began to grow anxious. He rode over to Sherman's position to talk with the colonel. He said he feared that Hunter was stalled and he might have to send Sherman's 69th New York over to aid the advance. Sherman, too, had worries about the progress of the attack, but they did not do more than talk over the situation before Tyler returned to his post.

Moments after he arrived, Tyler received a staff officer from McDowell. He brought orders to attack across the stone bridge at once. Tyler was puzzled. His original orders stated that he was not to cross Bull Run until Hunter's flank column had cleared the enemy from the other side of the bridge. "What does he mean?" asked Tyler. "Does he mean that I shall cross the stream?"

McDowell's messenger could not elaborate. "I give you the message exactly as it was given to me, he replied. "General McDowell says, 'Order General Tyler to press the attack.'" Tyler replied that, in that case, he had a mind to send Sherman over the stream. Within minutes he rode to Sherman once more and ordered him to cross and join Hunter's division. At once Sherman ordered his brigade, 3,400 strong, down to the crossing he had found earlier that morning.

"We crossed the stream, and ascended the bluff bank," Sherman wrote a few days later, "moving slowly to permit the ranks to close up." The men were confident of success as they crossed. "We sprung from the earth like the armed men of Cadmus," wrote one New Yorker. "On we rushed by the flank, over fields, through woods, down into ravines, plunging into streams, up again onto rising meadows, eager, excited, thrilled with hot desire to bear our share in routing the enemy." Once across Bull Run, Sherman's regiments moved through the woods that skirted the stream and then out into the open half a mile north of the Warrenton road, and on a direct line with the right rear of Bartow, a half mile in Sherman's front. The first sight that met the men emerging from the wood was the body of a man—no one noticed if he was a Confederate or a Federal—lying on his side, knees drawn up, fists and teeth clenched in the last tremor of pain before he had died. Already his face was starting to blacken in the heat.

Sherman did not give the men time to reflect on this first harbinger of the battle to come. There were more immediate concerns. For one thing, he had crossed where Hunter, Burnside, and

Porter did not expect him to. Worse, one of his regiments, the 69th New York, had two companies in gray uniforms. There was a real danger that Hunter's men might mistake Sherman for the enemy as they approached and fire on them. As a precaution, he therefore marched his men slowly as they approached the scene of action. He need not have worried. The first troops to see him coming were not Hunter's but Bee's, and the much feared mistaken identity actually worked to the Federals' advantage.[29]

Evans and Bartow with Alburtis had fallen back by the time Sherman crossed Bull Run. Only Bee's 4th Alabama was holding out. Bee had just ordered the regiment to fall back when Sherman's 69th New York approached within a few hundred yards on the east.

"We retired in good order through the woods on our left," wrote Captain Goldsby. The Alabamians descended the south slope of Matthews Hill and, as they approached Young's Branch, they saw off to their right the 69th New York "drawn up in close column in line of battle." Since the New Yorkers were actually some distance behind the line once occupied by Bartow, and some were in gray, Bee's men expected that they must be reinforcements, and "were confidently regarded by us as friends." Some form of signal was made by the 4th Alabama and, thinking that they saw the mystery regiment return it, the Confederates moved to re-form their line behind the New York unit. Then the 4th unfurled its Confederate colors. "They opened a murderous fire upon our ranks," wrote Goldsby. In the volley, the regiment's lieutenant colonel and major were both seriously wounded. With Colonel Jones dying, this left the 4th Alabama without a single field officer. Reeling in confusion and nearly surrounded, the regiment withdrew hastily, but not before firing a return volley which killed the lieutenant colonel of the 69th New York and wounded several others.

As the Confederates streamed away from the Federals' fire, Sherman rode across the hill to join Burnside and Porter. He found them near the Matthews house, and from there they watched as "the secessionists took to the woods and were seemingly retreating." McDowell was here, now, and he ordered Sherman at once to begin the pursuit with his fresh brigade. Meanwhile Sherman's regiments took position between Burnside and

Porter, and the advance resumed once more. McDowell, flushed with success, rode along the line shouting, "Victory! Victory! The day is ours."[30]

General Irvin McDowell had every right to elation. Despite a bad start in getting his divisions across Bull Run, the fight could not have gone better once they did cross. True, Burnside and Porter were badly handled by the enemy and might not do much more today, but Sherman was relatively fresh, and Tyler had hur-

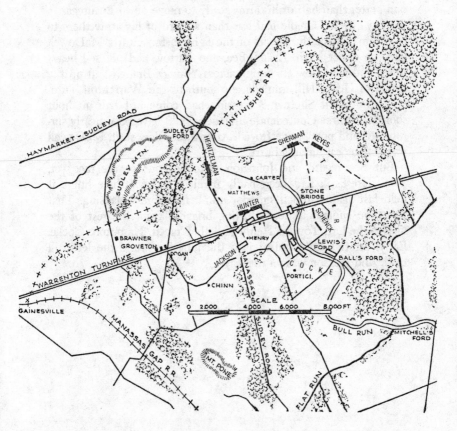

5. By 11:30 A.M. the battle is now general on the Confederate left. Hunter's division is hotly engaged and Heintzelman is coming into action. The Confederates are giving ground, falling back up the north slope of Henry Hill, where Jackson waits.

ried Keyes's brigade across right after Sherman. Heintzelman, meanwhile, had two of his three brigades across Sudley Ford and coming into line, while Howard had been ordered forward at last and would soon cross Bull Run. Of Tyler's and Heintzelman's divisions, only Schenck's brigade would be left on the north side of Bull Run at the stone bridge.

With this much manpower concentrated on the Confederates' already crumbling left flank, victory seemed assured. McDowell had better than half of his army ready to move down Beauregard's flank, while the Creole had less than a third of his army there to stop him. As for the effects of the fight so far, clearly McDowell had the upper hand. Evans, Bee, and Bartow had suffered heavy losses and were now streaming across Young's Branch and up the slopes of Henry Hill immediately south of the Warrenton Turnpike. Indeed, if Sherman's crossing had come just half an hour sooner, all three Confederate brigades would have been nearly surrounded and possibly destroyed. After a very slow start, McDowell was making capital in a hurry.

But Beauregard and Johnston were not out of the race yet. Their left flank had been badly mauled, but for three hours it held fast against much superior numbers before collapsing. That was time enough to start shifting brigades from the rest of the line to the left. Toward Henry Hill they raced. Hampton. Cocke. Early. Smith's train pulled into the junction while the left still held. And Jackson was on the way.

CHAPTER 10

"Trust to the Bayonet"

It would appear to many, as it did to the general himself, that so far this just had not been Beauregard's day. Every grand plan for the ruin of McDowell had come apart. The Federals refused to conduct their advance in a place and manner that the Creole expected, and meanwhile his own orders seemed to miscarry with alarming regularity. Indeed, by 10 A.M. that morning, the battle was almost entirely out of his control.

From their position on the hill behind Mitchell's Ford, Beauregard and Johnston could hear the sounds of the battle going on to their left. The generals' anxiety increased as the sounds continued, the din of musketry and artillery growing in volume as more and more soldiers joined the fray. Adding to Beauregard's concern, meanwhile, was the fact that he was not hearing similar sounds from his right, where Jones, Longstreet, and Ewell should be advancing on Centreville and engaging Miles in the bold stroke that was to win the battle. Then, shortly before 10:30, a messenger sent by Ewell rode up to the generals and delivered the *coup de grâce* to Beauregard's vaunted plan for an offensive victory. The Confederate right, far from attacking Centreville, was not even advancing toward it.[1]

In later days Beauregard would complain that the couriers he was using for his orders this day—there were a dozen or more—"were the worst set I ever employed." He did not know whether it was from incompetence or else over anxiety to do a good job and do it quickly. Whatever, his orders seemed repeatedly to miscarry, or else they were not delivered at all. He seems to have missed one other possible reason. "I always made my aides on the battle field, commit to memory my written orders, so that they could destroy them, if they ran the risk of capture, and yet be able to deliver them verbally," he wrote later. Indeed, so much reliance did Beauregard place on the memories of these aides that, a quarter century later, he still expected that they would be able to call his exact words to mind. In fact, of course, in the excitement of battle most of the aides could not remember a sentence verbatim for more than an hour or so.[2]

Now one of his most important messages had miscarried. Ewell, awaiting orders all morning, had finally sent to the next brigade in line, Jones's at McLean's Ford, to find out what was happening. Back came word that Jones had crossed Bull Run, having received his orders for the advance, and was now waiting for Ewell, who, he was told, had also been ordered forward. This was news to Ewell, for Beauregard's courier to him never did arrive, nor was he ever afterward identified.

It had been a frustrating morning for Ewell, too. The night before, sitting on his trunk in his chairless headquarters tent, Ewell told one of his staff that there would certainly be a great battle the next day. He much hoped to be in it. The original attack order called for him to make a diversion across Union Mills Ford to relieve any pressure on the Confederate center in its advance. This morning Ewell did order John B. Gordon of the 6th Alabama to make a reconnaissance across Bull Run, but then recalled him for fear of bringing on an engagement before the anticipated attack order was received from Beauregard.

Coming back to headquarters, Gordon found Ewell "in an agony of suspense. He was chafing like a caged lion, infuriated by the scent of blood." The general walked and paced back and forth. He mounted his horse, then absent-mindedly dismounted, only to mount again. To himself he constantly muttered, "No orders, no orders." Finally, expecting to get his orders at any minute, Ewell asked Gordon to share some crackers with him. "We will breakfast together here," he said, "and dine together in hell." Finally, fearing that something was not right, Ewell asked Gordon to send him an officer who would go to Jones to see what was wrong. No sooner did the officer appear than the general began a nonstop barrage of questions to be relayed, "slashing away with tongue and finger." The courier, totally confused, asked for more explicit information on his task, and Ewell exploded. Another man was found, and quickly he was dispatched to Jones. At the same time, another courier was sent to Holmes to see what he knew. Then, perhaps to relax, Ewell directed the placement of a battery to cover the ford. At that moment a woman rode up to him to report what she had seen of the Federal advance. Ewell was no romantic like Beauregard or Rosser. He had little use for such heroines, and abruptly told her there would be firing here soon. "You'll get killed," he said. "You'll be a *dead damsel* in less than a minute. *Get away from here! Get away!*" When Madam declined to leave, Ewell was astonished at her bravery. "Women," he said to Gordon, jerking his thumb in the lady's direction. "I tell you, sir, women would make a grand brigade—if it was not for snakes and spiders! They don't mind bullets—women are not afraid of bullets; but one big black-snake would put a whole army to flight."

Finally back came the word from the couriers. Holmes had heard nothing. He, too, had not gotten orders from Beauregard. But Jones had, and sent Ewell a copy which clearly showed that that general was supposed to be moving on Centreville. Ewell wasted no time. He immediately started his brigade across the ford, sent word to Holmes to follow, and then dispatched a courier to tell Beauregard of the delay, and why.[3]

Beauregard was almost distraught. Everything had crumbled. His anticipated attack was not materializing. His left flank was crumbling. Unbeknownst to him at this moment, his troops were suffering from the confusion of their flags and uniforms with those of the enemy despite his earnest efforts to have every Confederate wear a piece of red flannel or a badge to mark friend from foe. And now, just after getting the bad news from Ewell, Beauregard saw Captain Alexander approaching from his signal tower. He had just seen a huge cloud of dust several miles off to the northwest, just such a cloud as was made by the wagon train of a large army. Though it was in fact made by Johnston's own trains, Alexander, and now Johnston and Beauregard, feared that it meant Patterson was coming from the Shenandoah and would reach the field within a few hours. Already Johnston had been badgering Beauregard with his conviction that everything available must be sent to the left, where the fighting was. The appearance of this new threat made him certain. No longer maintaining his pose as a subordinate, Johnston announced to Beauregard that he must reinforce the left. Then he said, "The battle is there. I am going."[4]

Beauregard was finally convinced too. It is not clear whether he regarded Johnston's announcement as a direct order from a superior. Regardless, he at once sent a directive to Holmes, Early, and Bonham to move toward the battle on the left. He also ordered Longstreet, Jones, and Ewell to recross to the southern bank of Bull Run in order to defend. Not long afterward, however, still ever hopeful of the grand sweep to Centreville, Beauregard once more sent the three brigades back to the other side of the run. In all this dry, hot day, the shoes of those brigades were never dry. As for Beauregard, he feared that he, too, was washed up. "My heart for a moment failed me! I felt as though all was lost," he wrote two years later. "I wished I had fallen in the battle of the 18th; but I soon rallied, and I then solemnly pledged my life that I would that day conquer or die!" Then he rode off to join Johnston and make what they could of the embattled left flank.[5]

All the while that Beauregard agonized over his lost orders and lost opportunities, the Federals were pressing their advantage, though not with the vigor that might have won them a quick victory. Actually, in comparison with the men in the commands of Evans, Bee, and Bartow, the men of Hunter's and Heintzelman's divisions had not performed all that well. Burnside and Porter had sent their attacks in piecemeal, a regiment at a time, thus subjecting each one in turn to heavy enemy fire. Thus, by the time that Burnside delivered a final attack and the Confederates were withdrawing across Young's Branch, that officer no longer regarded his brigade as an effective fighting force. Indeed, much of it had simply broken up, the men withdrawing without orders to sprint through the woods back to Sudley Ford. Only the 2d New Hampshire remained organized, and Burnside would lead it personally through the remainder of the battle.

Meanwhile, two of Porter's regiments were badly mauled. The 8th and 27th New York Infantries were both disorganized, the former particularly. And when Heintzelman came on the field, he quickly found that some of his units could not stand the fire. He sent the 1st Minnesota to support the wavering Burnside, and then took the 5th and 11th Massachusetts to pass through Porter and strengthen the line along the Warrenton pike. But here the fire from Imboden's guns quickly broke their ranks and threw the regiments into some confusion.

But of course, Sherman was on the field now, and fresh for the battle, while Willcox's brigade would soon be across Sudley Ford and on its way to join Heintzelman. Howard was coming, and so was Keyes. As for artillery, the Federals had already clearly established their superiority on the field. Whereas the Confederates had only two of Latham's guns and four of Imboden's, the Federals had fourteen guns of various descriptions on the field, among them Griffin's battery of Porter's brigade. And as soon as Heintzelman arrived, Ricketts' formidable battery of six ten-pounder rifled guns was sent to the front, where it severely discomfited Evans and Bee.

By noon or shortly thereafter, McDowell's line was stable and ready to move forward across Young's Branch to meet the scattered Confederates grouped in clusters and knots on the slope and crest of Henry Hill. Sherman's brigade was right on the Sudley Springs road. On his left was what remained of Burnside's command, and Keyes, having crossed Bull Run, formed on the left of Burnside. Griffin and Ricketts with their batteries were in position behind Keyes. Porter, meanwhile, having re-formed most of his command, stood west of the Sudley Springs road, on Sherman's right. Heintzelman was rapidly pulling Franklin and Willcox toward the right of Porter, in the absence of any distinct orders from McDowell. Thus, the Federal line was extending by the right flank, not the left, which was the original intention. But it hardly seemed to matter. The gathering strength here was overwhelming. McDowell's adjutant echoed the sentiments of many in the front line who now believed that the rebels were beaten and the battle nearly over. Riding to Tyler, who crossed with Keyes and was now on the battle line, Fry exclaimed, "Victory! victory! We have done it! we have done it!"[6]

But before that victory was complete, there remained the matter of those Confederates on Henry Hill. McDowell still had to

push his way through or around them in order to cut off
Beauregard and Johnston from Richmond. Some of those rebels
were stubborn, particularly some of the reinforcements just now
arriving.

The first reinforcements to arrive, just before Evans, Bee, and
Bartow were driven back to the hill, were Hampton and his legion. Theirs was a hurried morning. Barely did the South Carolinians get off their train from Richmond before the sounds of battle
started. There was only time for "a handful of crackers and a cup
of coffee" before an order from Beauregard sent Hampton off to
relieve Evans. Riding at the head of his command, Hampton led
the Legion in a three-hour march toward the sound of the firing,
finally approaching the fight in the vicinity of Bee's left. Bee, who
had assumed over-all command of the regiments here engaged,
placed Hampton on his left in reserve. But Hampton would not
stay inactive. He quickly formed his men in line on Henry Hill,
and then marched them down its northern slope to meet the
enemy advancing down Matthews Hill toward Young's Branch. It
was at this point that the rest of the Confederates finally gave
way, while Heintzelman was just starting to prolong the Federal
right around the Confederate left. Thus, for a time Hampton's
Legion was all that remained in that part of the field to oppose
Heintzelman. The South Carolinians were conscious of their soli-
tude. "My sensations as . . . for the first time I saw the enemy in
order of battle moving upon us who seemed to stand there alone,"
wrote one legionnaire a few days later, "were very curious and
hard to describe." At once, the combined artillery of the enemy
seemed turned upon this one unit alone. From three sides the
shot seemed to come. One man, glancing to his right, saw a puff
of smoke from an enemy gun. "I kept my eye in that direction,
and in a few seconds saw the ball coming exactly where I was
standing." He stepped aside and watched as the ball just missed
him but killed three comrades nearby and cut off the foot of his
lieutenant.[7]

By this time the rest of the Confederates had completely withdrawn, excepting only the 4th Alabama, now standing leaderless
off to the right. At the urging of Bee and Bartow, Hampton finally
pulled his command back up the slope of Henry Hill. The remnants of the other brigades had fallen back behind the Robinson

house, just south of the Warrenton road and several hundred yards up the slope from Young's Branch. Hampton, in falling back, formed on their left. It had been a costly holding action for Hampton. His lieutenant colonel had been killed, and Hampton's own horse was shot from under him. It was a great relief to get to the protection of a small hollow and clump of trees behind the Robinson house. It was even more comforting to see, off to the left behind the Henry house, what appeared to be a full brigade, fresh, dressed in battle line, and ready for the battle. Jackson had arrived.[8]

The peculiar general from the Shenandoah had been up at least since 4 A.M. that morning, when he received an order from Longstreet that he needed a reinforcement at Blackburn's. There was an early reveille for the men that morning, and a hasty breakfast. Then came preparations for the battle to come. White cotton fabric was torn into hundreds of strips to be tied around hats and arms so that one friend might recognize another. "We presented the appearance of so many lunatics," complained one Virginian. Worse was to come when a watchword and signal were given out. Upon encountering an unidentified soldier, they were to strike the left breast with the right hand and shout, "Our homes." "They failed to tell us," complained one boy, "that, while we were going through this Masonic performance, we thus gave the other fellow an opportunity to blow our brains out."

About 7 A.M., having spent the night sleeping on a carpenter's bench in a shed, Colonel Alexander Chisolm bore a message from Beauregard to Jackson ordering that officer to take his brigade to support Bonham and Cocke between Ball's and Mitchell's Fords. But then Jackson heard the attack over on the left. Like Bee and Bartow, he did not wait for orders to march to the scene of the fighting, but on his own inititative set out for the front, notifying Bee by courier that he was coming. It was about 11:30 when his brigade finally approched, moving up the south slope of Henry Hill. After informing Bee of his arrival, Jackson ordered Imboden's battery, and one of his own, to take position in the center of the hill while he placed his regiments on either side and behind them. Then, determined to await either orders or the attack of the Federals now swarming down Matthews Hill, Jackson had his men lie down just behind the crest.[9]

"The firing in our front was terrific," wrote one Virginian, "and why we did not render immediate and timely assistance to Bee I could never learn." Instead, the men just lay there in the thin, wiry grass that sparsely covered the slaty ground. Over their heads flew the shot and shell of the enemy, but they made no reply. Instead, they saw the disheartening sight of Bee's men fleeing off to their right, very few stopping or re-forming before they reached the other side of the hill, and there most of them milled about in utter confusion or else continued their flight. Only Hampton and his command stood their ground before retreating slowly to the Robinson house. How good it was, then, that Jackson had those batteries loudly firing back at the enemy. He added to the moral effect this provided by bringing Pendleton's battery into line with the others. Pendleton himself sighted the guns and fixed their range. "Fire, boys!" he shouted, "and may God have mercy on their guilty souls!"[10]

Now it was time for the birth of a legend. As the Confederates on Hampton's right were retiring in disorder, men in Jackson's right-flank regiment saw a rider approach. "He was an officer all alone, and as he came closer, erect and full of fire, his jet-black and long hair, and his blue uniform of a general officer made him the cynosure of all." He asked what command this was and was directed to Jackson, then standing off to the left. The officer was Bee, and he rode hurriedly to Jackson to tell him what had happened with his command.

"General, they are beating us back," cried Bee.

Jackson was laconic. "Sir, we'll give them the bayonet."[11]

The commissions of both as brigadiers dated from the same day, yet Bee seems to have regarded Jackson's statement as an order. Certainly he did not question it. Instead, he saluted and immediately rode back toward the remnant of his command, now in the ravine at the back slope of Henry Hill. Of all of the men who had taken part in the early fighting that day, only the 4th Alabama had retained some sense of order, and that was not much. "Everything was in great confusion," one Alabama officer later wrote; "the disorder is indescribable . . . the regiment was cut to pieces." With all of the field officers killed or wounded, the several company captains spoke briefly, and it was agreed that the senior captain, Thomas Goldsby, should now command. But he was somewhere back on the field looking for his wounded brother. At that moment, Bee rode up to the regiment.[12]

Seeing no officers that he recognized, he asked, "What regiment is this?"

"Why, General," someone replied, "don't you know your own troops? This is all that is left of the 4th Alabama."

With what the now returned Goldsby called "an expressive gesture," Bee told them that "this is all of my brigade that I can find —will you follow me back to where the firing is going on?" As Goldsby described the scene a few days later, the men responded heartily, "To the death."[13]

But Bee certainly said something else before he led the Alabamians back toward the front. Just what it was that he said has been argued over for more than a century and may never be settled with certainty. Goldsby, who was either on the scene or else heard what was said from those who were, mentions nothing beyond Bee's request for the men to go back to the fighting. But others present would tell a newspaper correspondent within the next day or two that Bee concluded saying, "There is Jackson standing like a stone wall. Let us determine to die here, and we will conquer. Follow me." Three days later Colonel Chesnut of Beauregard's staff told his wife in Richmond that Jackson's men "stood so stock still under fire that they are called a stone wall!"

Scores of others would claim to have heard the remark, or a variant of it, and without doubt Bee said something to that effect. Beyond the accepted fact that he said it, however, lies the problem of just what he meant. Most witnesses regard it as a compliment to Jackson's tenacity in standing under the hot fire of the enemy. But Jackson's men were lying down behind the crest, subjected to nothing more than some shelling, most of which went harmlessly over their heads. Could the "stone wall" metaphor have had some other meaning? At least one responsible officer, Major Thomas Rhett, of Jackson's staff, claimed ever after that a few hours later Bee painfully detailed to him his anger that, while he and Bartow were being mauled by the Federals, Jackson had stood on the hill—like a stone wall?—instead of coming to their aid, and that the destruction of his command was largely the fault of the Virginian.[14]

Whatever the case, Bee said it, thereby giving "Stonewall" Jackson and the Stonewall Brigade to the ages. He then proceeded to give himself up for the cause.

Bee took a position at the head of the 4th Alabama's left and led the men back toward the enemy, straight into the combined fire of Griffin's and Ricketts' guns. Its effect was terrible. The company that Bee was leading personally was cut off from the rest of the regiment. The men were "exposed at every step to a galling fire," wrote Goldsby. "Not knowing our friends from our enemies, exposed to a murderous fire, with no opportunity of returning it, we marched back, reformed our line, and awaited orders." They would get no more orders from Bee, though. The company he led got barely a hundred yards before it began to break for the rear. Bee was seen riding all around and through the men trying to rally them, but with no success. Finally, at least one Virginian with Jackson believed that he saw the general turn his horse toward the enemy and deliberately ride alone into the Federal fire. Within minutes, Bee took a mortal wound and was taken to the rear by one of his aides. A few hours later he died.[15]

All this had come to pass when Johnston and Beauregard finally drew rein at the crest of Henry Hill sometime just before 12:30. They found Jackson's regiments still in place behind the crest, and Hampton's Legion standing well over by the Robinson house. The scattered remnants of Evans' and Bartow's men could be seen for some distance behind the lines, and the 4th Alabama was to the right rear of Hampton.

Frantically, Johnston and Beauregard rode here and there trying to rally the knots of disorganized men into a line once more, but with little success. "We came upon the field not a moment too soon," Johnston would recall. "Our presence with the troops under fire, and the assurance it gave of more material aid, had the happiest effect on their spirits." Poor Evans was found, almost alone, with no one left to command. And then Johnston looked over to the right and saw "a regiment in line with ordered arms and facing to the front, but 200 or 300 yards in rear of its proper place." He rode over to the outfit and asked who they were. It was the 4th Alabama. With all of their field officers, and now Bee, gone, they did not know what to do. Johnston found the regimental color-bearer. "Sergeant," he said, "hand me your flag." Sergeant Robert Sinclair politely declined. "General, I cannot give up my flag, but I will put it wherever you command." Placing the sergeant by his side, Johnston led him and the rest of the regiment over to the right of Jackson's brigade and put the Alabamians into the line once more, assigning one of Bee's staff to act as the regiment's commander.[16]

This action had a beneficial effect upon those other disorganized troops on the right and rear. Seeing the line starting to reform on the Henry crest, elements of Evans' command began to return to the front line to take position on the right of the 4th Alabama. Seeing this, Bartow, too, began regaining control of his two Georgia regiments, now milling in confusion some distance in rear of the Robinson house. First about sixty men of the 8th Georgia, a fourth of them officers, re-formed on their own and marched back toward the front line. Beauregard passed them as they marched, crying, "I salute the gallant 8th Georgia Regiment!" The men's hearts swelled with pride at the compliment. At almost the same time, the 7th Georgia, much more intact, rallied under the efforts of Bartow. Its colonel, Lucius J. Gartrell, asked where they should go. "Follow me, and I will show you where," yelled Bartow, seizing the regimental banner. Under a heavy fire from the Federals, who had now crossed Young's Branch and were on their slow way up Henry Hill, Bartow joined with the remnant of the 8th Georgia and reported to Beauregard. The general told him to take his command around to Jackson's left, and Bartow did so. Putting the men in line, he told them, "Gen. Beauregard expects us to hold this position, and, Georgians, I appeal to you to hold it." A moment later, with the enemy getting closer and the fire hotter, he turned to give the colors back to their bearer when a Federal bullet pierced his heart and he fell from his horse, clasping the wound with both hands. If one of the Georgians may be believed, he gasped, "They have killed me; but, boys, *never* give it up." Carried immediately from the field, the popular colonel died only minutes later.[17]

Bartow had met Beauregard just after the latter had made a peculiar request of Johnston, or at least he claimed to have made a request. He asked Johnston to leave the immediate front and allow him to conduct the fight there. Johnston, as senior officer and the general commanding the entire army, should go to the rear and direct the movements of the other brigades then hurrying to the battle. In effect, Johnston should act in over-all command of the whole battle, while Beauregard directed the fight here on the left. According to Beauregard, Johnston objected to leaving the fight, until he was reminded that one of them had to direct the movements on the rest of the field and that, as he was senior general, the responsibility lay with the Virginian.

Johnston would tell a different story. He admitted that Beauregard, being a junior officer, claimed the right to direct the fight here on the left, but insisted that he assigned the post to him rather than being persuaded into it, and also that he, Johnston, still made all the major decisions in the conduct of the fight. "I gave every order of importance," he recalled.[18]

Whatever happened, Johnston now left Henry Hill and the battle there to Beauregard while he rode to Portici, the home of Francis W. Lewis, roughly a mile southeast of the Henry house. From this vantage point he could see a good portion of the field of fighting as well as the stone bridge and the Federal positions there. It also gave Johnston good lines of communications with the rest of the army's brigades, most of which were hurrying toward the field now, and who would naturally pass close to Portici on the march. This would enable Johnston to direct them to the most advantageous place in the Henry Hill line at the last moment.

Even as Johnston left the line, more of the reinforcements so hurriedly ordered forward earlier that day began to arrive. Soon after Beauregard sent Bartow to Jackson's left, the men in Jackson's line saw a "fussy old officer" on horseback lead a small column of troops along their rear. "I am Col. Smith, otherwise Gov. Smith, otherwise Extra Billy Smith," he said, and he was looking for a place in the line. He was sixty-five years old, knew nothing about soldiering, and today, as on most hot days, he was probably protecting himself from the sun by riding under an umbrella. All along the way here he had encountered other regiments standing without orders, itching to move to the fight. As he neared the field, one still-organized company of the 4th South Carolina of Evans' brigade joined him, and later on he picked up Bee's two companies of the 11th Mississippi. These, with the three companies of his own regiment, the 49th Virginia, made up the column he led, about 450 men. Meeting Beauregard, he saluted and asked for orders.

"Colonel," said the general, "what can you do?"

"Put us in position and I'll show you," replied Extra Billy.

At once Beauregard sent Smith into position on the left of Bartow's 7th Georgia. In passing, Smith mentioned that he had passed Eppa Hunton's 8th Virginia, another regiment of Cocke's brigade, back near the Lewis house, and that Hunton was anxious to get into the fight. Beauregard at once sent for Hunton, at apparently the same time that Johnston was ordering him forward. On his arrival, Hunton was ordered to join Hampton as a reserve on the right of the line between Jackson and the remnant of Evans' men and the 4th Alabama. He was also ordered to help stop the continued straggling from those played-out troops. This reserve could act as protection against an advance across the stone bridge by Schenck. In a few minutes, Bee's 2d Mississippi had rallied and reported to Beauregard for assignment, and he sent them to the left of Smith's 49th Virginia. Immediately afterward Colonel Fisher's 6th North Carolina arrived on the scene and took its place in the line on the left of the Mississippians. Fisher's line reached nearly down to the Sudley road, forming the extreme left of Beauregard's infantry. Across the road, meanwhile, to protect that flank, lay the recently arrived Virginia cavalry led by Colonel Stuart.[19]

It was shortly after 1 P.M., now, and Beauregard's line was essentially complete. The fruits of a morning of ordered and unordered movements were finally ripe. From a situation an hour or so before where the Confederate left was in confused and hopelessly outnumbered retreat, Beauregard and Johnston now had a substantial line of nine full regiments in a good position on Henry Hill, with Hunton's regiment and remnants of several other reformed commands forming an acceptable reserve. Beauregard believed he now had about 6,500 men in the line, and thirteen guns. In fact, he was a little stronger than he realized, but still faced heavy odds in the Federals advancing against him. Aware of this, he rode all along the line trying his best to "infuse into the hearts of my officers and men the confidence and determined spirit of resistance to this wicked invasion of the homes of a free

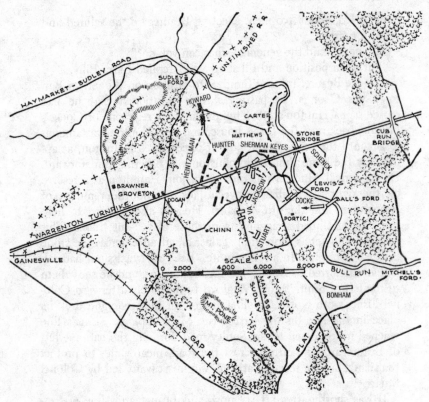

6. *Between 1 P.M. and 2, McDowell spends his brigades in a piece-meal fashion, while Jackson, aided by Hampton and a few remnants of the brigades of Evans, Bee, and Bartow, stoically resists the assaults. Sherman has joined the battle, while Stuart and other Confederate units are hurrying toward the beleaguered Jackson.*

people which I felt." More reinforcements were on the way, he cried. The line must hold until they arrived. Beauregard firmly believed that his work was well done, for the men cheered him wherever he went. He tried not to notice that here and there tired and frightened men still fled to the rear.[20]

At this moment two Federal batteries were seen to leave the enemy lines, rumble down Matthews Hill, cross the branch, and start their way up Henry Hill's northwest slope. Obviously,

McDowell was renewing his already very successful attack, and the Confederates must prepare to meet it. The cry of "attention" ran down Jackson's line, and he told one of his staff to inform the men that the Federals were advancing and "that when their heads are seen above the hill, let the whole line rise, move forward with a shout, and trust to the bayonet. *I am tired of this long range work.*"[21]

Jackson was not the only one weary of firing from a distance. McDowell, sensing victory, wanted to ensure it, and he felt he knew how. At this time, with all of the war's lessons still in the future, generals the world around still held to the Napoleonic notion of how to conduct a battle. First the artillery is to soften the enemy line and silence opposing guns, then the infantry should advance, knock a hole in the hostile line, and through that pour cavalry to demoralize and scatter the enemy into utter defeat.

Now, with significant reinforcements coming on the field, McDowell decided to soften the already shaky enemy with a concerted attack from his two powerful batteries, Griffin and Ricketts. He directed his chief of artillery, William F. Barry, to order the two batteries forward, across Young's Branch, and up the slope of Henry Hill almost to the crest, within a few hundred feet of Jackson's line. At once Barry sought out Griffin to convey the order. Already that officer had moved his guns forward some distance—one gun was now disabled—and was firing at the enemy on the crest. Now Barry told him that he was to advance roughly to the spot where Imboden's battery had been earlier that morning. The battery would be far in advance of the infantry. Griffin noted this instantly. "I hesitated about going there," he said, "because I had no support."

Barry, however, assured Griffin that he would have adequate support from the foot soldiers. Griffin persisted. He asked if the infantry could not go first, secure a position on the hill, and then let the two batteries come into position behind them. This done, the infantry could then pull back behind the guns, and there would still be a firm line of attack. Surely this was preferable to sending two lone batteries out on their own. Barry was adamant. Besides, he said, the 11th New York, the Zouaves, were coming up at the double-quick and they would run to support the field guns. Griffin had a premonition that the New Yorkers would not support him, that they would break. Barry disagreed. "Yes, they will: at any rate, it is General McDowell's order to go there."

"I will go," Griffin concluded, "but mark my words, they will not support us."

Dutifully, Griffin limbered his guns and set off across the Warrenton Turnpike and Young's Branch. The lieutenant to whom he gave the order to lead the battery mistook their objective point, and Griffin had to make the battery turn around and retrace its steps before it rolled up the slope of Henry Hill to a place on gently sloping ground just immediately southwest of the Henry house, and only a few hundred yards from the Confederate line. Ricketts, who had been behind Griffin, was the first to reach the spot, thanks to Griffin's misdirection. "I had scarcely got into battery," Ricketts recalled, "before I saw some of my horses fall and some of my men wounded by the sharpshooters." He believed that the sharpshooters' fire was coming from the Henry house itself, and determined to stop it. "I turned my guns upon the house and literally riddled it."[22]

Sharpshooters were arrayed around the modest frame house, but Ricketts had no idea who was really in it. It had been the home of Dr. Isaac Henry, once a surgeon's mate on the old frigate *Constellation*, and it was now the residence of his aged widow, Judith Carter Henry. They called the place Spring Hill Farm, and Mrs. Henry, her daughter Ellen, a son John, and a hired Negro servant, Lucy Griffith, were the only ones in the house at dawn on July 21. The old widow was bedridden, and when the first shots were fired on Matthews Hill and an occasional ball began to fall about the house, the family tried to get Mrs. Henry safely back to Portici. The battle grew too quickly around them and it became impossible to move her. They did carry her to a springhouse not far from the main building. It afforded more protection, but the old lady begged to be taken back to her own bed.

They got her back only minutes before Ricketts brought his guns into battery on their slope. John Henry was outside somewhere. Ellen, as soon as the shelling began, stood inside the fireplace chimney for protection, only to have her hearing permanently impaired by the reverberations of the explosions nearby. Lucy Griffith ducked under the widow's bed. But for the Widow Henry, there was no protection. Before long a shot from one of

Ricketts' guns entered the house, struck the bed and shattered it, and sent flying splinters, one of which injured Lucy Griffith. The old widow was thrown to the floor with wounds in her neck and side. One of her feet was almost entirely blown off. On through the afternoon, despite great pain and suffering, she tried to comfort her distraught daughter. Well before the sun went down on July 21, Mrs. Henry died. Outside, while the battle raged, her son John lay face down on the ground, occasionally raising his head to cry tearfully, "They've killed my mother."[23]

Mrs. Henry was probably already lying in her blood on the floor of her home when Griffin's battery reached Ricketts and took its position on his left. Now there were eleven big guns sending their shells at the Confederates and their artillery in the center of Jackson's line. It was about 2 P.M., and for nearly an hour there had been a comparative lull in the battle as McDowell, Beauregard, and Johnston brought up their reinforcements and adjusted their lines. It was as if they were in the eye of a hurricane. After the morning's intense fighting, a peculiar calm had come. But the eye of the storm was moving all the time, and sooner or later there must be more conflict, more terrible even than that of the morning. For now, it would center on these two unprotected batteries.

True to his word, Major Barry went off to bring up the 11th New York. They, of course, had crossed at Sudley Ford sometime earlier, passing the house there, formerly a hotel, where refugees from much of the countryside had gathered to escape the battle. Mostly ladies, they stood on the long piazzas and at the front windows watching the long lines of blue-clad soldiers as they marched by. Once they reached the Matthews Hill line, the Zouaves along with the 14th New York—Brooklyn's "Red-legged Devils"— formed in line of battle on the right and rested for a few minutes. Then came the order to advance, Barry personally conducting them.

As they moved down Matthews slope, the Zouaves saw ahead of them a small creek—Young's Branch—and on the other side another hill topped with a small white house, the Widow Henry's. Just below the house there was a cornfield, while behind it was an irregular wood with brush and scrub pines extending down on their right toward the creek.

"Down the hill we marched," wrote a Zouave, "over the fence

into a road, across the creek, passing some skirmishers of the 14th, and then, climbing another fence, gained the foot of the hill on the other side." The crossing of the fences and creek disrupted the 11th's line somewhat, but order was quickly re-established, "and up the hill we pushed at double quick. Up, up, not a single enemy in sight, not a shot from his side. Up, up till we gained the top and then . . ."[24]

The Zouaves may not have seen the enemy, but the enemy saw them, and waited. One of Bartow's men, just behind the crest, looked across the fields and slope and saw "a body of soldiers in crimson uniform emerge from a piece of woods." He was much impressed. "What a beautiful sight they were, as with well preserved line they moved across the undulating field! I knew they were Yankees, and my heart sank as I saw them move along in such a beautiful line." The men in Jackson's line felt much the same, though some noted wryly that the red uniform pants made the Zouaves easy marks. Still, they held their fire until the New Yorkers had come abreast of the two Federal batteries and gone slightly beyond. Then Jackson allowed them to open fire, and the result was devastating, though perhaps less so at the very first fire. "I recollect their first volley," a Virginian later wrote of his fellow Confederates. "It was apparently made with guns raised at an angle of forty-five degrees, and I was fully assured that the bullets would not hit the Yankees, unless they were nearer heaven than they were generally located by our people." After that fire, however, another man of the brigade declared that "we literally mowed them down."[25]

Here another of those confusions that plagued the day cost some lives in the 33d Virginia, Jackson's left-flank regiment. They were stationed mostly concealed in the line of woods and scrub on the 11th New York's right, and it was against them that the 14th New York was advancing. That morning the 33d Virginia had been given its own signal to tell friend from foe, the right hand placed palm out against the forehead and the watchword "Sumter." As the 14th New York approached, Colonel Arthur C. Cummings, of the 33d Virginia, seemed at first unsure of their identity. He had just reached the field and was not entirely familiar with the course of the battle thus far. Stepping forward, he raised his hand to his forehead and called out the watchword. An officer of the New York outfit appeared to return the signal, and Cummings consequently ordered his men to hold their fire. When scattered shots rang out, he called, "Cease firing, you are firing on friends." At the same instant a volley poured forth from the 14th New York. "Friends, hell!" muttered a man in the ranks.[26]

As for the Zouaves, that first volley from Jackson, however wildly aimed, sent a shock through the entire regiment. The bullets came "crashing through the cornfield, singing and whistling around our ears, making the air blue and sulphurous with smoke." Their colonel cried, "Down, every one of you." They hit the ground just in time to miss the second volley, after which, without orders, individual men began to rise and fire while others crawled to get closer to the enemy. Some broke ranks and went to the rear. The two right companies of the regiment, much demoralized in this fashion, withdrew back to the foot of the hill only to encounter a new hazard: Confederate cavalry.[27]

"Jeb" Stuart awoke that morning to the sound of distant firing on the Confederate left. "Hello! What is that?" he said to one of his staff. They soon found out. Stuart spent the morning in making reconnaissances across Bull Run, then took a position some distance in the rear of the battle line and awaited orders. Growing fearful that his command would not get into the fight, he repeatedly sent word to the front that he was ready for action, and even rode personally to talk with Jackson and others. As the afternoon wore on toward 2 P.M., Stuart impatiently paced back and forth in his anxiety, when finally a staff officer appeared with orders from Beauregard to come into action at once and attack where the firing was "hottest." At once the command mounted and rode toward the battle, passing a temporary field hospital with the surgeons at their grisly work.

Finally they emerged from the woods on the left of Fisher's 6th North Carolina. Through the smoke of battle they could see, "in strong relief against the smoke beyond, stretched a brilliant line of scarlet. It was the Zouaves. Stuart prepared to charge at once, then remembered that there was a Confederate regiment, Wheat's Tigers, dressed in similar garb. "Are those our men or

the enemy?" he asked an aide. Then they saw the Stars and
Stripes at the head of the Zouaves, and the question no longer
needed an answer. Stuart ordered the charge.

The Confederate horsemen rode down on the New Yorkers just
as they were falling back in the face of Jackson's fire. The Zouaves
and the 14th New York—a red-trousered regiment—turned to
meet the new threat and sent a volley into the advancing host.
"A sheet of red flame gleamed," wrote a Confederate officer. It
had an awful effect, but the horsemen rode on, right through the
Federal infantry "cutting right and left with their sabers." One
officer tried to jump his horse over a Zouave, but the hooves
struck the man in the chest and sent him flying. Before the New
Yorker could recover, the Confederate leaned down from the saddle, stuck the muzzle of his carbine in the hapless man's stomach,
and pulled the trigger. "The carbine blew a hole as big as my arm
clear through him." Then the Zouaves took their toll, bayoneting
riders from their saddles as they passed. Stuart led his command
back through the Federal line to the woods once more, well
pleased with what he regarded as the complete demoralization of
the enemy. The Zouaves, meanwhile, felt they had forced the cavalry back, and re-formed to try to get back to the rest of their line,
now attempting to support Ricketts and Griffin.[28]

The attacks of individual Confederate units in this part of the
fight could not have been better timed, though their sequence was
purely accidental. Stuart happened to reach the field at just the
right time. Now Cummings decided to disobey orders, and his
timing could not have been more perfect.

Before the Federal attack, Jackson had told Cummings to
watch out for enemy artillery fire, and to wait until the Yankee
foot soldiers were within thirty yards before he charged them with
the bayonet. This was fine, but then the 14th New York appeared
in Cummings' front and, between desultory fire from them and
an occasional shell from Ricketts and Griffin, Cummings saw that
part of his regiment was getting confused. Fearful that the men
would break if they had to stay in place, idle, while the enemy
moved against them, he decided to order them to attack. As a
result, while the rest of Jackson's brigade was waiting for the Federals to get within thirty yards, the 33d Virginia moved out alone.
"The men moved forward rapidly with a yell," recalled Cum-

mings. They struck at exactly the right time. The 14th and 11th New York, already battered by the fire from Jackson, had pulled back behind the two batteries, and the right companies of the Zouaves in particular had withdrawn to the base of the hill where they were just recovering from their bout with Stuart. This left Griffin and Ricketts almost on their own.[29]

On reaching their position on Henry Hill, Griffin and Ricketts anxiously looked for their promised supports. With relief they saw the 14th New York come up to contest with the Confederates for possession of the woods on the right, while the 11th took position behind the batteries. A small battalion of marines accompanied the Zouaves, while Franklin's brigade, or a portion of it, came up toward the left of the batteries and the Zouaves and lay down. Franklin's 5th and 11th Massachusetts had rallied from their earlier discomfiture that morning, as had the 1st Minnesota. One of his regiments, however, the 4th Pennsylvania, had turned back that very morning, its enlistments expired. Porter had augmented Franklin with the 27th New York, and Sherman lent his 69th New York.

This was the line that was to support the batteries. But before Franklin's command came into place, Ricketts saw trouble over on his right, where the 11th New York was thoroughly demoralized. Fearing their rout, Ricketts personally rode to the regiment. "I rode up to them and said something cheering to them," he later claimed. One of the Zouaves heard it differently. "For God's sake, boys, save my battery," one heard him cry.[30]

While Ricketts was trying to rally the Zouaves, and while Franklin was still on his way up Henry Hill, the Federal guns had done their task well. The Widow Henry was not their only casualty. Griffin, to get a better field of fire, had taken two of his guns from Ricketts' left and brought them around to his right. Soon afterward two guns from the Rhode Island battery joined the other batteries, and thirteen guns were pouring a steady hail of iron into Jackson's line, their fire centered on Imboden's battery, which they had earlier driven from the very spot where they were now firing.

Imboden, who had been in the fight almost from the beginning, had received a promise from Jackson that his battery could retire to rest and refit as soon as replacements came up. At the time, Imboden had but three rounds left to fire. During the lull before McDowell renewed the attack, Imboden and his gunners amused themselves by training their guns on Heintzelman's regiments marching on the Union right flank. Then, when Jackson informed Imboden that his relief was on the way, the captain decided to fire his last rounds before leaving. Imboden rammed home one charge himself, forgot to stand back far enough from the muzzle, and was knocked twenty feet or more by the muzzle blast, which caught him in the left side. Blood poured from his left ear, and for the rest of his life he remained deaf on that side.

By this time Imboden's battery had lost half of its horses and a number of men. Finally other batteries came into the line, and Jackson allowed the tired gunners to take their red-hot fieldpieces to the rear. He kept Imboden, however, on the line, detailing him to go from battery to battery, checking the fuses on the guns and making sure of their aim. At one point, while Ricketts and Griffin were pounding the Confederate line, Jackson raised his hand to give Imboden an order. At that instant a musket ball passed between the fore and middle fingers of the general's left hand, breaking the latter finger between the knuckle and the first joint. Wrapping the finger with a piece of cloth, Jackson said nothing about it and continued to direct the battle. Imboden, too, was spattered with blood. Splinters from shells had hit him in several places, inflicting superficial though painful wounds. Then, when Jackson finally sent him to the rear to join his battery, Imboden drew his saber and tried to halt a few men fleeing from the front. One crazed man attacked him with a bayonet, caught the sleeve of his jacket, and sliced open Imboden's left arm from wrist to elbow. Fortunate to get away with his life, Imboden rejoined his resting comrades, and for him the battle was over.[31]

Meanwhile Ricketts and Griffin continued to pound Jackson's line. When Imboden withdrew, Pendleton and Alburtis replaced him, as did Lieutenant Charles Squires with five guns of the Washington Artillery. Squires went looking for Jackson to report to him. He found the general "half sitting and half lying against the trunk of a small pine tree," wearing a shabby coat and an old blue United States army cap pulled low over his eyes. He wore a pair of old army boots, and when the lieutenant asked for orders Jackson did not by any movement or gesture indicate awareness of his presence. Only the general's lips moved, laconically directing the battery to its place in line. Shortly Beauregard rode past, cheering the men. "Hold this position and the day is ours," he cried to the artillerists. "Three cheers for Louisiana!" At that moment, one of the Federal shells exploded directly under Beauregard's horse, disemboweling the animal.[32]

Then, while so much of the contending foes' attention was focused on their immediate fronts, Cummings moved his regiment out of the cover they had enjoyed until now, crossed a fence, and then formed them in line and spoke a few words of encouragement before leading them in the charge. Griffin, on Ricketts' right, saw them emerge from the woods, and so did Major Barry. Griffin was sure it was an enemy regiment, and he ordered the two guns on Ricketts' right to turn and aim for Cummings. The cannon were loaded with canister—a scatter load much like a shotgun blast—and the gunners were just about to open fire when Barry ordered them not to. Mistaking the blue-clad 33d Virginia for part of the 14th New York, which, presumably, he had lost track of and assumed to be far in advance of its real position, Barry cried, "Captain, don't fire there; those are your battery support."

"They are confederates," yelled Griffin; "as certain as the world, they are confederates."

Barry was adamant. "I know they are your battery support."

Griffin remained skeptical but ordered his guns not to fire on them, and instead turned them once more toward the Henry Hill crest. Meanwhile, he watched as Cummings steadily marched his regiment fifty yards off to Griffin's right, then turned the regiment and marched it another forty yards toward the batteries. Increasingly worried, Griffin ordered his command to start limbering the guns to get away just in case. Then he turned his guns once more toward Cummings, certain it was the enemy. Barry told him yet again, "I know it is the battery support." The same confusion existed in the mind of Colonel Willis Gorman, leading the 1st Minnesota of Franklin's brigade. He brought his regiment up on the right of what remained of the 11th New York. Heintzelman was on the scene in person, sitting astride his horse somewhat in advance of the Zouaves. At first he did not see Cummings' regiment march out of its cover, but when he did, he immediately took them for the enemy, though Gorman thought the Virginians might be friends. Heintzelman ordered the Zouaves to charge.[33]

At the same instant that Heintzelman ordered his assault and that Griffin was preparing to fire on the mystery regiment, Cummings ordered the 33d Virginia to fire a volley into the guns. "That was the last of us," complained Griffin; "we were all cut down." Almost in an instant over fifty of his battery horses were slain, ensuring the impossibility of getting the guns back to safety. Men fell right and left, including Ricketts, who was shot out of his saddle and later captured. Griffin ran back to the Zouaves and begged them to come up to his support, but, after firing a desultory volley at Heintzelman's order, they declined to advance.

After only a few minutes, Griffin believed that every one of his cannoneers had been killed or wounded. More than half of his horses were killed. At once he and the officers of Ricketts' battery began the struggle to get some of their pieces off the field. The Rhode Island guns successfully retreated, and Griffin would manage to get one gun to safety with only two horses to pull it. Ricketts could not get away a single piece, thanks to having forty-nine of his horses killed on the spot. A few caissons were saved, and most of the men of the batteries found their way back across Young's Branch, but behind them they had to abandon ten prize field guns to the enemy. Cummings and his men swarmed around the pieces, jubilantly clambered over them, and some began to turn them toward the fleeing Federal gunners. It was a heady moment for the Confederates, and for the Federals a major setback that they could not allow to pass without strenuous efforts to regain what had been lost.[34]

Along with the fall of the batteries, the Zouaves and the 1st Minnesota had been completely routed from Cummings' front, and a mass of fugitives were seen racing down the slope of Henry Hill heading for safety. At the base of the hill, McDowell, Barry, and other officers frantically tried to rally the fleeing soldiers. The effect of seeing so many of their comrades demoralized and abandoning the field had a debilitating effect upon many of the soldiers who had yet to go into the fight, and their loss of heart would tell in the minutes to come.

When Cummings took Griffin's guns and Jackson saw what had happened, he at once ordered the rest of his brigade to charge. Before Jackson could move, a heavy musketry fire from Franklin's men drove Cummings and his regiment back to their cover, forcing them to abandon Griffin's guns, without being able to pull any of them back with them. Now Jackson moved forward, while Beauregard also ordered the units on Jackson's right to advance. He wanted to clear the Henry Hill plateau entirely of the enemy before McDowell could mount a spirited attack to recover his guns and lost ground. It would also buy more time until Johnston could get more reinforcements sent up to the front line, for as every few minutes passed by, more regiments arrived to bolster the thin, yet sinewy, Southern battle line. And they would be much needed, for now the battle for Henry Hill would begin in earnest. The morning had been McDowell's all the way. The early afternoon had seen fortune cast its gaze more favorably on Johnston and Beauregard. Now it was 2 P.M. or after. Both of the armies had converged the bulk of their strength on and around this hill, and now both were in a position to commit that strength to a sustained contest for possession of it. The hardest fighting yet seen on this continent was still to come this afternoon, and much would be decided by it.[35]

CHAPTER 11

"A TALE OF DEFEAT"

For the next two hours the battle raged indecisively on Henry Hill, neither side apparently gaining much but increased casualties. Beauregard attacked first. His right led the attempt to drive the enemy from the top of the hill. Hampton led the charge, assisted by the recently arrived 18th Virginia on his left and the 8th Virginia on his right. Forward they swept toward the Henry house, all the while receiving a heavy musketry fire and, apparently, some cannon fire from men of Ricketts' command who had returned to their pieces. "In the face of this my men advanced as rapidly as their worn-out condition would allow," wrote Hampton. They first fired a volley into the Federals in their front, and then he ordered them to race for the battery.

In the pell-mell rush forward, Hampton was hit in the head by a bullet that grazed across his scalp and put him out of action for a time. Beauregard is said to have taken the Legion's colors and led them on, though soon an officer of the Legion took over. On they rushed right up to the guns, driving the gunners away, while the Virginia regiments on either side of the South Carolinians drove back the enemy regiments trying to creep up the hill. "We came up in good order," wrote a man of the 18th Virginia, "amidst a hail of bullets, bomb shells & cannon balls, stepping over dead men & horses and in direct range of those belching cannons. The cannon balls struck all around us, the shells bursted at our feet, and the Minies sung their song of death around our ears." Then they saw the enemy fall back before them, and Beauregard came riding along the line shouting, "The day is ours. The day is ours."[1]

The general's jubilation was somewhat premature. Only the first charge across the Henry Hill plateau was his, for the Federals quickly began to group to come back up its slopes and regain what they had lost. McDowell was now down along Young's Branch, still suffering from his upset stomach, but now far more interested in his upset battle plan. The advance should not have bogged down so long here. Now the enemy had brought up reinforcements, and they would have to be forced back by strength rather than maneuver. He and Barry, as well as other officers, rode back and forth along the line trying to stop the men from leaving the ranks, re-forming disorganized regiments, grabbing unit flags and trying to rally and lead forward units that had lost heart in the battle. Somewhere along the creek Barry ran into Colonel William Averell, Porter's adjutant. "Halloo, Barry, is that you?" cried Averell.

"Yes."

"Where is Griffin?"

"I am afraid he is killed," said Barry. "I am to blame for the loss of that battle. I put Griffin there myself."

Not long afterward Barry stopped to water his horse in the branch. To his surprise, Griffin appeared before him, mounted, and watered his horse briefly as well. Griffin was in a foul mood.

"Major, do you think the Zouaves will support us?" he said in sarcastic reference to Barry's earlier promise of the 11th New York.

"I was mistaken." Barry was too dejected to counter Griffin's abuse.

"Do you think that was our support?" Griffin continued, prodding him over the mistaking of Cummings' regiment.

"I was mistaken."

"Yes," growled the angry artilleryman, "you were mistaken all around." Then Griffin rode off.[2]

By now a Federal counterattack was ready, though here, and for the rest of the night, McDowell and his commanders made the fatal blunder of sending in only a regiment at a time instead of attacking in brigade force. The result was that each advance sub-

jected the Union soldiers to a terrible fire from several regiments
in Beauregard's line. The worst of it fell on the men of Franklin's
brigade. He first brought up his 5th and 11th Massachusetts regiments, the latter somewhat disorganized. Yet both moved forward
and, aided by support from one of Willcox's regiments on the
right, they retook the two lost batteries momentarily. "The mangled artillerists rested beneath the guns," noted one of the Bay
Staters, who now had possession of the pieces. At once some of
the men began trying to manhandle the guns to the rear. On their
right, Willcox had led the 1st Michigan forward and had taken
Griffin's guns again. Griffin himself accompanied the charge and
shortly had three of the cannon slowly rolling down the slope toward safety.[3]

They never made it. While sequence and timing were much
confused at this stage of the battle, it appears that at this moment
Jackson led his first general attack, some minutes after Hampton
had moved on his right. "The charge of Jackson's men was
terrific," wrote a man of the 33d Virginia. "The enemy were
swept before them like chaff before a whirlwind." Jackson himself
was impressed by the severity of the fighting. His horse was
wounded, his uniform torn by bullets, and the battle, he said a
few days later, "was the hardest that I have ever been in."
Beauregard led at least part of Jackson's brigade, the 5th Virginia,
in the charge. "Give them the bayonet!" he cried. "Give it to
them freely!" All along the brigade's line the fight was hot.
William Woodward of the 5th Virginia, who the night before
had a premonition of death, fell beside the Henry house, killed instantly by a musket ball.[4]

Almost as soon as Jackson forced Franklin and Willcox away
from the contested batteries, the Federals came on once again. The
two Massachusetts regiments had been badly shaken by their
repulse, and now it was Heintzelman leading the 1st Minnesota
forward in their place. Already some of the Minnesota men had
fallen from sheer sunstroke in the stifling heat and dust. Now,
under Heintzelman's stern gaze, they marched up the hill holding
their fire until very close to the enemy. Then they blazed away,
forcing Jackson to abandon his so recently won fieldpieces. "It was
a trying time, I assure you," wrote one of the Minnesota men,
"the cannon balls & shells all around us." Still they managed to

drive Jackson back with the aid of other Federal troops on either side. Indeed, the Confederates withdrew so quickly that some Virginians were left stranded. One, who did not see the retreat, suddenly found himself alone, turned, and ran back toward friendly lines, all the time beating on his left breast and yelling, "Our Homes!"[5]

And so it seesawed back and forth for two hours. Meanwhile, on Franklin's left, Sherman began putting his units into the fight. He had kept them sheltered in a depression along the Warrenton road, but then an order came from McDowell to attack. Here Sherman, like the other brigade commanders, made the mistake of committing his regiments one at a time. First he sent the 2d Wisconsin up the north slope of Henry Hill, past the Robinson house and toward the Widow Henry's.

The Wisconsin men moved out of the shelter of the sunken road and stepped up the slope. "Men who had charged before us, straggled through our ranks," recalled one of them. "As we mounted the crest we were met by distinctive volleys of musketry." Here they encountered a problem. The crest was semicircular where they topped it, and, as the regiment had marched perpendicularly to the slope, the line was curved around it in such a way that the right of the outfit could not see the left. Unified command was thus impossible, and made even more so by the fact that their officer leading the charge, Lieutenant Colonel Harry W. Peck, had dismounted and was advancing on foot. It made him a less conspicuous target, but it also made him hard to find by those seeking orders.

On topping the hill, the regiment met a withering fire from Jackson's right and the troops beyond, including the remnant of the now used up Hampton Legion. "It was impossible to push our line forward against the evidently superior forces massed in our front," they found. Instead, they settled down to exchanging volleys with the enemy until a blue-clad officer ran along their rear ranks shouting for the men to stop firing. "You are shooting your friends," he cried. Many slackened their fire, then renewed it, only to see the same officer or another similarly clad run past shouting the same thing. Once again the men hesitated to continue their firing. The 2d Wisconsin was a gray-clad unit, one of the many that caused confusion on the field. Either the officer was a blue-

clad Confederate—there were many—who genuinely thought this
was a southern regiment attacking their own people, or else it was
a Federal officer who mistook the banner of the enemy on the hill
for the Stars and Stripes. The Confederate flag at this stage of the
war, when draped limply from its staff without a breeze to make it
billow out, was hard to distinguish from the United States
banner. In any case, the Wisconsin regiment kept up its fire, falling back once but then surging forward once more, until a heavy
flank fire from Jackson forced Peck to give the order to retire.
They did so in some confusion, not stopping the retreat until
across the Warrenton Turnpike once more.[6]

Now Sherman sent in his next regiment, the 79th New York.
"Up we rushed," wrote one of the Highlanders. "The first fire
swept our ranks like a quick darting pestilence." "Come on, my
brave Highlanders," shouted Colonel James Cameron, brother of
the Secretary of War. The first fire hit them halfway up the hill.
The regiment became confused, but the officers ran through the
ranks crying, "Rally, boys—Rally!" and the men responded. They
marched on, only to receive another heavy volley, which left
Cameron mortally wounded. The regiment staggered but on they
pressed. Then, as with the 2d Wisconsin, someone yelled that
they were firing on their own men. "Suddenly we saw the American flag waving," a Highlander wrote a week later. Either the
Confederates did it as a ruse, or else it was the same old confusion. Orders were given to cease firing. "As we lowered our arms,
and were about to rally where the banner floated, we were met by
a terrible ranking fire, against which we could only stagger." This
was all the regiment could stand. They halted, then began to fall
back. "As we passed down we saw our Colonel lying still, in the
hands of Death."[7]

This left the 69th New York. Twice they charged up the slope.
Twice they were repulsed, in part, they claimed, because of the
demoralization of the Highlanders before them. Sherman, down
at the foot of the hill, watched disgustedly as his brigade was used
up. "First one regiment and then another and another were
forced back," he wrote a few days later, "not by the bayonet but
by a musketry and rifle fire, which it seemed impossible to push
our men through." His own horse was hit in the foreleg, while
bullets creased his knee and struck his coat collar. Now, with

many of his staff officers injured or missing, he struggled desperately to keep some order in the confused mass of men that had been his brigade. They were on the verge of total demoralization. "I do think it was impossible to stand long in that fire," he wrote to his wife. "I did not find fault with them, but they fell into disorder—an incessant clamor of tongues, one saying they were not properly supported, another that they could not tell friend from foe." Sherman had been skeptical of the quality of these ill-trained volunteers from the first. "Each private thinks for himself," he complained. "If he wants to go for water, he asks leave of no one. If he thinks right, he takes the oats and corn, and even burns the house of his enemy. . . . No curse could be greater than invasion by a volunteer army. . . . McDowell and all the generals tried their best to stop these disorders, but for us to say we commanded that army is no such thing. They did as they pleased." Greatly depressed by what he saw before him, Sherman concluded, "Our men are not good soldiers. They brag, but don't perform, complain sadly if they don't get everything they want, and a march of a few miles uses them up. It will take a long time to overcome these things, and what is in store for us in the future I know not."[8]

The Federal line was becoming more and more jumbled now, as attacking regiments fell back in confusion and intermingled. Sherman's men were mixed with Franklin's, Franklin's with Willcox's, and so on. While Sherman was attacking on the left, Franklin's men meanwhile captured, then lost, the contested batteries once more in the face of Jackson's muskets. They were aided by Heintzelman, now leading the 1st Michigan, and once that regiment had been repulsed, he collected the remains of the 14th New York and led them forward, but they broke and ran at the first fire. Now Heintzelman took a painful wound which badly mangled his arm. Still he remained in the saddle while a surgeon attempted to remove the bullet. Then, riding back toward the field hospital, Heintzelman encountered Howard, just arrived with the only remaining fresh troops on the Federal right.[9]

It had been a long, hard, hot day for Howard, first detached as a reserve on the other side of Bull Run, and then hurried forward once more. And his brigade, like Hunter's and Heintzelman's other brigades, had gone the long way around to get to Sudley Ford.

Now they had been marching steadily through the very hottest part of the day, their canteens quickly emptied of what they scooped up at the ford, the dust from the road and the drifting battle smoke choking their lungs. They were double-quicked, and apparently Howard or his regimental commanders did not think to relieve the men of their packs, including two heavy blankets per man. "Our men began to fall out and could not go any farther," wrote one man of the 5th Maine. "I think there was at least one quarter of the men fell out before we got to the battle field."[10]

It was about 3 P.M. when Howard approached Young's Branch and received an order from McDowell to go to the right. In a ravine along the branch, several hundred yards west of Henry Hill, Howard formed his brigade in two lines, the 2d Vermont and 4th Maine in the first, and the 3d and 5th Maine in the second. As the regiments formed in line, Howard stood, mounted, in a position by which the men would pass in twos. He looked carefully into their eyes. "Most people were pale and thoughtful," he recalled. Some smiled at him. Then he ordered the front line forward toward the crest of Henry Hill.[11]

The two regiments swept forward, Howard leading them personally, and the very first sight that met them was Lieutenant Edmund Kirby of Ricketts' battery, his face covered with blood, fleeing from the battlefield. The sight of him quickly told the tale of what had happened to the batteries. It was hardly a vision to inspire confidence in the green troops hastening toward the sound of the battle. Then men of the 2d Vermont began to fall, while the 4th Maine on their right was briefly spared the first fire. Then both regiments caught it. "All was excitement and turmoil." The artillery thundered all around them, officers shouted their unheard orders, bullets and shells and men and horses shrieked. In the excitement, reason seemed lost. Men fired their rifles straight into the air rather than at the enemy. Others, frantic to reload and fire their next shot, forgot to put a musket cap in place, without which the rifles would not fire. Failing to notice this in the frenzy, they loaded again and again, until several charges lay one on top of another in the gun barrel. Others forgot to remove their ramrods after ramming home a bullet. When the rifle was fired, the ramrod shot forth like a steel arrow, sailing across the battlefield. The color-bearer of the 4th Maine went down. Colonel Hiram Berry seized the flag and bore it himself. His horse went down under him, and his clothing was riddled by enemy bullets, yet miraculously he survived. As for the Vermont men, they fired fifteen or twenty rounds in the face of a heavy Confederate fire.[12]

After seeing this line forward, Howard returned to bring up his second line. He had already lost part of the 5th Maine, thanks to a stray cannon shot and some retreating cavalry that panicked a portion of the regiment. The 3d Maine, however, was nearly intact, and now he led both forward. "It was a pretty hot place," Howard wrote a few days later. "The air seemed full of whistling bullets." In general, Howard found that he was simply too busy to give much thought to the danger about him, but when he did he found that "I felt at peace in my heart. You would think that a battle would be horrible & sickening, but the sense of personal danger & the effort necessary to master it, make one feel very differently from what he would anticipate."[13]

On went the second line. "We went up a rise and came upon the enemy lodged in the woods," wrote a boy of the 3d Maine. They were met with a shower of bullets as the 3d Maine relieved the Vermont regiment and the 5th Maine went over to the right of the 4th. They were ordered to fire but could see nothing but woods ahead to fire into. Volley after volley they sent into the trees. One officer, in desperation for a target, emptied his pistol firing at an enemy battery nearly a mile away. The men could see in the distance to their left the remains of Ricketts' and Griffin's batteries, but not distinctly enough to know what had taken place there. All this time, they were subjected to a heavy fire from Confederate batteries and unseen enemy riflemen. Howard sent the Vermont regiment back down the hill to act as a reserve, but shortly groups of the Maine men began to follow without orders. His line was breaking up. "Do you order us to retreat?" asked an officer of the 4th Maine. Howard said no, but then the colonel of the 5th Maine fell ill. Officers struggled valiantly to keep their men in line, but Howard saw that it was no use. He ordered the entire command to fall back to the valley at the base of the hill. The withdrawal, at first slow and orderly, soon broke into a near panic to get out of the enemy fire.[14]

Just as the battle had turned against McDowell, now it was

going splendidly for Beauregard and Johnston, though their losses, too, were heavy. After about an hour of fighting, around 3 P.M., they had succeeded in driving the enemy from their right front— Sherman's brigade—so that this portion of the line was fairly safe. Then the 18th Virginia from Cocke's command at the stone bridge arrived to take a position between Jackson and the Hampton Legion. This stabilized this part of the line for the remainder of the battle, though at least one officer on the field had serious objections to the conduct of the 18th and its officers. Samuel W. Ferguson, serving on Jackson's staff, found the 18th standing at ease some distance behind the battle line, making no motions whatsoever toward entering the fight. He begged them to go forward. "Don't you see the Palmetto Flag in the smoke, before you where Hampton is driving them back?" he cried. The men complained that they could not find their commander, who, they said, was off to the right. Riding in that direction, Ferguson found Colonel R. E. Withers, apparently taking shelter from the fire ahead. Along with Ferguson, he finally led the regiment forward into the line just in time to join in a final charge to retake the batteries from Franklin.[15]

Over on the more threatened left, Cocke's 28th Virginia and two of Bonham's regiments, the 2d and 8th South Carolina, were arriving to lengthen and strengthen that flank. Until now, Colonel Fisher's 6th North Carolina had held it valiantly but with heavy cost, including the life of Fisher himself. "The wonderful good fortune of my life will not desert me now," he had written to his sister just four days before. He led his regiment in several of the attacks that retook the contested batteries, and in one of them an enemy ball entered his brain and killed him instantly. The 6th North Carolina itself was roughly handled, for as they attacked Franklin and Willcox in their right front, Howard kept pushing around to their exposed left flank. During one of the assaults a blue-clad officer ran up to them and cried, as so many had on this field, that they were firing on their friends. Then he discovered his mistake and tried to get away but was brought down wounded. He turned out to be Orlando Willcox himself, with several months in a Confederate prison ahead of him. Every Tarheel fought with special vigor—or desperation—so conscious were they of their exposed position on this flank. Even the ill turned out. "I want a pop at the confounded Yankees and I intend to go while I can stand up," declared one invalid. He went into the fight only to be hit three times, and nearly murdered when a Federal who rushed past him almost shot him with his own pistol before a comrade urged the bluecoat to "Let the damned dog die as he is." That night the wounded man was brought away from the field, unconscious of the fact that, in the heat, flies had laid their eggs in the wounds. The same thing happened to others, including one North Carolinian who was wounded in the head. A few days later his head was infested with maggots, and he could only cry out in pain and delirium, "Worse, worser, worser." For five days he lived the hellish torment before the larvae consumed his brain.[16]

Thus it was a considerable relief to see the 28th Virginia and the two South Carolina regiments come on the field. They arrived just in time to meet Howard's attacks and relieve the decimated 6th North Carolina. It had so far been a dull morning for Bonham and his regiments. That morning Federal guns from Richardson's brigade had opened a desultory long-range fire on Mitchell's Ford, but there was nothing to hint of an attack, and through most of the day his men simply sat in their trenches trying to escape the stifling heat. Early in the morning the South Carolinians could look back on the hill behind them and see Johnston, Bonham, and Beauregard, with the last occasionally looking off toward the left through his field glasses. That morning the men awoke with a certain premonition that they would be in a fight that day, and the anxious activity of the generals, coupled with the early morning sounds of firing over toward the stone bridge, gave weight to the prophecy. By noon, there was no question that almost everyone in the army would see some firing. "While not actually engaged in my office," wrote Samuel Melton, one of Bonham's aides, "I was kept constantly engaged in dodging shells and cannon balls." Other than that, however, the chief occupation of the men at Mitchell's Ford was waiting. "Everything could be heard, & much seen, from my position," wrote Melton a few days later, "and such a day of anxiety, heart-rending spasms of anxiety, I hope never again to spend. The alternatives of joy and sorrow were shocking to me." They saw other troops pass by on their way to the front, among them Jackson, who stopped to ask directions of Kershaw. Then finally, just after noon, Bonham re-

ceived and transferred orders to send two regiments to the vicinity
of the Lewis house as reserve reinforcements for Jackson. He
quickly dispatched Colonel Joseph B. Kershaw and his 2d South
Carolina, and Colonel E. B. C. Cash with the 8th.[17]

Taking Captain Delaware Kemper's Alexandria Light Artillery
with them, Cash and Kershaw set off toward the battle. With
Kemper leading the way, they marched rapidly to the Lewis
house, Portici, and here they first encountered stragglers and demoralized men from the battle in large numbers. "We saw hundreds of our men retiring, crying that we were ruined, that the
battle was lost, and that nothing could save us from being cut
up," wrote one Camden boy of the 2d South Carolina. Old Edmund Ruffin was here too, and he was appalled at the straggling.
"This was my first acquaintance . . . of the class of 'skulkers' or
'stragglers' from battlefields." To explain their absence from the
front, the men claimed that they were wounded or exhausted.
"But I was struck with the strange fact, that of all these men reported as either wounded or worn down by exertion, not one was
sitting or lying, as if to rest." They were in too much of a hurry to
get away from the danger.[18]

On reaching Portici, Kershaw received orders from Johnston to
take the commands to the left of the Lewis place. Off they went,
but shortly they discovered that the battle had spread far to the
left of the place they had been assigned. On his own initiative,
Kershaw marched his command behind the battle line toward the
left, until he came to the 6th North Carolina and, on its left, the
28th Virginia. Kershaw put the 2d South Carolina into line next
to the Virginians, while Cash brought his regiment up on
Kershaw's left. Then the men lay down in the grass and brush,
while Kershaw suggested to the colonel of the 28th Virginia that
he put his regiment on Cash's left to further prolong their line as
Howard's regiments were moving against them.[19]

Now the accidental timing of the arrival of Confederate reinforcements, which had so far this afternoon worked to their advantage, gave the Southerners a great boost on their most vulnerable flank, the left. "At this moment," wrote Kershaw, "the head
of a regiment marching by a flank passed to the right of my regiment and partly over my right wing, led by an officer who was
said to be General Smith." It was E. Kirby Smith indeed, arrived

at last from the Shenandoah. Seldom in the history of warfare did reinforcements come at a more opportune moment.

Smith's train reached Manassas Junction between noon and 12:30 after a long wearying ride which included a few anxious hours that morning during which they could hear the firing in the distance ahead of them. "When our ears caught the sound of cannon," wrote a Marylander, "could you have seen every eye flash & every face brighten as the sound came nearer." Smith ordered them to drop their knapsacks where they stood, leaving them in a pile by the railroad. On arriving, Smith received orders to detach one of his regiments to guard Manassas. He left his smallest outfit, Colonel A. P. Hill's 13th Virginia. "Colonel Hill as well as his men were all disgusted," wrote a man of the regiment. "The war to close and we to have no part in it!" Still they remained behind as Smith double-quicked the rest of the brigade north on the Manassas-Sudley road.[20]

They found the road clogged in places by stragglers whom Smith and his staff had to force aside to make way for the brigade. "The dust was most distressing," wrote a man of the 1st Maryland, "so thick at times that it was impossible to see more than a few feet ahead of one." For six miles they had to stay on the rapid march. "Our pulses beat more quickly than our feet, as we passed on, the sounds of battle waxing nearer and nearer every moment." Men could not see their officers in the thick dust, and many dropped by the road from exhaustion. One brief halt was allowed. Those who happened to have water in their canteens drank it greedily. Those who did not picked blackberries for their moisture. A few sipped the muddy water left in hoofprints from the rain earlier that week.[21]

At length the brigade came near Portici, and one of Johnston's staff officers brought orders for him to take his brigade to the left of the line. Minutes later, at Smith's request, Johnston joined the brigade personally. "Take them to the front," yelled Johnston; "it is our left that is driven back: but the ground is new to me, and I cannot direct you exactly." His only orders were to "Go where the fire is hottest."[22]

Rushing forward through stragglers who cried "we were catching hell," and bypassing groups of two and three men who felt it necessary to leave the battle to accompany a comrade with nothing more than an injured finger, the brigade met their first Federals, prisoners going to the rear. Some of them had "Richmond or hell" written on their caps. Finally, at 4 P.M., Smith led his brigade past the southern slope of Henry Hill and off toward Kershaw's right flank. As his men passed over the South Carolinians who were lying on the ground, some of the Palmetto Staters raised their heads and cried, "Go in." Smith's men replied with some vigor that they should come in with them.[23]

At this moment, Kershaw rode over to see Smith and told him that this part of the line was fairly stable, but that the Federals—Howard—still seemed to be extending on their left. Could not Smith take his brigade there instead? As they spoke, a volley crashed toward them from Howard, and a shell exploded nearby. A bullet struck Smith in the left breast. "He fell in the most spectacular way," wrote a Marylander, "the reins falling from his grasp, he reeled in the saddle, threw out his arms and fell to the ground, seriously but not fatally wounded." At the same instant a private's canteen was hit. Feeling the warm water running down his leg, he at first thought it a stream of blood and promptly fainted. With Smith out of the action before he really got into it, the command devolved on Elzey. Expecting either promotion or death in the aftermath of the fight, Colonel Elzey said to Bradley Johnson, "Now for a yellow sash," referring to the sword belt sash of a general, "or six feet of ground."[24]

Elzey first sent the brigade's battery under Lieutenant Robert F. Beckham off to the far left, where it joined with Stuart's cavalry to get in Howard's left and rear if possible. Then, responding to Kershaw's suggestion to Smith, or else seeing the necessity of the situation himself, Elzey moved the brigade around behind the South Carolinians and put it in place on the extreme left of the army's infantry line. He had reconnoitered the move himself, and moved the brigade through a heavy wood in line, the 3d Tennessee on the right, the 1st Maryland in the center, and the 10th Virginia on the left. Emerging from the wood just west of the Manassas-Sudley road, almost immediately south of Henry Hill, Elzey came out in an open field and saw in his front, to the northwest, Howard's command only a short distance away, Stars and Stripes waving. Elzey and his staff studied the Federal position for a few minutes, not realizing that Howard had just finished ex-

39. The Wilmer McLean house, where Beauregard made his headquarters. *Courtesy of the Library of Congress*

40. Portici, the Lewis house, where Johnston established field headquarters to direct brigades into the battle. *Courtesy of the Manassas National Battlefield Park*

41. The prize, Manassas Junction. *Courtesy of the National Archives*

42. A view along the Sudley road with Matthews Hill in the distance.
There the first fighting occurred, and down those slopes the Federals
swarmed in the attack on Henry Hill in the right foreground. The
Warrenton road crosses in the middle distance. *Courtesy of the Library
of Congress*

43. (ABOVE) The
Matthews house, past
which Federals and Con-
federates battled in the
first hours of the fight.
*MOLLUS-Mass. Collec-
tion* 44. (LEFT) Brady's
one battle photograph,
showing Federal dead on
Matthews Hill. *Courtesy
of the Library of Congress*

45. A postwar view of a rebuilt Henry house on the left, and the ground over which Jackson, Bee, and Bartow fought so desperately. *MOLLUS-Mass. Collection*

46. A sketch of the Henry house sometime after the battle. *Courtesy of the Manassas National Battlefield Park*

hausting his brigade in attacks on the troops to the right. Then, eyes glowing, he called to the brigade, "Stars and Stripes! Stars and Stripes! Give it to them, boys!"

At once there was a volley. "A brisk and terrific fire was kept up for a few seconds," Elzey reported. Then he ordered a charge, Howard having disappeared. The men went forward with a cheer, but many of them got no farther than a cluster of blackberry bushes until officers shooed them onward. Even then, the men tried to grab the berries as they ran, often filling their hands with thorns. Coming to an open field, they could see nothing but the bodies of dead Federals and horses, so the line moved on toward a wood near Young's Branch. They halted, poured repeated fire into the woods, aided by Beckham's shelling from the left, and then moved against the thicket, meeting only token resistance. Once on the other side of the wood, they reached Young's Branch, but there was not a Federal in sight. Despite their thirst, however, the men declined to drink from the stream. On all sides, dead Yankees were lying and bleeding into its waters. Elzey did not realize it yet, but the right wing of McDowell's army, already damaged, had crumbled before him and a freshly arrived brigade on his right. Now Beauregard rode up, ecstatic. "Hail, Elzey!" he cried, "thou Blucher of the day."[25]

Beauregard had good reason to be jubilant. A few minutes before he had been almost panicked. He was making his field headquarters on the Henry Hill plateau, about one hundred yards behind the Widow Henry's house. While here, around 3 P.M., he received a message from Captain Alexander that a large dust cloud had been sighted to the southwest approaching his left. The signalman believed that it was Patterson's column coming from the Shenandoah. "I concluded that it might be Patterson," said Beauregard, but he reserved judgment for the moment. If it was Patterson, however, the game was up. Such a force coming against his already exposed and hard-pressed left would mean disaster. His only options would be to fight in the face of certain defeat, or else withdraw from the battle, leaving McDowell the victory, and Manassas Junction.

Shortly, a mile away, Beauregard could make out the head of a marching column under the cloud of dust. At its head he saw a flag drooping against its staff. It was impossible to tell if it was a

Union or Confederate flag. With the mysterious column coming ever closer to his left, the Creole was increasingly worried. He turned to Evans, just then by his side, and described the dilemma. If the soldiers were Federals, then he would have to notify Johnston and prepare to withdraw. After another look that still revealed nothing, "which tended to increase my doubt about the troops I saw," he decided that they must be Patterson's. He asked Evans to ride personally to Portici to give Johnston the news. But then, as Evans was riding off, Beauregard saw the Federal right pulling back from his left as though fearful of something. "Let us wait a few minutes," he called to Evans, "to confirm our suspicions before finally resolving to yield the field!" He looked anxiously once more through the still air of that hot battlefield. Then there came a gust of wind, he saw the flag at the head of the column billow out, and recognized it as the colors of a Confederate regiment of Early's brigade. Beauregard's anxiety turned to joy as he realized that, far from his own left being threatened with disaster, Early's appearance at this time and place made the enemy's position on that sector of the field untenable. Now Beauregard had victory at last in his grasp.[26]

It had been a busy, albeit unfruitful, day for Early thus far. At sunup that morning the men awoke in their bivouac near the McLean house, and not long after began to hear the sound of cannon near Blackburn's Ford. Shortly thereafter Early received orders from Beauregard to take his brigade forward to be ready to assist either Longstreet at Blackburn's Ford or Jones at McLean's Ford. He did so at once but remained only a short while before Longstreet asked for first one, and then another, of his regiments. Early found that Longstreet had crossed his entire brigade over the stream and was awaiting a signal to advance toward Centreville. Here Longstreet told him that Jones had crossed and was awaiting similar orders. Then Longstreet asked Early to cross part of his command to take a Federal battery, some distance in their front, which was giving the line a sharp shelling. Early was not enthusiastic about the proposition, when just then a courier arrived from Beauregard ordering all forces north of Bull Run to cross back to the south side. "I felt this as a reprieve from almost certain destruction," Early recalled.

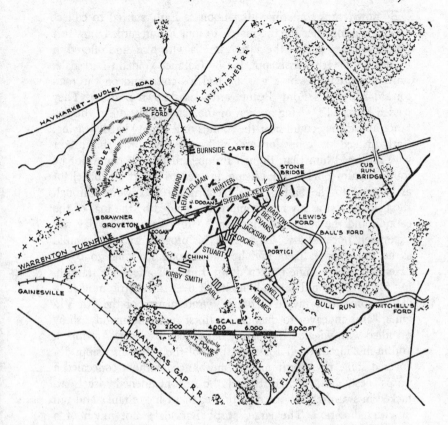

7. *For two hours, from 2 P.M. until 4, the battle for Henry Hill sways back and forth. Six full Federal brigades are engaged but still not co-ordinated. The Confederates rally well and, as Early's and Kirby Smith's brigades approach the field, they advance all along the line.*

It was now 11 A.M. As the brigades began to cross the stream, Early met General David R. "Neighbor" Jones, who told of an order just received from Beauregard. It called for Jones to move his brigade to the left of the line where the battle was going on. In a note at the bottom was written, "Send Early to me." A similar order had been sent to Early, but like so many other messages sent by the careless Beauregard, it never reached him.

By now it was sometime after noon as Early started to collect his brigade together for the march to join Beauregard. Longstreet wanted to keep part of the 24th Virginia with him, and offered in its place the 13th Mississippi, led by Colonel William Barksdale. Early accepted, and by 1 P.M. he had his command on the road toward Mitchell's Ford, Beauregard's last known position. They passed Mitchell's, seeing no sign of the general, but off in the distance ahead they could hear the sounds of a mighty battle waging. Early pressed his troops forward until he was met by a staff officer who informed him that, though Beauregard himself could not be found, reinforcements were being directed to report at Portici for assignment to the battle line. "I continued to advance through the fields as fast as my men could move, guided by the roar of the cannon and the volleys of musketry," wrote Early. "The day was excessively hot and dry." As a result, his progress was not as rapid as he would have liked, and he had a good six miles to cover. "Here and there some broken down, thirsty Confederate, famishing for water, would throw himself flat over some little mud puddle, in some little ravine or drain," wrote a man of the 7th Virginia, "and endeavor to quench his thirst from the muddy, slimy pit filled with wiggle-tails." Every berry bush passed was stripped, and in moving through a pasture, men of the 13th Mississippi discovered some ripe persimmons. One bunch of them concealed a wasps' nest, and when disturbed the heat-maddened insects attacked in swarms. Fifty men of the regiment broke ranks and ran in every direction. The large, portly Barksdale, not much of a horseman in the first place, rushed in to restore order, and rode right into the middle of the wasps. Onlookers would declare that the spectacle "beat a circus" for entertainment.[27]

One of Early's staff encountered an aide of Beauregard's who said that orders were for all reinforcements to go to the front at once. Shortly afterward, he met one of Johnston's staff who directed the brigade to move to the left of the line, and Early immediately turned his column in that direction, meeting Johnston a few minutes later. Early asked the general to show him his assigned position, but Johnston was too busy, saying that he should move to the extreme left of the line and attack at once. Not long before, Johnston had met Kirby Smith's advance, and he seemed to sense that these two brigades together on the left could stabilize the threatened line and perhaps even turn the tables on the enemy. In particular, certainly reflecting on earlier mistakes made that day, Johnston implored Early to be careful of whom he opened fire upon. Enough Confederates had already been killed by their friends, and by failing to recognize the enemy when spotted.[28]

By this time, Beauregard had seen Early's column and soon would sigh in relief when he recognized the flag at its head. It was nearly 4 P.M., Early's brigade having taken almost three hours to cover their six-mile march, no mean feat in that heat. He moved his brigade around behind the woods then occupied by Elzey, and as he approached an open space at the extreme left of the infantry line, he received a message from Stuart. The cavalry-man and Beckham's guns were off some little distance farther to the left, harassing Howard's brigade, and Stuart now sent to no-tify Early of where he was and that he felt the Federal flank was about to break. If Early could hurry into the fight, he believed the enemy would give way and retreat. Early quickly moved his bri-gade into a prolongation of Elzey's brigade, while Stuart and the fieldpieces moved farther yet to the left. At once the infantry came under some fire from the enemy, but within minutes Early saw Elzey's brigade on his right advance through an open field into a wood. In Early's own front he could see a line of the enemy before him on a crest sometimes called Bald Hill. He sent his bri-gade forward toward the crest at the same time that Stuart and Beckham reached a position on the enemy's exposed flank and began pouring shells into it. With little or no resistance, the Fed-erals fled the hill, and by the time Early's brigade topped it and he allowed the men to stop for a brief rest, he could see thousands of Federal troops on the Warrenton Turnpike and beyond in full retreat. Early, thinking that the sight of his thinly spread line fooled the enemy into thinking his numbers much larger, de-clared, "We scared the enemy worse than we hurt him." It was the truth, but it mattered little now, for from all appearances McDowell's was a beaten army.[29]

Early and Elzey struck at exactly the right moment without knowing it. Howard's attacks had been blunted and his line was already shaky when Elzey came into line. Then, while the Maine regiments were facing that brigade from their position atop Bald

Hill, Early appeared. "In a short time," wrote a boy of the 5th
Maine, "a bout a thousand men marched down from a nother direction . . . they marched with in 50 or 60 rods without firing or
being fired upon. they then opened fire on us and we on them at
the same time a mask[ed] batery opened on us from the side hill
that we knew nothing about. a nother [Beckham's] opened on us
about a half mile on the back side." The brigade was already
shaky, Howard struggling to hold the men in the ranks. Then
came the appearance of Early and the fire of Stuart and Beckham.
"It was evident that a panic had seized all the troops in sight,"
wrote Howard. An officer cried by his side that his men would not
stand. Surgeons yelled at the fleeing to help save the wounded.
Men ran everywhere yelling, "The enemy is upon us! We shall all
be taken!" Even the wounded Heintzelman, riding and swearing
mightily along the rear of the brigade, could not stop the rout.
Howard's brigade slowly melted into the Warrenton Turnpike,
and then fell back toward Sudley Ford and other crossings.[30]

Beauregard, seeing the advantage gained on his left, made one
of the very few decisions he would make this day that would
beneficially affect the battle. Sensing that the whole Federal line
was shaky, he ordered a general charge all along the line from the
8th Virginia, near the Robinson house, to Early's command. At
this moment, Cocke arrived with the 19th Virginia and joined
Early, and in tandem with Stuart they set out in pursuit of the
crumbling Federal right flank. In front of the other Confederate
regiments in the line, the Federals fell back consistently with little
or no stout resistance. "There were no fresh forces on the field to
support or encourage them," wrote Adjutant James B. Fry, "and
the men seemed to be seized simultaneously by the conviction
that it was no use to do anything more and they might as well
start home."[31]

Stragglers and discouraged men had been indiscriminately leaving the battle line and moving to the rear all day. Their officers
tried repeatedly to force them back up into the line, but with little success. Instead, they hurried toward Sudley Ford or one of the
other fords above the stone bridge. In passing the fresh troops
who met them on the road, they most often told a tale of woe, at
the same time indicating that the battle was hot and turning
against them. This hardly put the fresh brigades in the best frame

of mind for going into their first fight. McDowell's brigade commanders contributed to the increasing number of fugitives by committing their commands only a regiment or two at a time. When one was beaten back, it often forced those behind it into some confusion. And the sight of Federal troops repeatedly being repulsed by the enemy was a potent ingredient in the demoralization of McDowell's men. Finally, Sherman, Willcox, Franklin, and Howard had fought hard and marched hard on a miserable day. After the showing they had put up, there was no shame in being defeated. Even Burnside's brigade, and particularly the 2d New Hampshire, had fought a good fight. The humiliation came only afterward. Then, with the battle done, what should have been an orderly retreat became a disgraceful panicked rout.

Several regiments were already breaking up when Howard came on the field. Perhaps at this point McDowell should have recognized that the battle on this field was lost, and used Howard's fresh men as a rear guard to cover the withdrawal of the rest of the troops south of Bull Run. But he did not. Instead, Howard's men were still among the last to leave the field, but only because most of the rest of the line was already collapsing when Elzey and Early turned his flank. Perhaps part of McDowell's reason for holding out as long as he did in the futile attempt to turn Beauregard's left was that, during the last hour of the battle, he also had a brigade in motion trying to turn the Confederate right. If either should succeed, the Federals might still have a victory.

It was about 10 A.M. that Keyes's brigade, following Sherman, was ordered to cross Bull Run north of the bridge. Keyes formed his command on Sherman's left, and for the next four hours or more engaged in the general but ineffective attacks on the Henry Hill position, Keyes striking principally in the vicinity of the Robinson house. Then at 2 P.M., orders came from Tyler, himself now across Bull Run, to advance and take an enemy battery, probably Latham's. Keyes promptly sent two regiments forward, up the hill into a withering enemy fire from the guns and their infantry supports. After only a hundred yards, Keyes had the men fall flat on the ground. Then they advanced once more, only to see the battery move back toward the Henry house. "We went up that hill shouting and yelling as if two thousand demons had been suddenly let loose from Pandemonium," wrote a man of the 3d

Connecticut. The yelling did not help, for the regiments stalled before the withering enemy fire, and Keyes could not go farther. Tyler came up and the two stood just behind the firing line and talked over the situation. Tyler had not received any further orders from McDowell, nor did he really want any. That left him on his own, and a bold stroke now that might win the day would therefore rebound to his credit, and not McDowell's. Deciding that the stone bridge was an important position, Tyler resolved to take possession of it. It had been an important spot early in the day, but only because McDowell hoped to cross much of his army over it instead of marching the long way around. But now all of Heintzelman's, Hunter's, and Tyler's divisions were already across Bull Run, except for Schenck's, and the bridge really had little import left except as a possible avenue of retreat. At this time, however, Tyler believed that the Federals were beating Beauregard at every point.

Tyler ordered Keyes to start moving his regiments by the left flank, between Henry Hill and Bull Run, down toward the stone bridge. Once Keyes had secured the bridge and the Warrenton road, he would then order Schenck to cross and together the two brigades would deal a mighty blow to the enemy right flank and rear. Without much difficulty, Keyes got his command across the Warrenton road and nearly a half mile south of it. Then he faced the men right again and tried once more to push up the slope of a hill, this time charging up the back slope of Henry Hill. There were two troublesome Confederate fieldpieces shelling his men, but the fire was not well aimed. Tyler himself was about to lead the men forward when an aide came riding up to him in a frenzy.

"The army is in full retreat towards Bull Run!" he cried.

Tyler did not believe him. "Ride with me to the rear line," urged the staff officer. Tyler did so. "To my astonishment," he would recall, "I saw the Army was retreating towards Bull Run." At about this same time Lieutenant Emory Upton rode to Keyes with orders from McDowell to retire to the right, back across the ford that Keyes and Sherman had crossed earlier. The army, he said, was beaten. The men of the brigade, as Keyes marched them back toward the crossing, suspected nothing until they came out of a wood. "As we emerged from the woods one glance told the tale; a tale of defeat, and a confused, disorderly and disgraceful retreat. The road was filled with wagons, artillery, retreating cavalry and infantry in one confused mass, each seemingly bent on looking out for number one and letting the rest do the same." These were mostly Sherman's men, with some of Franklin's. All semblance of regimental and brigade organization was lost in the retreat. At the moment, Keyes's was the only well-organized Federal command south of Bull Run, and he kept it that way until they crossed the stream and became mixed with the rest of the pan-

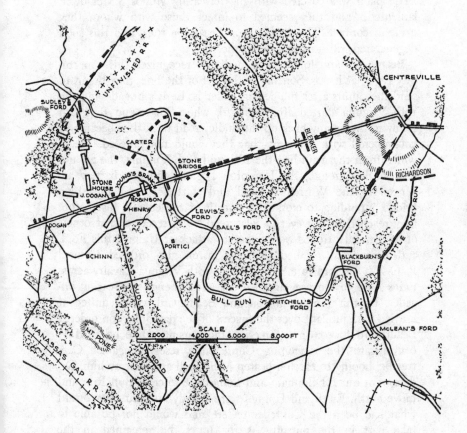

8. *The timely appearance of Elzey, leading Kirby Smith's brigade, and Early at the right place discourages McDowell's right flank, and the men start to withdraw. Retreat quickly becomes panicked rout as the Confederates mount a largely ineffectual pursuit.*

icked army. Schenck's brigade was waiting on the other side, and here Tyler halted Keyes to rest.[32]

The retreat began between four o'clock and four-thirty. The only troops McDowell could get to rally and stand on the slopes of Henry Hill while the rest of his right and center withdrew were Sykes and his regulars, and they stood the test bravely, while the remainder of the men of Franklin's, Willcox's, and Howard's brigades pulled back across the Warrenton road toward Sudley Ford. "The plain was covered with the retreating groups," McDowell lamented, "and they seemed to infect those with whom they came in contact. The retreat soon became a rout, and this soon degenerated still further into a panic."[33]

Beauregard and Johnston immediately recognized this opportunity for what it was. Starting at the left of the line, they began to send their units after the fleeing Federals. Early's brigade and the 19th Virginia started after Howard, while Stuart and Beckham followed the enemy back up the Sudley road until they became so encumbered with prisoners that they could not proceed. Meanwhile, from the main line the 18th and 28th Virginia, the 2d and 8th South Carolina, the Hampton Legion, and one battery advanced to the Warrenton road and started toward the stone bridge, intending to cross it in pursuit of the enemy. Just before they reached it, however, a false report was received that others of McDowell's troops were about to attack at Union Mills Ford, and Beauregard recalled them. Johnston also ordered Colonel R. C. W. Radford to take part of his 30th Virginia Cavalry across Ball's Ford to move against Keyes's and Schenck's retreating brigades. By this time, Johnston and Beauregard were reunited at Portici, each jubilant over the success of the day. Johnston ordered Beauregard to continue directing the pursuit, while he tried to concentrate the remaining Confederate reserves against Centreville, hoping to catch a beaten McDowell and destroy him. Orders went out for Bonham and Longstreet to cross Bull Run and move north. Ewell and Holmes were already on their way toward what had been the Confederate left, and would not be able to take part in the pursuit. As for Jones, he remained in the McLean's Ford area, still guarding against a possible attack by Richardson or Miles. In fact, Richardson stopped Bonham and Longstreet from pressing their advance toward Centreville, aided by the same false intelligence of an attack at Union Mills. Bonham and Longstreet also disagreed with one another, and from all these influences they finally retired back to the other side of Bull Run, perhaps missing an excellent opportunity to see some fighting, but not really missing anything more. Even if they had pushed past Richardson to get close to Centreville, by the time they did so it would have been nearly dark, not time enough to do more than start a fight.[34]

While Jackson and most of the other remnants of regiments on Henry Hill were ordered to mass in the vicinity of Portici under Jackson's command, the only other attempt at seriously pressing the enemy was Radford's crossing against Keyes and Schenck. Radford rode up to his men and cried to them, "General Johnston says the enemy are in full retreat and you must intercept them between the Stone Bridge and Centerville." The men were overjoyed that finally they would see their part in the battle. Guided by Colonel Chisolm of Beauregard's staff, Radford and his command rode down to Bull Run, crossed over, and turned north toward the flank of Tyler's brigades now on the road back toward Centreville. Before they reached Cub Run, Radford struck. Keyes saw the whole episode. "Then a scene of confusion ensued which beggars description. Cavalry horses without riders, artillery horses disengaged from the guns with traces flying, wrecked baggage-wagons, and pieces of artillery drawn by six horses without drivers, flying at their utmost speed and whacking against other vehicles. . . ." He saw men throw down their rifles as if they were snakes. "The rush produced a noise like a hurricane at sea." The attack by Radford was repulsed, but his cavalry continued to spar at the retreating mass all the way to Cub Run, doing much to maintain the panicked state of McDowell's men.[35]

It was Confederate artillery, which had done so much today, that finally ensured that the Federal rout would remain chaotic. Kershaw, Cash, and Hampton, along with Kemper's battery, resumed their pursuit toward the stone bridge after it was determined that the Union Mills Ford scare was a false one. They crossed the bridge and moved toward Centreville until they came upon a Federal line of defense on the hill which overlooked the suspension bridge over Cub Run. Here Kershaw and the others also found Radford's cavalry, who had just been repulsed by the enemy rear guard. At once, Kershaw, the senior officer on the field, formed his regiment and the Hampton Legion on the right of the road, and Cash's regiment on the left. Kemper and his battery were placed on the road itself. Then the whole line moved forward, encountering no substantial resistance from the rapidly retiring enemy.

Finally Kershaw's line crested the ridge and saw before it, several hundred yards off, the remnants of Keyes and Schenck—with some of Sherman's men undoubtedly—falling back in utter haste toward the bridge. At the same time, the remnants of the other Federal regiments, who had retreated by way of Sudley Ford and the other upstream fords, were coming in on the road from Sudley Ford which struck the Warrenton Turnpike just this side of the bridge. Both bodies of Federals collided at the entrance to the bridge at almost the same time, and just as Kershaw allowed Kemper to open fire. The effect was electric. Rout became bedlam. Kemper's first shot, fired by the venerable Edmund Ruffin, struck in the middle of the bridge just as a team was pulling a wagon across. In pain and panic the horses upset the wagon on the rickety bridge, effectively blocking it to all further traffic. "The whole mass of fugitives," wrote Ruffin, "immediately got out of the track, & all escaped who could, on foot & as quickly as possible." All of the wagons and artillery not already across the bridge were abandoned. Kershaw gloried in the spectacle. "Many of the soldiers threw their arms into the creek, and everything indicated the greatest possible panic." Perhaps a dozen more rounds were fired by Kemper, each increasing the desperation of the Federals, who waded and swam across the run any way they could to reach the other side and safety. After concentrating his fire on those who had retreated along the Warrenton road, Kemper turned his guns on the men coming down from Sudley Ford. In both cases, the dispersal of the enemy was complete. By now darkness was approaching. It was sometime after 7 p.m., and Beauregard sent Kershaw an order directing him to return to the stone bridge. Since Longstreet and Bonham had gotten nowhere and the rest of the army was too far back on the other side of Bull Run to assist, it was foolish to send Kershaw any farther forward. There had been victory enough for one day. Before he left, however, Kershaw helped get much of the abandoned ordnance and

stores safely back to the rear, and he left Cash's regiment at Cub
Run until well after midnight to handle the business of getting
the rest of the captures in hand.[36]

There was one other peculiar form of abandoned goods besides
the guns and wagons, and those unfortunate men who could not
get to the other side of Cub Run in time to escape. A considerable number of Washington's civilians, ladies, businessmen,
members of Congress, had come out in their buggies with bulging
picnic hampers, intent upon seeing the entertainment as McDowell drubbed the rebels. Instead, many of them were hopelessly
caught in the panic and trapped on the south side of Cub Run.
"Many distinguished citizens came over from Washington to wit-
ness the grand performance of their army," wrote a South
Carolinian four days later, "many of whom were captured and
frightened to death by our advancing army." In among the rifles
and knapsacks, and abandoned articles of uniform and equipment, the Confederates now and then found a lady's slipper or a
parasol. Senator Henry Wilson of Massachusetts had sat by a
roadside passing out sandwiches to fellow spectators. When the
rout commenced, he got in his buggy and tried to fight his way
through the sea of fugitives back to safety. He fell behind, however, and a Confederate emptied his shotgun into the back of the
senator's buggy, thinking he had killed him—hoping so at least.
He had not, but Wilson soon lost his buggy and had to comman-
deer a horse which he rode bareback to safety. Congressman Albert G. Riddle of Ohio tried valiantly to rally some of the demoralized Federals.[37]

Meanwhile, the soldiers themselves looted the knapsacks and
wagons left behind, and rejoiced in every manner of booty,
though not without some reservations. Men were warned not to
eat the food found in Federal knapsacks for fear that it had been
poisoned and left behind intentionally. Other Confederates would
ever after claim that they found a wagon filled with manacles—
handcuffs. The estimates of the numbers found ranged from 6,000
to 30,000, but whatever the number—or the veracity of the report
itself—the rumor that the enemy had intended to manacle them
like convicts or slaves infuriated the Southerners. But for now
they reveled in their finds. "Baggage lay as thick as the rocks on
the Pike," wrote a Virginian. "Wagons were broken in every fence

corner, guns, trunks, clothes &c blocked up the road." It was good
to be alive, and grand to be victorious. Certainly, at the moment
it was wonderful to be a Confederate.[38]

Even McDowell might have agreed with this. He was among
the last to get across Cub Run, and his dismay at seeing what had
become of his army must have been overwhelming. Courageously,
however, he set about trying to get those few organized commands left to form some kind of line below Centreville. Keyes
and Schenck were still in fairly good order, and so was that part of
Burnside's command which had fallen out of the battle early in
the day. With them, he started to form a front to meet any Confederate probes coming from the direction of the Warrenton
road. Then he rode south toward Blackburn's Ford to find out
what had become of his left flank, Miles and his division, and
Richardson's brigade of Tyler's division.

It had not been a good day for them. Miles's orders that morning were to make a show in front of Blackburn's Ford in order to
keep Beauregard from crossing there and threatening the left
flank while the main part of the army crossed at Sudley Ford.
However, thanks to the delay of the marching columns early in
the morning, Miles's own brigades, Blenker's and Davies', did not
get on the road for several hours, by which time Richardson had
already moved well down toward Blackburn's and opened a desultory artillery fire against Longstreet on the other side. Miles, when
finally he did get going, injudiciously left Blenker at Centreville
and sent only Davies to join Richardson. Davies further weakened
himself when he left two of his regiments to guard a road by
which Confederates coming from McLean's Ford or Union Mills
Ford might move on his left.

Finally Davies joined Richardson and assumed command of the
field. Here they kept up their artillery fire throughout the morning and into the afternoon, all the while constructing barricades
and earthworks in case of an enemy advance. Sometime before
noon Miles himself rode toward his front, first encountering the
regiments Davies had left behind. Miles, ill and drinking more
than he should, became infuriated that these units had been left
behind. He upbraided Davies when he found him and, his mood
growing blacker with every hour and every additional swallow of
brandy, he then left to find Richardson.

As morning turned into afternoon, Richardson could see that

Confederate troops were leaving the lower fords on Bull Run and moving toward the main battle. When Miles joined him, he, too, saw what was happening. Perhaps the Confederate right was thus weakened sufficiently for them to fight their way across the ford in their front and strike a telling blow where Beauregard could just now least stand it. Miles chafed at being left in reserve while the other generals fought today. Now he decided to advance on his own responsibility. Richardson would have none of it, however. He cited specific orders from McDowell that his brigade was not to attack anyone. This stopped Miles momentarily, but he still ordered that Richardson and Davies demonstrate against the enemy. A few regiments went forward but were forced back quickly.

Miles, meanwhile, went back to Centreville, and here he learned of the disaster on McDowell's right. One of Heintzelman's staff asked if Blenker could not be sent toward the stone bridge to try and stop the rout. Miles, apparently too ill and intoxicated to keep his reason, brushed the man aside saying, "I know all about the fight. You can't give me any information. I have something else to attend to." Shortly he saw through the fog, however, and he ordered Blenker to move toward Cub Run, while ordering Davies and Richardson to pull back toward Centreville. Davies got caught when Bonham and Longstreet pushed across Bull Run under orders from Beauregard to move on Centreville. He put his battery in a good position, and by its fire alone managed to stop the Confederates and disorient them long enough to pull away and march toward Centreville, where Richardson had already gone unmolested.

When Davies and Richardson met, both were puzzled by what had happened, neither greatly trusting the judgment of a man with as much liquor on his breath as Miles. Just then word came from McDowell that they were to take a position south of Centreville to prevent an enemy advance from the direction of Blackburn's Ford. They did so less than a mile south of the town, and here Miles once more rejoined them. He objected to their positioning of the regiments and began shifting things to suit himself. In passing the 12th New York, the outfit that was routed at Blackburn's Ford three days before, he growled at them, "You are now where I want you. Stay there, damn you, and die there."

One of Richardson's colonels objected to the way Miles was

acting, and sent an officer to Richardson. "We have no confidence in Colonel Miles," he said. Richardson asked why. "Because he is drunk," came the reply.

It was at about this same time, if not before, that McDowell learned of Miles's condition. He at once sent an aide to give Richardson command of the line below Centreville, telling him that Miles would be relieved of command. Richardson began overseeing the line at once, and meanwhile McDowell now rode to Miles to see what had been going on. "Colonel Miles," he said, "I find you have everything here in great confusion. You are relieved from the command of your troops." Then, leaving a saddened Miles behind him, McDowell went to Richardson's position to see what was being done. Sometime later Miles went to the line south of Centreville and, ignoring McDowell's orders, tried once more to direct Richardson's troops. The colonel was not about to stand for it. "Colonel Miles, I will do as I please," he said. "I am in command of these troops." To Miles's questioning stare, Richardson said bluntly, "Colonel Miles, you are drunk." Miles muttered something about arresting Richardson, who dared him to try it, then turned away.[39]

With Richardson and Davies south of Centreville, Blenker on the Warrenton Turnpike, and the remnants of Schenck and Keyes placed here and there along the line, McDowell had re-established at last a defensive perimeter on the high ground south and west of the town. It was almost dark now, and there would not be light enough for any further Confederate pursuit. McDowell must consider whether to try to stand and hold his ground or continue the retreat to Falls Church, or even Washington. He called a council of his officers just after dark and put the proposition to them. The majority opted to withdraw to Washington. McDowell, whose illness and fatigue caused him to doze during the meeting, had the operation begun immediately. With half of his army already streaming in a confused mob toward the capital, there was little else he could do. They had lost the fight, and their spirit.[40]

CHAPTER 12

ROUT AND RESOLUTION

For every long face in that weary army that marched and ran through the night and all the next day toward Washington, there was a smiling, jubilant one south of Bull Run. It was almost too much to believe, despite all the brag and boast before the battle over what they would do with the Yankees when they met them. Johnston and Beauregard and their Southern chivalry had won a crushing victory. McDowell was almost destroyed, and Manassas and Richmond were saved. There was no question that the infant Confederate States of America would have a long and healthy life.

Even before the firing was done, a tall, black-clothed figure rode on a horse through the stragglers and up to the lawn at Portici, where he met Johnston. It was President Davis. A military man who would rather have been a general-in-chief than a chief executive, he could not stand the uncertainty of Richmond and came instead this day to the battlefield. He actually rode in the pursuit toward Sudley Ford for a time, talking with the soldiers and cheering them on, before starting to find Johnston. As they shook hands, Davis asked, "How has the battle gone?" The general was only too happy to tell him. Sometime later the two rode back to Manassas and Beauregard's headquarters, where the President pumped Johnston for every detail of the fight. About 10 P.M. Beauregard came in off the field and found the two seated at his little wooden table. Davis warmly congratulated the Creole, who then gave some details of the battle the others had not heard.

At length, Davis said, "I think the news of our victory ought to be communicated, at once, to the War Dept. at Richmond." The generals agreed, and Davis wrote out a telegram. "Night has closed upon a hard-fought field," he began. "Our forces have won a glorious victory." There followed a few sketchy and inaccurate details of the fight, after which Davis personally signed it rather than handing it to the generals for signatures. Beauregard silently boiled at this, fearing that Davis, by signing the telegram, was trying to imply that he had commanded there, when in fact he had arrived when the battle was done. "My conclusion was however," Beauregard would write, "that we had to deal with an ambitious man." Davis faced re-election in a few months, and the Creole was sure Davis wanted the credit for this victory to help him win another at the polls.[1]

This done, Davis asked what manner of pursuit was being conducted. He was told of the false report of an advance at Union Mills Ford which had stopped all pursuit forces except Kershaw. Was it too late to start after the enemy now? he asked. Then news came in from an officer who claimed to have gotten close enough to Centreville to see that it was being abandoned. This was a perfect opportunity. Davis himself began writing an order for Bonham to pursue at once, but then it was learned that the officer had only been as far as Cub Run. Now the men decided that, without better information, they should not risk sending Bonham forward in the dark. Instead, Davis wrote—or claimed that he wrote—an order for Bonham to pursue at dawn the next day. Beauregard, however, only understood that Bonham was to make a reconnaissance, which is what was eventually done.[2]

Weather the next day made any sort of pursuit inpractical anyhow, as a heavy rain began in the morning and continued all day, swelling the streams and turning dusty roads into mires. And, though many would be loath to admit it, an effectual pursuit was out of the question anyhow. The Confederate army was nearly as disorganized and battered as McDowell's. Only Ewell, Holmes, Early, and Jones had seen no action, yet they were much wearied by their long march in the heat and dryness as they tried to reach the left. Most of the other brigades were cut up badly by the fighting; some, like those of Bee and Bartow, Evans and Hampton, were particularly disorganized. And even if a pursuit had been mounted, the Federals retreated too fast with too much head start.

But this could hardly dampen the spirits of the men in the camps in and around Manassas and along Bull Run on the day after the battle. The search across the battlefield for the treasures the enemy left behind went on all day and for several days thereafter. The cannon were the big prizes. In all, McDowell lost twenty-seven of them, eleven alone from Ricketts' and Griffin's batteries. The Rhode Island battery of Burnside's also lost five of its thirteen-pounders, and the giant thirty-pounder Parrott rifle was left behind as well, along with four guns each from two other batteries, most of them abandoned after the Cub Run bridge was blocked. The 71st New York also lost its two howitzers.[3]

The other things the men found were almost equally delightful. As much as one hundred rounds of ammunition for each cannon were left behind in caissons and limber chests. Forges, battery wagons, teams of horses, equipments of all kinds, over five hundred rifles, and half a million rounds of ammunition for them were picked up from the field. Even hospital stores and rations were left behind, chiefly by regiments that dropped their knapsacks before going into battle without having time to retrieve them in the rout. For weeks thereafter the Confederates would scour the hillsides and ravines for more of the items abandoned by the fleeing enemy. Much was found in the first few days by those assigned the odious task of burying the Federal dead where they fell. In the stifling July heat, the bodies of men and horses quickly bloated and then started the inevitable putrification. Long before all were buried, the smell that would attend so many battlefields in this war began to sour the nostrils of the living.[4]

It was also a time for Johnston and Beauregard to tally their own losses. They would eventually report 387 killed, 1,582 wounded, and 13 missing and probably killed or captured. Since such reports were inevitably inaccurate, largely because of men who felt their wounds too slight to report or else due to inaccurate surveys, it is certain that total Confederate casualties ran somewhat over 2,000: while Beauregard's and Johnston's combined armies totaled nearly 30,000, there were so many troops, such as those of Holmes, Ewell, and Early, who saw no fighting at all, and others, such as those of Longstreet, who saw only limited action, that the real brunt of the battle was borne by only about 17,000. This made total Confederate losses just under 12 per cent of those engaged. This hardly tells the whole story, however. Bee's small brigade lost better than 16 per cent in casualties. In Jackson's brigade, the percentages were even higher for some regiments. The 33d Virginia, which first took the batteries of Griffin and Ricketts, had losses of 30 per cent. Jackson's total losses were 525, about 16 per cent. Among the commands of Beauregard's army, the losses were less severe, though many still suffered much. Hampton lost as much as 20 per cent of his command.

Beyond this, the loss in leaders was substantial. Not one of Johnston's four brigade commanders emerged unwounded. Bee and Bartow were both killed. Smith was badly injured, though he would survive, and Jackson had a finger broken and almost severed by a musket ball. In addition, Colonel Gardner of the 8th Georgia was wounded, Jones of the 4th Alabama was killed and his other field officers wounded, Fisher of the 6th North Carolina was killed, and Imboden took several slight injuries, though none of them put him out of action. In Beauregard's Army of the Potomac, all of the brigade commanders managed to survive unscathed, but Hampton was wounded and his lieutenant colonel killed, Roberdeau Wheat was seriously injured, and a host of lesser field and company officers fell in the battle.[5]

In large part, the casualties told the tale of who did the fighting. Jackson and Bee took the greatest losses and bore the brunt of the fight along with Evans, whose casualties were miraculously few considering that his troops were engaged all day. Indeed, Evans was virtually alone in the first crucial hours when McDowell's flanking advance had to be stopped to provide time for Confederate reinforcements to arrive. Had Evans not held in those early hours of the battle, the chances of Johnston and Beauregard establishing a good defensive line anywhere north of Manassas were almost negligible. Characteristically, Evans was the first to admit this. He told one of his headquarters people that there was "no use for other Generals to brag about what they did in the battle—that he inaugurated that fight, he and Gen. Bee fought it through and he and Bee whipped the fight before any reinforcements came." Graciously sharing the credit for the victory, Evans finally conceded that "the fight was really won by God Almighty and a few private gentlemen." Bee, of course, did not live to boast of his command's part in the fight, but Jackson did. Though braggadocio was utterly foreign to his character, he relaxed enough to write to his wife with pardonable pride that, "Whilst great credit is due to other parts of our gallant army, God made my brigade more instrumental than any other in repulsing the main attack." He cautioned her not to say this to anyone else, however. "Let others speak praise," he said, "not myself." Somewhat more generous to the Almighty than Evans, Jackson declared that "all the glory is due to *God alone*."[6]

It had been a close thing for the Confederates all day, but the longer they stayed in the battle, the better their position became, thanks to the constant arrival of reinforcements at the right place and the right time. It was the coming of Elzey and Early which finally turned the battle in their favor, though they saw comparatively little fighting. Before they arrived McDowell was already stalemated, his army too exhausted and disorganized to hope any longer for a victory. But if the appearance of these two fresh brigades had not put the tired Federals into a panicked retreat, McDowell might have re-formed at Centreville and stayed there. Given a direct, short line of access to Washington for fresh supplies and equipment, and with a reserve division of new troops available there under Runyon, McDowell could have refitted his army for another attack across Bull Run long before Johnston and Beauregard could be ready to meet it. Indeed, within days after the battle the Confederates would be going hungry for lack of rations. Thus, Early and Elzey did more by their simple appearance on the field than their force of numbers would have accomplished anywhere else in the line.

The fact that these brigades arrived on the field where they did, and when they did, is but one indication of which of the Confederate commanders deserves the lion's share of the credit for the successful defense. Beauregard, who had already shown himself an impractical grand strategist in the days before the battle, proved himself an equally mediocre tactician in the fight itself. From the very beginning he never really had a firm grasp on the fighting. Instead of influencing it, he merely reacted to it. Evans, Bee, and

Jackson found and took their own positions, thereby establishing
the line that the battle would take for the rest of the day. Upon
reaching the scene, Beauregard oversaw the placement of some of
the regiments that Johnston forwarded to him, but even here it
was Kershaw who, on his own, extended the Confederate left to
blunt Howard. And it was Johnston who directed Elzey and Early
to that part of the field in which their appearance so frightened
the enemy. In fact, Beauregard acted chiefly as a dime novel general, leading the charge of an individual regiment, riding along
the line to cheer the troops, accepting the huzzas of the soldiers
and complimenting them in turn. The closest he came to a major
tactical decision was his fleeting intention to withdraw from the
Henry Hill line when he briefly mistook Early's advance for Patterson's arrival.

Meanwhile, it was Johnston, behind the lines, who exerted a far
greater influence on the battle. With a maturity which Beauregard lacked, he accepted the less glamorous role of noncombatant
and quietly but steadily did the job that won the battle. Steadily
throughout that hot afternoon he called up regiments and brigades from the south and dispatched them toward the front. It
was Johnston who pointed Kershaw to the left of the threatened
line, and who personally rode out in search of Smith to direct him
and Elzey to their positions, as he did with Early as well. Johnston did not know the terrain well. Indeed, it is probable that he
saw the countryside around Henry Hill for the first time when he
and Beauregard rode there to see how Evans and Bee were doing.
Still, through couriers and his own personal observation from the
high ground around Portici, Johnston kept informed of the progress of the battle, and sent units where they were needed most.

Thus it was unfair—though often typical of Civil War battles
—that the public acclaim went to the wrong man. Johnston,
though widely complimented for his part as over-all commander
of the victorious army, received far less acclaim than the much
more romantic figure Beauregard. It helped that the Creole was
still dear to Confederate hearts from his Sumter success. Now the
Southern public selected him to be lionized once more as the hero
of yet another great victory. Horses and boats and babies were
named for him. Composers named their songs after him. Newspapers gave him titles derived from the heroes of ancient Rome.

In the South in the weeks after the battle, he was the greatest
hero Confederates had yet known, his popularity threatening even
to eclipse that of President Davis. Indeed, many began to suggest
that this great general might make a great chief executive in the
coming elections, a thought well calculated to make Davis wary of
Beauregard. For now, however, all was cordiality between the two.
Davis sealed it by promoting Beauregard to the rank of full general on the day after the battle.

Even as Davis was handing Beauregard his promotion, the rank
and file of the army were themselves putting pen to paper. There
was a high rate of literacy in these first regiments raised in the war
that would not be found in later years, when the ranks were filled
more with the poor and uneducated. These men sensed that they
had taken part in something special, the largest battle ever yet
fought in North America, and surely the first and last battle of
this war. They hurried to put their thoughts and recollections into
writing for those at home. "Everybody is writing," declared a man
in Jackson's brigade, "who can raise a pencil or sheet of paper."
The letters themselves were much the same. "We have won a glorious victory here to day," a man of the 4th Virginia wrote late
that Sunday. "I saw the fiercest torrent of destruction and wrath
that I ever expect to see again," wrote an officer on Beauregard's
staff. Bonham's aide, Samuel Melton, wrote his wife that "We
have gained a glorious victory to-day, praise be to God." "We
have at last had a grand battle," wrote a South Carolinian, "perhaps the largest that was ever fought on this continent, and our
exertions and bravery were crowned with a victory that was only
equal to our efforts." More modest was Captain E. P. Alexander,
whose signal work contributed considerably to the success of the
Confederate army. "How grateful," he wrote, "we should be to
the God in whom we trusted & who has given us the victory."

Surely all were grateful for the victory. Most were glad just to
be alive. And that night after the battle, all of the men were
exhausted. Colonel John L. Manning, a volunteer aide on Beauregard's staff, tried to write a few details of the fight to his wife in
the darkness of headquarters a few hours after the conflict ended.
In his weariness, his pen faltered, smearing ink, making letters he
had not intended. Still he wrote proudly, and magnanimously.
"Untill the enemy became demoralized they fought well," he

wrote. Then he could say no more. "I cannot write more tonight. My eyes close of themselves from weariness."[7]

There were thousands of men and women throughout the South who anxiously awaited those letters. Their first news of the fight usually came by telegraph and was promptly passed on to the newspapers. Never again during the war did a battle get such fulsome coverage in the press as did this one. They could not decide what to call the battle—Young's Branch, Stone Bridge, Bull Run, Manassas, or Manassas Plain—but they published letter after letter from soldiers and correspondents who were in the fight. For those who had sons or fathers in the army, the great anxiety was to learn if he had been killed or wounded, and to many cities and homes the news was tragic. "Our city is filled with mingled exultation and sorrow at the news of the recent triumph," wrote a man in Savannah, Georgia. "Colonel Bartow and some of our best young men have fallen, and our city is filled with mourning."[8]

Richmond, of course, was most anxious of all, as evidenced by Davis' inability to remain there on the day of the battle. Probably the first civilian to know the outcome was Mrs. Davis, sent a wire by her husband after his arrival. She told most of her friends, and then took upon herself the task of telling Mrs. Bartow of her husband's death. Secretary of War Leroy P. Walker paced the War Department most of the day, damning his bad luck in being a cabinet minister rather than an officer in the Army. Through the day the rest of the Cabinet gathered there, along with many other prominent citizens, waiting for the few meager dispatches from Manassas. Nothing indicated which way the battle was going. Finally, Attorney General Judah P. Benjamin went to Mrs. Davis' hotel and there learned the contents of the President's telegram to her, which apparently was sent before the official announcement of the victory. Benjamin carried the news back to the War Department. "Then joy ruled the hour," wrote a clerk. Soon thereafter the victory announcement was received from Manassas and, as Beauregard feared, it gave many the impression that Davis "had directed the principal operations in the field." Lee was well pleased. "That indeed was a glorious victory & has lightened the pressure upon our front amazingly," he wrote his wife. As Richmonders flocked out to Manassas in the days following the battle, they congratulated the living, brought succor to the wounded whom they found "in every village on the railroad from Manassas to Richmond," and grieved for the dead, many of them badly buried. One shocked civilian wrote in horror that "the air was awful." War, for all its splendid glory, was beginning to show its grimmer side.[9]

How much grimmer are the horrors of war to the loser. Military writers before and after this war have used the cliché that a defeated army retires to "lick its wounds." Of wounds and killed and missing McDowell had plenty. But that was not the worst of it. How did an army retrieve its pride from utter humiliation? No one, not McDowell or Scott, or Lincoln or Washington City, had ever seen such a spectacle as was presented in the days following the battle. Thousands of totally demoralized soldiers, most of them dirty and hungry, many without arms or even uniforms, constantly trudged across the Potomac bridges into the capital or collapsed behind the earthworks at Alexandria.

Washington's first word of the disaster came with the speed of the telegraph wire, even as it was happening. Scott had received a few dispatches during the day, all of them encouraging. At 4 P.M., before the rout began, McDowell had an officer wire Scott that he had "driven the enemy before him." But then, not long afterward, came a telegram which conveyed all the panic and desperation of McDowell's defeated army. "The day is lost," it said. "Save Washington and the remnants of this army. . . . The routed troops will not reform." Ironically, just a few hours earlier Scott had sent to McDowell confirmation that Johnston had left the Shenandoah.[10]

Scott was incredulous but soon faced the situation. "We are not discouraged," he wired McDowell that night. At once he began forwarding troops toward Fairfax Court House, hoping that McDowell would rally there or at Centreville. But after a while he realized that the army was not going to stop retreating before it reached Alexandria at the least, and he stopped sending any more regiments. At 1 A.M., July 22, he wrote of "A most unaccountable transformation into a mob of a finely-appointed and admirably-led army." Scott still expressed his confidence in McDowell, but at the same time McClellan was ordered to leave his command and come to Washington, probably as a potential successor. By evening of July 22, McDowell was back in Arlington, and most of the rabble that had been an army were in the vicinity.[11]

Lincoln took the first news of the defeat in silence, and kept the intelligence to himself until he was asked by a congressman if the news was good or bad. Into his ear the President whispered, "It's damned bad." Still, when he met with McDowell the next day, Lincoln said he still had confidence in the general. Scott, too, did not immediately blame McDowell. He blamed himself for allowing the politicians to force him into sending an unready army out to fight a battle. The only person everyone seemed to be ready to blame without qualification was Patterson, and certainly he deserved much of it. His tardiness, vacillation, lack of will in the face of his subordinates, and moral cowardice were inexcusable. McDowell, with much less experience, had manfully advanced to the enemy and engaged him without wasting near as much time and energy as Patterson used just in trying to make up his mind. It was no loss to the Union that this was one old soldier who would now be allowed to fade away.[12]

McDowell and his officers were almost unanimous in their conclusions on the disaster. Only Tyler would blame McDowell. The others would agree for the most part with the most articulate of their number, Colonel Sherman. "Bull Run Battle was lost by us," he wrote six years later, "not from want of combination, strategy or tactics, but because our army was green as grass." "The Rebel army was little if any better," he continued, "and the attacking force was sure to be beaten, unless its antagonist ran off." Yet he concluded that, "Though a source of great disgrace it was no misfortune, for we then realised that organization & discipline were necessary." Already skeptical of the worth of volunteer soldiers and officers, Sherman was now convinced that the war had to be fought in large part by Regulars. At least the men in charge should be Regulars, and he never really altered that view.[13] Rational though he was, Sherman keenly felt the humiliation of defeat. "I am sufficiently disgraced now," he wrote three days after the battle, "I suppose soon I can sneak into some quiet corner."

McDowell himself blamed Patterson and, indirectly, Scott for allowing Johnston to make his junction with Beauregard. But assigning the blame was, for now, rather academic. The battle had been lost, and it was time to tally the cost. It was high. Reports showed 460 men killed, 1,124 wounded, and 1,312 missing and presumed killed or captured. That came to 2,896 total casualties and, allowing for error and inadequate reporting, the total probably ran somewhat in excess of 3,000. As with the Confederates, the tally showed who did the heaviest fighting. Sherman's brigade had the highest battle losses, 312 killed and wounded, and total losses of 605. Porter was next, with 464 total casualties, followed closely by Willcox with 432. Conversely, Davies suffered only three. The 79th New York of Sherman's brigade alone lost 198, though 115 of these were men captured or missing. It was Franklin's 1st Minnesota that stopped the most enemy lead. All told, 155 men of that regiment were killed or wounded.

Beyond this, the loss in leaders was severe. Hunter and Heintzelman had both been wounded, the former rather severely. The only brigade commander injured was Willcox, who was at first presumed to be killed. Among the regimental officers, Colonel Cameron of the 79th New York and Colonel John Slocum of the 2d Rhode Island died on the field, while the lieutenant colonels of the 11th and 69th New York were mortally wounded. The injuries among McDowell's officer corps were not as many or as grave as those of the Confederates, but they were much felt just the same, particularly by Secretary of War Simon Cameron, who had a brother to lament.[14]

No one substantially faulted McDowell's generalship in the battle. Sherman claimed that Bull Run "was one of the best-planned battles of the war," and McDowell planned it entirely on his own. His battle orders and plans were far more erudite than Beauregard's, and much better thought out. His design for the fight was excellent, missing only the strong defensive position open to the rebels at the Henry Hill line, and this McDowell could not know about with the faulty maps available. His deployment of Miles's division and Richardson's brigade achieved the desired result. Richardson alone held about 10,000 Confederates out of the main action.

McDowell's fault, of course, lay in overestimating the ability of his raw troops to move quickly on the morning of the battle, and in not gathering—or at least trying harder to gather adequate information on the roads to Sudley Ford and the other fords. Such information might not have exhausted Hunter and Heintzelman before they ever entered the fight. As for just how much influence McDowell personally exerted on the firing line, accounts are sketchy, but he certainly committed the same error that his brigade commanders made in attacking by regiments only rather than in brigade strength. Of course in the early hours of the fight, a brigade strength attack might have defeated his purpose. He did not want a general engagement. He only wanted to push his way past the Confederates to cut them off from Richmond. Too large an attack might bring on such a major battle, whereas smaller regimental assaults should answer the task of pushing the enemy aside to clear the Warrenton road for Tyler's advance. But when the course of the battle changed, and it became obvious that this was going to be a major engagement, certainly McDowell's tactics should have changed accordingly. Of course, at this early day in the war, few if any on either side knew how to fight what would be a more modern war than any yet seen on the globe. No one can be faulted for a lack of prescience. This would be a new kind of war, one to be mastered by learning firsthand, not by the light of past experience.[15]

As for the present experience, the men in the camps around Washington were not as prolific in their written outpourings to home. After all, they had little to boast of other than safety. "I have had a chance to *smell powder*," wrote a Maine boy. "I have just arrived from that terrible battlefield," wrote another upon reaching the District of Columbia. Most presumed, as did a man of the 3d Michigan, that "i suppose you are anxious to hear about the battle." Most wrote soberly of what they had experienced. "I can truly say that I have seen all the horrors of war," said one. Another, from the battered 1st Minnesota, wrote that "I am one of the fortunate ones that escaped from the disaster." Most of the details of the battle they covered with pride, since they felt themselves the victors until 4 P.M. As for the story of the retreat that became a rout, the men wrote with surprising candor. "My courage never feiled me until they commenced to drive us before them —I could have sold myself for about 3 shillings." Another, a man of the 5th Massachusetts, confided that "we were lucky dogs to get off as well as we did."[16]

The news the boys wrote home, along with the agonizingly

full reports in the press, hardly raised spirits in the North. "Today will be known as *BLACK MONDAY*," wrote a New Yorker, referring to the day the news of the disaster reached the city. "We are utterly and disgracefully routed, beaten, whipped by secessionists." The disappointment was heightened by exaggerated reports of soldiers that the rebels mutilated and murdered the wounded. "Scrape the 'Southern Gentleman's' skin, and you will find a second-rate Comanche underneath it," wrote a civilian who believed the stories. The populace did what Scott and Lincoln did not. They quickly began to blame the generals. Schenck, Patterson, McDowell, and Tyler were all vilified, McDowell even being accused of drunkenness. Politicians and civic leaders, incredulous that the army they had raised could be beaten, demanded scapegoats. Scott and McDowell seemed the prime candidates. The thirst for blood may even have been encouraged by a new medium which brought the image of the battle more to life even than a correspondent's account. Those who had stereopticon viewers would soon be able to see photographs of parts of the battlefield made on the spot, some of them while the battle raged. Mr. Mathew Brady of Washington had taken his camera along with the army. "I know well enough that I cannot take a photograph of a battle," he told someone on the march, "but I can get a little glimpse of some corner somewhere that will be worth while. We are making history now, and every picture that we get will be valuable." Soon the few views he got of the field were much in demand. It did not help that several of them showed Federal dead sprawled on the slope of Matthews Hill.[17]

Still, most people of the Union did not lose heart in the task before them. Rather, the defeat gave them a renewed sense of purpose. National pride and honor had to be avenged. "If the North be not cast down and discouraged by this reverse," wrote one, "we shall flog these scoundrels and traitors all the more bitterly for it before we are done with them."[18]

Much this same reaction was feared by intelligent men of the Confederacy. Their victory, wrote one War Department clerk, would stimulate the North "to renewed preparations on a scale of greater magnitude than ever." The purposeful declaration of one disgruntled Federal soldier spoke well for his nation. "I shall see the thing played out," he wrote, "or die in the attempt."[19]

With the great battle done, there came a time of rest and rebuilding for both armies. The scene in the Confederate camp was almost as bad as that in McDowell's, if not worse. Camp sanitary conditions rapidly deteriorated to the point that Beauregard's adjutant, Colonel Thomas Jordan, feared the army would bury itself in its own filth. As for provisions, suddenly the Commissary Department in Richmond seemed to cease functioning. Ten days after the battle, Captain Alexander complained, "We can do nothing now for want of provisions, for our army is actually *almost starving*." The army's organization remained chaotic for days. New troops arriving found that "The confusion that reigned about our camps for the next few days was extreme. . . . Men of all arms and all commands were mixed in the wildest way. A constant fusillade of small arms and singing of bullets were kept up, indicating a superfluity of disorder, if not of ammunition." Many were actually wounded by the wild firing in celebration that went on for some days. The problems were all compounded by the fresh regiments that arrived for several days after the fight, most of them terribly disappointed that they had missed what would be surely the last battle of the war. There was no food and no shelter and no sanitation facilities for these new men. Beauregard actually had to ask Davis to stop sending men, complaining that "some regiments are nearly starving."[20]

In time the problems were alleviated, and the army settled into a routine of drill and training, and the endless monotony of camp life. The armies and the generals remained at Manassas and the vicinity well into March of 1862 before another Federal advance, this one overwhelming, forced them to abandon the area without a fight. Repeatedly Beauregard and Johnston, their officers and men, rode and walked over the battlefield, reliving for all who would listen the day of glory and triumph. Back in the camps, the men enjoyed what they could of a warm summer and a lovely autumn. "You have no idea of the wonderful state of idleness in which we live," Captain Alexander wrote late in August. In Ewell's headquarters he could be found lying listlessly on his couch reading a book on tactics, while men of his staff slept, wrote home, read novels upstairs, or just did nothing. Aside from inconsequential skirmishes, there was no real action in that theater for seven months, the chief military exploit being Johnston's and Beauregard's design of a new battle flag for Confederate regiments that would preclude confusing it with the Stars and Stripes. It was a red square, with a blue St. Andrew's cross adorned with one white star for each Confederate state. It would be in use for the rest of the war by all of the Southern armies. On October 22, Johnston was assigned command of the newly created Department of Northern Virginia, encompassing all of Virginia north of the James River and including the Shenandoah. In the newly created department, the Army of the Potomac passed the first winter of the war, still flush in the euphoria of victory. How many more war winters there would be no one in that army could know.[21]

No one in the army around Washington knew either, but more and more they began suspecting that it would not be such a quick little war after all. An army of amateurs had taken the field and met its match. Next time it would take an army of professionals—still volunteers, but trained and disciplined as American soldiers never had been before. The work began in earnest on August 15, when the old Northeastern Virginia command became the Department and Army of the Potomac. By the time these men and the thousands who joined them marched again in March of 1862, the Union had forged the largest, best-equipped, and best-trained army ever seen on the continent. It was an army forged in the defeat at Bull Run and tempered by many defeats to come, defeats which, in the end, hardened it into near invincibility. Ironically, just as the Union army came to adopt the title of its opponent at the first battle, so did the Confederate army that it faced eventually change is designation to the Army of Northern Virginia. It was a war of ironies.

Just as much lay ahead for the armies, so it did for the chief actors in this first scene of the drama. Some met ignominy. Miles was investigated by a court of inquiry and found guilty of drunkenness, though with extenuating circumstances. He never held a really important command again, and was finally killed while commanding a garrison at Harpers Ferry in September 1862. As for Blenker and Davies, both became generals, though neither particularly distinguished himself. From McDowell's Third Division, Franklin, Willcox, and Howard all became generals as well, and Howard would three years hence command an army, the

Army of the Tennessee. Franklin served out the war as a contentious and difficult subordinate, toppling himself from high commands until he was shelved in 1864. Willcox eventually rose to corps command and proved himself the best officer of the three, but only after he spent more than a year in a Confederate prison. And an artillerist from Franklin's brigade, Captain Ricketts, recovered from his wounds and was appointed a brigadier for his services in the battle. He rose to command a corps in the fighting in the Shenandoah in 1864.

Another artilleryman, this one from Porter's brigade of Hunter's division, rose to wear a general's stars. Charles Griffin became one of the premier corps commanders of the Union Army, and a commissioner at the surrender at Appomattox in 1865. Others in Hunter's command saw equal or greater rises. Porter became a brigadier but had to leave the army because of bad health. Sykes, whose Regulars stood so well, climbed to a major generalcy and a corps command. And Burnside would one day command this very army as a major general. At Fredericksburg, in December 1862, he would lead it to one of the greatest disasters met by any Union army in the war. A tragic figure who lacked both confidence in himself and any genuine talent, he was shifted about for the remainder of the war until finally relieved of command for poor generalship. Hunter himself would become a major general, and would have many commands, most of which he led either to defeat or else to tarnished victory. His chief distinction was to become one of the most hated Yankees in all the Confederacy, thanks to his views on emancipation. His fellow division commander, Heintzelman, was not hated at least, but he was largely ignored. After showing little acumen in several field and department commands, he finished the war serving on courts-martial.

Of the First Division, General Tyler stayed in the Army until 1864, achieving nothing and spouting much venom at McDowell, for whom he developed an intense dislike. Keyes and Schenck both exercised corps command later in the war, but both resigned their commissions before the peace. Ayres, whose battery never made it into the main action, developed into one of the finest division commanders in the service, ending the war as a major general. But the star of this division, as indeed of the whole army that fought on July 21, was Sherman. As the years of strife went forward, he became one of the two great leaders of the Union, and one of history's outstanding generals. In July 1861 he was an obscure colonel, certain that disgrace would dog him the rest of his days. By war's end, he was William Tecumseh Sherman, the very image of Mars himself.

Poor McDowell. He became the scapegoat. His command lasted just four weeks after his defeat. Then, as suspected, McClellan superseded him and began building the Army of the Potomac. McDowell commanded a division and then a corps in that army, and then led a corps in another army in which his performance was adjudged inferior. He finished the war in command of the Pacific coast, where he stayed after the war to become a park commissioner in San Francisco. Few more tragic figures would emerge from the war. Anything but a success in the first battle of the war would certainly doom the defeated commander. It was McDowell's unhappy lot to be the first in a series of Federal experiments to find the right man to lead the Union to victory. No one could know that the man who was needed was an obscure colonel training a regiment out in Illinois while McDowell fought his battle. It was a man to whom McDowell had taught tactics at West Point two decades before, Ulysses S. Grant.

There were great captains of the future south of the Potomac as well. Two of the Confederates would go on to command armies of their own in the days ahead. Early, as a lieutenant general, was one of the fightingest corps commanders in the South until given an independent command in the Shenandoah in 1864. He led a celebrated raid which passed through Maryland, and actually opened fire on the defenses of Washington itself before being driven back. After the war, no ex-Confederate worked harder to win by the pen what had been lost by the sword. He remained cantankerous to the very end. As for the wounded Kirby Smith, he rose to the rank of full general and finished the war commanding the Department and Army of the Trans-Mississippi, that Confederate territory west of the great river. So firmly did he rule that the land was called "Kirby Smithdom."

For the other brigade commanders at Manassas, varying degrees of achievement awaited. Ewell became a lieutenant general, as did Longstreet and Holmes. The first two, along with A. P. Hill of

the 13th Virginia, proved to be three of the four foremost corps
commanders in Virginia, part of the very soul of the Army. The
fourth man, of course, was "Stonewall" Jackson, the most inspired
soldier in the Army. He too became a lieutenant general. But he
became what none of the others ever achieved: a legend. Just as
Sherman was the one great leader to emerge from the Union army
at Bull Run, so was Jackson the one genius in the rough that the
Army of the Potomac would contribute. For all of posterity he
would need even less to identify him and his greatness than Sherman. One need only say "Stonewall."

Stuart enjoyed a rapid ascension, becoming a lieutenant general
and the premier cavalryman of the Army, though he, like Jackson,
would not survive the war. Imboden rose to brigadier, serving
competently in secondary theaters of the war. Elzey was promoted
brigadier for his "Blucher of the day" service at Manassas, and
served with distinction until a serious wound took him out of active service for the rest of the war. The engagingly egotistical
Shanks Evans fought well on several more fields, rising to brigadier before his evil temper and drinking habits brought him twice
before courts-martial, and ended his service in obscurity. The gallant Major Wheat recovered from his wound, just as he boasted
he would, only to be killed the following year in a battle against
McClellan. Bonham resigned his commission to take a seat in the
Confederate Congress, rejoining the Army only in the last months
of the war. As for Jones, later battles brought him the distinction
that was denied him by his inactivity at Manassas, but in 1863 his
recurrent heart problem brought him death at the age of thirty-
seven.

Philip St. George Cocke, who was principally responsible for
selecting the line of defense that the Confederates used through
the successful campaign, was appointed a brigadier once more in
October. His health was ruined by his arduous services, however.
As winter came on, he left the Army and went home. There, the
day after Christmas, 1861, he committed suicide.

Neither Johnston nor Beauregard ever lived up again to what
was expected of them after Bull Run. Eventually they quarreled
over the conduct of the battle, and both quarreled with President
Davis over just about everything. Beauregard was sent to Kentucky
in January 1862 to assist the army that eventually fought the Battle

of Shiloh in April. The battle ended with him commanding the army, but then, his health failing, he spent most of the rest of the war commanding the coastlines of South Carolina and Georgia, coming north briefly to fight at Petersburg, Virginia, in 1864, where he saved the city from capture by Grant. At war's end, he was once more serving under Johnston. Few who showed so much promise in the early days of the conflict proved to be greater disappointments. Always grand, always eloquent, he was just never a first-rate general.

Johnston was a better one, though he, too, could not live up to expectations, thanks chiefly to that same quirk that kept him from bagging any birds when hunting with Hampton. If he did not fight a pitched battle, a loss could not tarnish his reputation. Remaining in command of the army around Manassas, he tried to fight against McClellan in the Peninsular Campaign in March–May 1862, but a serious wound at Seven Pines put him out of action for months. Command of his army then went to another architect of the Bull Run victory, General Robert E. Lee. Johnston, meanwhile, went west to try to relieve besieged Vicksburg in 1863, and later took command of the Army of the Tennessee for most of what would be its epic campaign against Sherman from Dalton, Georgia, to surrender in North Carolina. His campaign was one strategic retreat after another, all skillfully executed, but all a great disappointment to the Confederacy. Just as contentious as Beauregard and Davis, he made many enemies of onetime friends. But at the same time, he made a fast friend of a former enemy. He and Sherman met for the first time when Johnston surrendered to him in April 1865. They became very close in the years ahead. When Sherman died on February 14, 1891, Johnston came to New York to march in the funeral procession as an honorary pallbearer. Bareheaded, he stood in the cold, and damp, and wind. When admonished to put his hat on for fear he might take ill, Johnston, eighty-four years old, replied, "If I were in his place and he were standing here in mine, he would not put on his hat." He caught a cold. It taxed his weak heart. And five weeks later he was dead.

And the battlefield? Few would ever agree on what to call it, Bull Run or Manassas. The battle done, the farmers returned to their fields and the people to their homes. The streams and runs

washed the blood from their banks. The rebuilding began, and
the endless march of Nature went on. But it was not to go on
without one more interruption. In August of 1862 the armies
came here once more. This time the Confederates were led by
Lee, but there were familiar names among his subordinates: Jackson, Longstreet, Jones, Evans, Hill, Ewell, Early, Stuart. And
across the lines fought other men who had been here before.
Names like Schenck, Ricketts, Heintzelman, Sykes, and McDowell were on the order of battle. Ranks and relative positions had
changed, but the field was the same. As a year before, it was
Henry Hill that proved the key to the battle, though this time the
Federals held it, and the Confederates were north of the Warrenton road. But as a year before, it ended in Union defeat, though
this time there was no rout. Never again would this Army of the
Potomac turn to rout.

Then finally the armies were gone for good, the fighting moved
south for the duration. Once more the land was given back to its
people, and the people to the land. The bridge was destroyed, and
the Henry house burned. The earthworks and explosions of artillery had changed the face of the land. The mark of war would be
a long time in fading. But it did fade, until it was almost gone,
leaving the peaceful hills and valleys of Manassas at rest by the
waters of Bull Run. Many would not live to see it this way again,
and at least one man simply would not wait. Wilmer McLean saw
part of his home ruined when an artillery shell tore through the
roof and almost extinguished Beauregard and his staff as they ate.
McLean decided not to wait around for more battles to be fought
around him. He would find a safer place, a retreat where the war
would not come again to disturb him. But still the armies found
him one more time.

He moved to Appomattox Court House.

DOCUMENTATION BY CHAPTER

INTRODUCTION

1. Milledge L. Bonham to P. G. T. Beauregard, August 27, 1877, Milledge L. Bonham Papers, South Caroliniana Library, University of South Carolina, Columbia, S.C.; Louis A. Sigaud, "Mrs. Greenhow and the Rebel Spy Ring," *Maryland Historical Magazine*, XLI (September 1946), p. 173; U. S. War Department, *War of the Rebellion: Official Records of the Union and Confederate Armies* (Washington, 1880–1901), Series I, Volume 51, Part 2, p. 688. This last source is hereafter cited as O.R., with series, volume, part, and page numbers given as I, 51, pt. 2, p. 688.

CHAPTER 1

1. Roy P. Basler, ed., *The Collected Works of Abraham Lincoln* (New Brunswick, N.J., 1953), IV, pp. 261, 271.
2. Douglas S. Freeman, *Lee's Lieutenants* (New York, 1943–44), I, p. 712n.
3. O.R., I, 2, pp. 23–27, 37–42.
4. Warren W. Hassler, Jr., *Commanders of the Army of the Potomac* (Baton Rouge, 1962), pp. 3–5; James B. Fry, *McDowell and Tyler in the Campaign of Bull Run* (New York, 1884), pp. 7–9; U. S. Congress, *Report of the Joint Committee on the Conduct of the War* (Washington, 1863), Part 2, p. 37 (hereafter cited as C.C.W.); O.R., I, 2, p. 653.
5. O.R., I, 2, pp. 653–55, 659; I, 51, pt. 1, p. 400.
6. *Ibid.*, I, 51, pt. 1, pp. 389–90, 396.

CHAPTER 2

1. O.R., I, 2, pp. 776–77, 780, 785–87; I, 51, pt. 2, pp. 19, 29.
2. O.R., I, 2, pp. 784–85; Staunton, Virginia, *Vindicator*, April 26, 1861.

3. James I. Robertson, Jr., *The Stonewall Brigade* (Baton Rouge, 1963), pp. 7–8, 11; *O.R.*, I, 2, p. 862; Mary Anne Jackson, *Memoirs of Stonewall Jackson* (Louisville, Ky., 1895), p. 168.

4. Joseph E. Johnston, *Narrative of Military Operations* (New York, 1874), p. 16; W. W. Goldsborough, *The Maryland Line in the Confederate Army* (Baltimore, 1900), pp. 10–11; John N. Opie, *A Rebel Cavalryman with Lee, Stuart and Jackson* (Chicago, 1899), pp. 19–20.

5. George W. Hopkins to his mother, May 24, June 8, 9, 1861, George W. Hopkins Papers, A. L. P. Vairin Diary, May 21, June 1, 1861, Mississippi Department of Archives and History, Jackson, Miss.

6. Goldsborough, *Maryland Line*, pp. 19–20; "Work of a Confederate Woman," *Confederate Veteran*, IX (July 1901), p. 322.

7. *O.R.*, I, 51, pt. 2, p. 66; Blanton Duncan to Thomas J. Jackson, October 22, 1861, Dabney-Jackson Collection, Virginia State Library, Richmond.

8. *O.R.*, I, 2, pp. 798–99, 819; Jubal A. Early, *War Memoirs* (Bloomington, Ind., 1960), pp. 2–3; Lee A. Wallace, comp., *A Guide to Virginia Military Organizations* (Richmond, 1964), pp. 115, 120, 127.

9. George A. Gibbs, "With a Mississippi Private in . . . the Battle of First Bull Run," *Civil War Times Illustrated*, IV (April 1965), pp. 42–43.

10. William M. Owen, *In Camp and Battle with the Washington Artillery* (Boston, 1885), pp. 8–13.

11. John B. Gordon, *Reminiscences of the Civil War* (New York, 1904), pp. 26–28; Ezekiel Armstrong Diary, June 13, 1861, Mississippi Department of Archives and History.

12. James B. Suddath, "From Sumter to the Wilderness," *South Carolina Historical Magazine*, LXIII (January 1962), p. 2; Thomas Pitts to "Lizzie," May 28, June 10, 1861, Pitts-Craig Papers, Emory University Library, Atlanta; D. Augustus Dickert, *History of Kershaw's Brigade* (Newberry, S.C., 1899), pp. 32–34; Jesse W. Reid, *History of the Fourth Regiment of S.C. Volunteers* (Greenville, S.C., 1892), pp. 10–11.

13. John Coxe, "Wade Hampton," *Confederate Veteran*, XXX (December 1922), p. 460; John Coxe, "The Battle of First Manassas," *Confederate Veteran*, XXIII (January 1915), p. 24.

14. *O.R.*, I, 2, pp. 806, 817, 824, 841, 845, 846–47; I, 51, pt. 2, pp. 79, 82.

15. *O.R.*, I, 2, pp. 831, 865, 879–80; I, 51, pt. 2, pp. 102, 104, 105, 108; Francis W. Pickens to Bonham, July 7, 1861, Bonham Papers, South Carolina.

16. *O.R.*, I, 2, pp. 60–64, 872–73, 886, 895, 896; I, 51, pt. 2, pp. 113–14, 123.

CHAPTER 3

1. C.C.W., p. 38.
2. O.R., I, 51, pt. 1, pp. 396, 399, 408.
3. John C. Gregg to "Friend Heber," May 28, 1861, Peter Schmitt Collection, Calendar of Stephen L. Lowing Papers, Allen M. Giddings Collection, Western Michigan University Library, Kalamazoo, Mich.; Charles P. Haydon Diaries, April 30, May 25, 1861, Michigan Historical Collection, University of Michigan, Ann Arbor, Mich.
4. Charles C. Perkins Diary, May 24, June 7, 1861, in possession of Frederick Clark, Marblehead, Mass.
5. J. Pine to Mrs. Alfred Pine, May 16, 1861, North Family Papers, Cornell University Library, Ithaca, N.Y.; Seymour Hall, "A Volunteer at the First Bull Run," War Talks in Kansas (Kansas City, Mo., 1906), p. 150.
6. Pine to Alfred Pine, June 21, 1861, North Family Papers; Thomas S. Allen, "The Second Wisconsin at the First Battle of Bull Run," War Papers Read Before the Commandery of the State of Wisconsin (Milwaukee, 1896), p. 376; Nathan Foster to his wife, June 12, 1861, Clarrissa Haas and Stanley Oswalt Collection; Gregg to "Friend Heber," June 11, 1861, Schmitt Collection, Western Michigan University; Haydon Diary, June 8–9, 1861.
7. Gerald S. Henig, ed., "The Civil War Letters of George S. Rollins," Civil War Times Illustrated, XI (November 1972), p. 21; Haydon Diary, June 10, 1861; Perkins Diary, June 18, 19, 1861; Foster to his wife, June 12, 1861, Haas and Oswalt Collection; Gregg to "Friend Heber," June 11, 25, 1861, Schmitt Collection; Augustus Woodbury, A Narrative of the Campaign of the First Rhode Island Regiment (Providence, 1862), pp. 26–27.
8. O.R., I, 2, pp. 652, 657–58, 660–62; I, 51, pt. 1, p. 392; Robert Patterson, A Narrative of the Campaign in the Valley of the Shenandoah in 1861 (Philadelphia, 1865), p. 31.
9. O.R., I, 51, pt. 1, pp. 397–98.
10. Ibid., I, 2, pp. 670–71.
11. C.C.W., p. 79; O.R., I, 2, pp. 657, 685.
12. O.R., I, 2, pp. 187, 686, 687, 691, 692–93; C.C.W., pp. 79–80.

CHAPTER 4

1. Pickens to Bonham, July 7, 1861, Bonham Papers, South Carolina.
2. O.R., I, 2, pp. 896, 901–2, 907; John Esten Cooke, Wearing of the Gray (Bloomington, Ind., 1959), p. 73.
3. Alfred Roman, The Military Operations of General Beauregard in the War Between the States (New York, 1884), I, pp. 66–69; O.R., I, 2, p. 907; Sigaud, "Rebel Spy Ring," pp. 174–75.

266 DOCUMENTATION BY CHAPTER

4. T. Harry Williams, *P.G.T. Beauregard, Napoleon in Gray* (Baton Rouge, 1955), p. 70; John B. Jones, *A Rebel War Clerk's Diary* (New York, 1961), p. 28.

5. O.R., I, 2, pp. 943–44.

6. U. P. Bonney to Eli W. Bonney, May 29, 1861, Eli W. Bonney Papers, Duke University; J. R. Winder, "Second South Carolina at First Manassas," *Confederate Veteran*, XVII (January 1909), p. 28.

7. William Scarborough, ed., *The Diary of Edmund Ruffin* (Baton Rouge, 1977), II, p. 55; A. P. Aldrich to Mattie Aldrich, June 23, 1861, Bonham Papers, South Carolina; Frederick S. Daniel, *Richmond Howitzers in the War* (Richmond, 1891), pp. 19–20; Pitts to "Lizzie," June 25, 1861, Pitts-Craig Papers; Ben Ames Williams, ed., *A Diary from Dixie* (Boston, 1949), pp. 58–59.

8. Richard S. Ewell to Bonham, June 21, 1861, Bonham Papers, South Carolina; Gordon, *Reminiscences*, pp. 38–39; Thomas R. Lightfoot, "Letters of the Three Lightfoot Brothers, 1861–1864," *Georgia Historical Quarterly*, XXV (1941), pp. 394, 396.

9. Natalie J. Bond, ed., *The South Carolinians. The Memoirs of Col. Asbury Coward* (New York, 1968), pp. 14–15; Gibbs, "Mississippi Private," p. 44.

10. James Longstreet, *From Manassas to Appomattox* (Philadelphia, 1896), pp. 32–33; Loehr, *First Virginia*, pp. 8, 9; G. Moxley Sorrel, *Recollections of a Confederate Staff Officer* (New York, 1905), p. 17; Alexander Hunter, *Johnny Reb and Billy Yank* (New York, 1905), pp. 46, 47.

11. Early, *Memoirs*, pp. xl, 3–4; Dickert, *Kershaw's Brigade*, p. 46; Richard Bryant to his wife, June 29, 1861, Bryant Family Papers, Virginia State Library; George J. Hundley, Reminiscences of the First and Last Days of the War, Virginia Historical Society, Richmond; Joseph Sessions to Lida Sessions, July 7, 1861, Joseph F. Sessions Papers, Mississippi Department of Archives and History; Micah Jenkins to his wife, July 11, 1861, Micah Jenkins Papers, Duke University; Charles W. Squires Memoir, Southern Historical Collection, University of North Carolina, Chapel Hill; Longstreet, *Manassas to Appomattox*, pp. 34–35.

12. Williams, *Diary from Dixie*, p. 62.

13. Roman, *Beauregard*, I, p. 77; Williams, *Beauregard*, p. 71; Early, *Memoirs*, pp. 4–5; O.R., I, 2, pp. 447–48.

14. Roman, *Beauregard*, I, pp. 81–87; John L. Manning to his wife, July 7, 1861, Williams-Chesnut-Manning Papers, South Caroliniana Library; Williams, *Diary from Dixie*, pp. 82–83.

15. E. P. Alexander to his wife, July 10, 1861, E. Porter Alexander Papers, Southern Historical Collection; Maury Klein, *Edward Porter Alexander* (Athens, Georgia, 1971), pp. 32–33.

16. Bonham to Beauregard, August 27, 1877, Bonham Papers, South Carolina; O.R., II, 2, p. 1308; Roman, *Beauregard*, I, p. 89;

Rose Greenhow, *My Imprisonment and the First Year of Abolition Rule at Washington* (London, 1863), p. 16.

CHAPTER 5

1. O.R., I, 2, pp. 124–30, 664–65, 695; Samuel P. Heintzelman Diary, June 10, 1861, Samuel P. Heintzelman Papers, Library of Congress, Washington, D.C.
2. O.R., I, 2, pp. 125, 700; I, 51, pt. 1, p. 404.
3. O.R., I, 2, pp. 718–21.
4. James H. Stine, *History of the Army of the Potomac* (Philadelphia, 1892), pp. 9–10; C.C.W., pp. 36–37, 55, 62.
5. Heintzelman Diary, June 29, 1861, Heintzelman Papers; C.C.W., p. 36.
6. O.R., I, 2, p. 726; I, 51, pt. 1, pp. 411, 413–14.
7. Lucius E. Chittenden, *Invisible Siege* (San Diego, 1968), p. 119.
8. Heintzelman Diary, July 10, 1861, Heintzelman Papers; C.C.W., p. 38; Donald Mitchell, *Daniel Tyler, A Memorial Volume* (New Haven, Conn., 1883), p. 49.
9. C.C.W., p. 38; Heintzelman Diary, July 11, 14–16, 1861, Heintzelman Papers.
10. O.R., I, 2, pp. 707–8, 709, 711–12.
11. *Ibid.*, pp. 717–18, 725.
12. *Ibid.*, pp. 729–30, 735.
13. Johnston, *Narrative*, p. 17; O.R., I, 2, pp. 889–90, 907–8, 910, 923–24.
14. Pickens to Bonham, July 7, 1861, Bonham Papers, South Carolina; Williams, *Diary from Dixie*, p. 175.
15. Johnston, *Narrative*, pp. 19, 24–25; O.R., I, 2, pp. 934–35; I, 51, pt. 2, p. 143.
16. O.R., I, 2, pp. 187, 962.
17. Johnston, *Narrative*, pp. 27–30; O.R., I, 51, pt. 2, pp. 153–54; I, 2, pp. 185–86.
18. O.R., I, 2, pp. 967, 969; Johnston, *Narrative*, pp. 30–31.
19. Williams, *Diary from Dixie*, pp. 85, 126.
20. R. H. Beattie, Jr., *Road to Manassas* (New York, 1961), pp. 84–85; O.R., I, 2, pp. 157, 158, 179–85.
21. O.R., I, 2, pp. 159–61; C.C.W., pp. 55–56.
22. O.R., I, 2, pp. 161–62, 163–64; C.C.W., p. 195; Patterson, *Narrative*, pp. 53–55.
23. C.C.W., p. 56.

CHAPTER 6

1. O.R., I, 2, pp. 303, 304.
2. Sullivan Ballou to Sarah Ballou, July 14, 1861, Civil War Letters Collection, Chicago Historical Society.

3. Martin A. Haynes, *A History of the Second Regiment, New Hampshire Volunteer Infantry* (Lakeport, N.H., 1896), pp. 19–20; C. B. Fairchild, comp., *History of the 27th Regiment N.Y. Vols.* (Binghamton, N.Y., 1888), p. 9; Woodbury, *First Rhode Island*, pp. 76–77.

4. Elnathan B. Tyler, *"Wooden Nutmegs" at Bull Run* (Hartford, Conn., 1872), pp. 56–57; C.C.W., p. 39.

5. Alfred S. Roe, *The Fifth Regiment Massachusetts Volunteer Infantry* (Boston, 1911), p. 65; Edwin S. Barrett, *What I Saw at Bull Run* (Boston, 1886), p. 12; George W. Bicknell, *History of the Fifth Regiment Maine Volunteers* (Portland, Me., 1871), pp. 22–23; Oliver O. Howard, *Autobiography* (New York, 1907), I, pp. 147–48; Oliver O. Howard to Lizzie Howard, July 18, 1861, Oliver O. Howard Papers, Bowdoin College Library, Brunswick, Maine.

6. O.R., I, 2, p. 304.

7. Heintzelman Diary, July 17, 1861, Heintzelman Papers.

8. Mitchell, *Tyler*, pp. 50–51; Tyler, *"Wooden Nutmegs,"* pp. 61–63; Allen, "Second Wisconsin," pp. 380–81; William Todd, *The Seventy-Ninth Highlanders* (Albany, 1886), pp. 20–21.

9. Perkins Diary, July 17, 1861; C.C.W., p. 39; Haydon Diary, July 17, 1861, Michigan Historical Collection; George D. Wells to "Dear S.," July 17, 1861, George D. Wells Letterbook, East Carolina University Library, Greenville, N.C.

10. Woodbury, *First Rhode Island*, pp. 79–80.

11. O.R., I, 2, pp. 447, 449–50, 453; Dickert, *Kershaw's Brigade*, pp. 55–56.

12. Woodbury, *First Rhode Island*, pp. 80–83; Perkins Diary, July 17, 1861; William T. Lusk, *War Letters* (New York, 1911), p. 52.

13. John H. Burrill to his parents, July 20, 1861, in possession of Perry E. Jamieson; William M. Thompson, *Historical Sketch of the Sixteenth Regiment N.Y.S. Volunteer Infantry* (n.p., 1886), p. 7; Newton M. Curtis, *From Bull Run to Chancellorsville* (New York, 1906), pp. 38–39.

14. Heintzelman Diary, July 17, 1861, Heintzelman Papers; Barrett, *What I Saw*, p. 13.

15. C.C.W., p. 39.

16. *Ibid.*, p. 39; O.R., I, 2, pp. 305, 307–8, 328–29; Mitchell, *Tyler*, p. 50; James B. Fry to Heintzelman, July 18, 1861, Heintzelman Diary, July 18, 1861, Heintzelman Papers.

17. General Orders No. 120, July 16, 1861, Thomas Jordan Papers, Chicago Historical Society; O.R., I, 2, pp. 980–81.

18. Roman, *Beauregard*, I, p. 90; O.R., I, 2, pp. 980–81.

19. General Orders No. 41, July 17, 1861, Jordan Papers.

20. O.R., I, 51, pt. 2, p. 176.

21. Bonham to Beauregard, August 25, 1877, Bonham Papers, South Carolina.

22. Thomas Pitts to Lizzie Pitts, July 17, 1861, Pitts-Craig Papers.

23. Pitts to Lizzie Pitts, July 20, 1861, Pitts-Craig Papers; Robert W. Shand, "Incidents in the Life of a Private Soldier," 1907-8; L. P. Foster to Mary Ann Foster, July 19, 1861, James R. McKissick Papers; Samuel W. Melton to Mary Melton, July 20, 1861, Samuel W. Melton Papers, South Caroliniana Library; Scarborough, *Ruffin*, pp. 70-72; Emmet Seibels to Bonham, February 13, 1862, Bonham Papers, Duke University, Winder, "Second South Carolina," p. 28.

24. O.R., I, 51, pt. 1, p. 24; Charles T. Jones, "Five Confederates, The Sons of Bolling Hall in the Civil War," *Alabama Historical Quarterly*, XXIV (February 1962), p. 144; J. A. Gardner to Amanda Gardner, July 27, 1861, Amanda Gardner Papers, Duke University; Francis W. Chamberlayne Memoir, 1900, Chamberlayne Family Papers, Virginia Historical Society.

25. O.R., I, 51, pt. 2, p. 177; Roman, *Beauregard*, I, p. 92.

26. A. R. Chisolm to George P. Smith, April 15, 1901, A. R. Chisolm, Notes on Blackburn's Ford, Alexander R. Chisolm Papers, New-York Historical Society.

CHAPTER 7

1. O.R., I, 2, p. 310; George M. Finch, "The Boys of '61," G.A.R. *War Papers, Department of Ohio* (Cincinnati, 1891), I, pp. 253-54.

2. C.C.W., p. 199; Mitchell, *Tyler*, pp. 51-52.

3. O.R., I, 2, p. 313; Henry F. Lyster, "Recollections of the Bull Run Campaign," *War Papers Read Before the Michigan Commandery of the Military Order of the Loyal Legion* (Detroit, 1888), I, pp. 7-8.

4. O.R., I, 2, pp. 310, 313; C.C.W., p. 199; Mitchell, *Tyler*, pp. 52-53.

5. O.R., I, 2, p. 311; Warren H. Cudworth, *History of the First Regiment Massachusetts Infantry* (Boston, 1866), pp. 41-42; William L. Haskin, comp., *History of the First Regiment of Artillery* (Portland, Me., 1879), p. 146.

6. Jerome J. Robbins Diaries, July 18, 1861, Michigan Historical Collection.

7. Cudworth, *First Regiment*, p. 42; Wells to "Dear S.," July 19, 1861, Wells Letterbook.

8. John Setright to "Dear cousin," July 28, 1861, John T. Setright Papers, Michigan Historical Collection; O.R., I, 2, pp. 328-29; John G. Barnard, *The C.S.A. and the Battle of Bull Run* (New York, 1862), pp. 48-49; Fry, *McDowell and Tyler*, pp. 28, 29; C.C.W., p. 162; Mitchell, *Tyler*, p. 53.

9. Mitchell, *Tyler*, pp. 53-54; C.C.W., pp. 199-200; Henry E. Noyes, "A Few Guns Before the First Gun at Bull Run," *Journal of the Military Service Institution of the United States*, XLIX (1911), p. 415; G. W. Miller to his parents, July 20, 1861, John F. Lane Collection, Western Michigan University, Kalamazoo; Haydon Diaries, July 18, 1861, Michigan Historical Collection.

10. Mitchell, *Tyler*, p. 54; *O.R.*, I, 2, p. 311; William R. Wells to "Dear Friends," July 23, 1861, William R. Wells Papers, Southern Historical Collection.

11. John C. Gregg to "Friend Heber," July 25, 1861, Schmitt Collection; Perry Mayo to his parents, July 23, 1861, Mayo Family Papers, Michigan State University, East Lansing, Mich.

12. Wells to "Dear Friend," July 23, 1861, William R. Wells Papers; *O.R.*, I, 2, p. 313; Cudworth, *First Regiment*, p. 45.

13. *O.R.*, I, 2, p. 313; Cudworth, *First Regiment*, p. 45; Perkins Diary, July 18–19, 1861.

14. Haydon Diary, July 18–19, 1861, Michigan Historical Collection; Daniel G. Crotty, *Four Years Campaigning in the Army of the Potomac* (Grand Rapids, Mich., 1874), p. 22; Gregg to Heber, July 25, 1861, Schmitt Collection.

15. *C.C.W.*, pp. 20–21; *O.R.*, I, 2, p. 313; Mitchell, *Tyler*, p. 54; Lyster, "Recollections," p. 9; Gregg to Heber, July 25, 1861, Schmitt Collection; Miller to parents, July 20, 1861, Lane Collection.

16. William T. Sherman, *Memoirs* (New York, 1875), I, pp. 209, 214.

17. M. A. De Wolfe Howe, *Home Letters of General Sherman* (New York, 1909), p. 200.

18. Lusk, *Letters*, p. 53; Todd, *Seventy-Ninth Highlanders*, pp. 24–25.

19. Mitchell, *Tyler*, p. 54; *O.R.*, I, 2, pp. 306–7, 314; Fry, *McDowell and Tyler*, pp. 29–30; Haydon Diary, July 18, 1861, Michigan Historical Collection; Howe, *Home Letters*, pp. 201–2.

20. Cudworth, *First Regiment*, pp. 50, 52; Haydon Diary, July 18, 1861, Michigan Historical Collection.

21. Owen, *Washington Artillery*, pp. 25–26; Peter Hairston to Fanny Hairston, September 4, 1861, Peter Hairston Papers, Southern Historical Collection.

22. *O.R.*, I, 2, p. 441; Early, *Memoirs*, p. 6.

23. *O.R.*, I, 51, pt. 1, p. 33; Loehr, *First Virginia*, p. 9.

24. Alexander Hunter, *Four Years in the Ranks*, p. 34, Virginia Historical Society; Hunter, *Johnny Reb*, pp. 52–55.

25. *O.R.*, I, 2, pp. 461–62; Longstreet, *Manassas to Appomattox*, pp. 38–39; William Morgan, *Personal Reminiscences of the War of 1861–5* (Lynchburg, Va., 1911), pp. 53–54.

26. *O.R.*, I, 2, p. 462; Longstreet, *Manassas to Appomattox*, p. 39; Loehr, *First Virginia*, p. 9.

27. Early, *Memoirs*, pp. 7–8; Squires, Memoir.

28. Squires, Memoir; Longstreet, *Manassas to Appomattox*, pp. 39–40; Early, *Memoirs*, p. 8; *O.R.*, I, 2, p. 462; James Franklin, "Incidents at the First Manassas Battle," *Confederate Veteran*, II (October 1894), p. 292.

29. Loehr, *First Virginia*, pp. 9–10; Longstreet, *Manassas to Appomattox*, p. 40; Early, *Memoirs*, p. 8; Manning to his wife, July 18, 1861, Williams-Chesnut-Manning Papers.

CHAPTER 8

1. Chisolm, Notes on Blackburn's Ford, Chisolm to Smith, April 15, 1901, Chisolm Papers.
2. Johnston, *Narrative*, p. 33; Bradley T. Johnson, *A Memoir of the Life and Public Service of Joseph E. Johnston* (Baltimore, 1891), p. 45; Magnus H. Thompson, "The Strategy of Stonewall Jackson," *Confederate Veteran*, XXX (March 1922), p. 93; O.R., I, 51, pt. 2, pp. 188–89.
3. Gilbert E. Govan and James W. Livingood, *A Different Valor, The Story of General Joseph E. Johnston* (Indianapolis, 1956), pp. 46–47; O.R., I, 2, p. 478.
4. Johnston, *Narrative*, pp. 33–34.
5. Johnson, *Johnston*, p. 46; Robert U. Johnson and Clarence C. Buel, eds., *Battles and Leaders of the Civil War* (New York, 1887), I, p. 229.
6. Jackson, *Jackson*, p. 175; Opie, *Rebel Cavalryman*, p. 25; D. B. Conrad, "History of the First Battle of Manassas and the Organization of the Stonewall Brigade," *Southern Historical Society Papers*, XIX (1891), p. 87; Susan P. Lee, *Memoirs of William Nelson Pendleton* (Philadelphia, 1893), pp. 147–48; Charles C. Wight Reminiscences, Virginia Historical Society.
7. N. H. R. Dawson to Elodie Dawson, July 18, 1861, N. H. R. Dawson Papers, Southern Historical Collection.
8. O.R., I, 51, pt. 2, pp. 188–89; Bradley T. Johnson, "Memoir of First Maryland Regiment," *Southern Historical Society Papers*, IX (1881), p. 482; Bradley T. Johnson, "Memoir of the 1st Md. Regiment," January 1863, Bradley T. Johnson Papers, Duke University.
9. Williams, *Diary from Dixie*, p. 69; "Work of a Confederate Woman," *Confederate Veteran*, IX (July 1901), p. 323.
10. Johnston, *Narrative*, pp. 37–38; Roman, *Beauregard*, I, p. 91.
11. Chisolm, Notes on Blackburn's Ford, Chisolm Papers.
12. Jackson, *Jackson*, p. 177; Wight Recollections; George Baylor, *Bull Run to Bull Run* (Richmond, 1900), p. 20; Conrad, "Battle of Manassas," p. 87.
13. Johnston, *Narrative*, p. 37; clipping, "The 7th and 8th Georgia Regiment at Manassas," July 3, 1861, M. J. Solomons Scrapbook, Duke University; B. M. Zettler, *War Stories and School-day Incidents for the Children* (New York, 1912), p. 58.
14. Thomas Goldsby, "Fourth Alabama Regiment—Official Report," July 29, 1861, clipping in Solomons Scrapbook; Johnston, *Narrative*, p. 38.
15. Johnson, "Memoir," p. 482; James McHenry Howard, *Recollections of a Maryland Confederate Soldier* (Baltimore, 1914), pp. 34–35; Goldsborough, *Maryland Line*, p. 22.
16. Keller Anderson, "Kentuckians Defend Their State," *Confederate Veteran*, XVI (November 1908), p. 597; Maud Brown, *The University Greys* (Richmond, 1940), p. 19.

17. Lee, *Pendleton*, p. 148; Cary I. Crockett. "The Battery That Saved the Day," *Field Artillery Journal*, XXX (January–February 1940), pp. 29–30.

18. J. E. B. Stuart to his wife, June 13, 1861, J. E. B. Stuart Papers, Duke University; William W. Blackford, *War Years with Jeb Stuart* (New York, 1945), pp. 19–24.

19. Richard Habersham to Bernard and Emma Habersham, July 19, 1861, Habersham Family Papers, Library of Congress; James Griffin to his wife, July 19, 1961, James Griffin Papers in possession of R. Bransford.

20. John Coxe, "The Battle of First Manassas," *Confederate Veteran*, XXIII (January 1915), pp. 24–25.

21. Johnston, *Narrative*, pp. 38–39; General Orders, July 20, 1861, Joseph E. Johnston Papers, Henry E. Huntington Library, San Marino, California.

22. Early, *Memoirs*, pp. 10–12; Owen, *Washington Artillery*, p. 30.

23. Johnston, *Narrative*, pp. 39–41; Special Orders, July 20, 1861, Williams-Chesnut-Manning Papers.

24. Roman, *Beauregard*, I, p. 97.

25. O.R., I, 2, pp. 779–80; Freeman, *Lee's Lieutenants*, I, pp. 50–51.

26. Johnston, *Narrative*, p. 41.

27. C.C.W., pp. 163–64, 191, 229–31; Patterson, *Narrative*, pp. 57–58; Beattie, *Road to Manassas*, pp. 104–5.

28. O.R., I, 2, pp. 165–68, 171, 172; C.C.W., p. 232.

29. O.R., I, 2, pp. 330, 743–44.

30. O.R., I, 2, pp. 330–31; Barnard, *Bull Run*, pp. 49–50.

31. Heintzelman Diary, July 19–20, 1861, Heintzelman Papers.

32. William T. Sherman to John Sherman, July 19, 1861, William T. Sherman Papers, Library of Congress; C.C.W., pp. 23, 34, 40, 167; Heintzelman Diary, July 19, 1861, Heintzelman Papers.

33. O.R., I, 2, p. 745.

34. C.C.W., p. 39; Heintzelman Diary, July 20, 1861, Heintzelman Papers.

35. Howe, *Home Letters*, p. 202; Heintzelman Diary, September 1, 1861, Heintzelman Papers; Howard, *Autobiography*, I, p. 152; Mitchell, *Tyler*, pp. 56–57; C.C.W., p. 207.

36. O.R., I, 2, p. 318.

37. C.C.W., p. 24.

38. Howe, *Home Letters*, p. 202; Howard to his wife, July 20, 1861, Howard Papers; Howard, *Autobiography*, I, p. 152.

39. New York *Times*, July 24, 1861.

CHAPTER 9

1. O.R., I, 2, p. 362.

2. Finch, "Boys of '61," pp. 255–56; Robert M. Johnston, *Bull*

Run, Its Strategy and Its Tactics (Boston, 1913), p. 166; O.R., I, 2, p. 362.

3. Mitchell, *Tyler*, pp. 57–58.

4. Finch, "Boys of '61," p. 256.

5. Sorrel, *Recollections*, p. 93; Thomas Pelot to Lalla Pelot, September 15, 1861, Lalla Pelot Papers, Duke University Library.

6. Reid, *Fourth Regiment*, pp. 23–24; O.R., I, 2, pp. 558–60; T. B. Warder, *Battle of Young's Branch, or Manassas Plain* (Richmond, 1862), pp. 42–43, 45.

7. O.R., I, 2, p. 348.

8. *Ibid.*, p. 59; *Confederate Veteran*, V (June 1897), p. 298, (December 1897), p. 621.

9. Howe, *Home Letters*, p. 206.

10. O.R., I, 2, p. 559; Klein, *Alexander*, p. 39; E. P. Alexander, *Military Memoirs of a Confederate* (New York, 1907), p. 30.

11. O.R., I, 2, p. 383; Charles G. Halpine to Margaret Halpine, July 2, 1861, Charles G. Halpine Papers, Henry E. Huntington Library.

12. Woodbury, *First Rhode Island*, pp. 88–89.

13. *Ibid.*, pp. 90–92; Haynes, *Second Regiment*, pp. 23–24.

14. C.C.W., p. 161; Woodbury, *First Rhode Island*, pp. 91–93.

15. O.R., I, 2, p. 518; Freeman, *Lee's Lieutenants*, I, pp. 54–56.

16. O.R., I, 2, p. 489; Freeman, *Lee's Lieutenants*, I, p. 56.

17. O.R., I, 2, p. 559.

18. O.R., I, 2, pp. 384, 385, 395; Woodbury, *First Rhode Island*, pp. 93–94; David Hunter, *Report of Military Service* (New York, 1892), p. 9.

19. O.R., I, 2, pp. 384, 390; Dangerfield Parker, "The Regular Infantry in the First Bull Run Campaign," *United Service*, XII (1885), p. 526.

20. O.R., I, 2, p. 559; "Major Chatham Roberdeau Wheat," *Confederate Veteran*, XIX (September 1911), p. 427; Frank Wheat to his wife, July 26, 1861, John T. Wheat Papers, Southern Historical Collection.

21. Goldsby, "Report," Solomons Scrapbook; Crockett, "Battery That Saved the Day," p. 30; Johnson and Buel, *Battles and Leaders*, I, p. 232.

22. Goldsby, "Report," Solomons Scrapbook.

23. Zettler, *War Stories*, pp. 60–62; "7th and 8th Georgia at Manassas," Solomons Scrapbook.

24. O.R., I, 2, p. 489; Zettler, *War Stories*, pp. 62–63.

25. "7th and 8th Georgia at Manassas," Solomons Scrapbook; Robert M. Myers, *The Children of Pride* (New Haven, Conn., 1972), p. 726; letter from unidentified soldier of the 7th or 8th Georgia, July 21, 1861, Museum of the Confederacy, Richmond; Warder, *Young's Branch*, p. 41; Jones, *Diary*, pp. 36–37.

26. Rufus Hollis Memoir, p. 1, Tennessee State Library and Archives, Nashville; Goldsby, "Report," Solomons Scrapbook; Dawson to Elodie Dawson, July 21, 1861, Dawson Papers; "Joe P. Angell," *Confederate Veteran*, XVIII (March 1910), p. 133; Jones, *Diary*, pp. 36–37.

27. O.R., I, 2, p. 384.

28. Heintzelman Diary, September 1, 1861, Heintzelman Papers; O.R., I, 2, p. 402; Lewis H. Metcalf, "So Eager Were We All," *American Heritage*, XVI (June 1965), pp. 36–37.

29. Howe, *Home Letters*, pp. 206–7; Mitchell, *Tyler*, p. 59; C.C.W., p. 43; Lusk, *Letters*, p. 57; Todd, *Seventy-Ninth Highlanders*, p. 34.

30. Goldsby, "Report," Solomons Scrapbook; Howe, *Home Letters*, p. 207; Todd, *Seventy-Ninth Highlanders*, p. 34.

CHAPTER 10

1. Roman, *Beauregard*, I, pp. 101–2; Freeman, *Lee's Lieutenants*, I, pp. 59–60.

2. O.R., I, 51, pt. 2, p. 199; Beauregard to Early, April 14, 1884, Jubal A. Early Papers, Library of Congress.

3. Campbell Brown Reminiscences, Brown-Ewell Papers, Tennessee State Library; Gordon, *Reminiscences*, pp. 38–42.

4. Jordan to Early, July 8, 1861, P. G. T. Beauregard Papers, Duke University; A. C. Myers to William P. Miles, June 17, 1861, William Porcher Miles Papers, Southern Historical Collection; Alexander, *Military Memoirs*, pp. 32–34.

5. O.R., I, 51, pt. 2, p. 689.

6. C.C.W., p. 201.

7. Richard Habersham to Emma Habersham, July 26, 1861, Habersham Family Papers; James Lowndes to "Cousin Mattie," August 2, 1861, James Lowndes Papers, South Caroliniana Library.

8. Manly W. Wellman, *Giant in Gray: A Biography of Wade Hampton* (New York, 1947), pp. 62–63.

9. O.R., I, 2, p. 481; Opie, *Rebel Cavalryman*, pp. 26–28; Chisolm, Notes on Bull Run, Chisolm to Smith, April 20, 1901, Chisolm Papers.

10. Opie, *Rebel Cavalryman*, p. 30; Randolph Barton, "Stonewall Brigade at Louisville," *Confederate Veteran*, VIII (November 1900), p. 482; Jones, *Diary*, p. 39.

11. Conrad, "First Battle of Manassas," pp. 89–90; Charleston, South Carolina, *Mercury*, July 25, 1861.

12. Dawson to Elodie Dawson, July 24, August 29, 1861, Dawson Papers; Samuel W. John, "The Importance of Accuracy," *Confederate Veteran*, XXII (August 1914), p. 343.

13. John, "Importance," p. 343; Goldsby, "Report," Solomons Scrapbook.

14. Charleston, South Carolina, *Mercury*, July 25, 1861; Williams, *Diary from Dixie*, p. 88; Freeman, *Lee's Lieutenants*, I, pp. 733–34.

15. Goldsby, "Report," Solomons Scrapbook; Dawson to Elodie Dawson, July 24, August 9, 1861, Dawson Papers; Opie, *Rebel Cavalryman*, pp. 30–31.

16. Johnston, *Narrative*, p. 48; J. A. Chapman, "The 4th Alabama Regiment," *Confederate Veteran*, XXX (May 1922), p. 197.

17. "7th and 8th Georgia Regiments at Manassas," Solomons Scrapbook; Warder, *Young's Branch*, pp. 42–48; O.R., I, 2, p. 492.

18. O.R., I, 2, pp. 475, 492; Johnston to Bradley Johnson, September 30, 1887, Johnson Papers.

19. Barton, "Stonewall Brigade," p. 483; William Smith, "Reminiscences of the First Battle of Manassas," *Southern Historical Society Papers*, X (1882), p. 437; O.R., I, 2, pp. 492, 545.

20. O.R., I, 2, pp. 492–93.

21. Opie, *Rebel Cavalryman*, p. 31; Henry Kyd Douglas, "Stonewall Jackson and His Men," *Annals of the War* (Philadelphia, 1879), pp. 642–43.

22. C.C.W., pp. 168–69, 243.

23. Eleana H. Henry, Some Events Connected with the Life of Judith Carter Henry, Virginia Historical Society.

24. J. K. McWhorter, "Caring for the Soldiers in the Sixties," *Confederate Veteran*, XXIX (October 1921), p. 410; Metcalf, "So Eager Were We All," p. 37; C.C.W., p. 144.

25. Zettler, *War Stories*, pp. 67–68; Opie, *Rebel Cavalryman*, p. 31; Baylor, *Bull Run*, p. 21.

26. John O. Casler, *Four Years in the Stonewall Brigade* (Guthrie, Okla., 1893), p. 27.

27. Metcalf, "So Eager Were We All," p. 37.

28. Blackford, *War Years*, pp. 24–32; Metcalf, "So Eager Were We All," pp. 37–38.

29. A. C. Cummings, "Thirty-Third Virginia at First Manassas," *Southern Historical Society Papers*, XXXIV (1906), pp. 368–69; A. C. Cummings to Johnston, December 27, 1870, Joseph E. Johnston Papers, William and Mary College Library, Williamsburg.

30. O.R., I, 2, pp. 384–85; C.C.W., p. 243; Metcalf, "So Eager Were We All," p. 38.

31. C.C.W., p. 169; Johnson and Buel, *Battles and Leaders*, p. 235; Crockett, "Battery That Saved the Day," p. 32; Jackson, *Jackson*, pp. 177–78.

32. Squires Memoir, Southern Historical Collection; Owen, *Washington Artillery*, pp. 36–38.

33. C.C.W., pp. 169, 216; O.R., I, 51, pt. 1, pp. 212, 394, 407; Heintzelman Diary, September 1, 1861, Heintzelman Papers.

34. C.C.W., p. 169; Casler, *Four Years*, pp. 28–29.

35. O.R., I, 2, p. 495.

CHAPTER 11

1. O.R., I, 2, p. 567; Wellman, *Hampton*, p. 64; Benjamin I. Scott to Fanny Scott, July 25, 1861, Scott Family Papers, Virginia Historical Society.

2. C.C.W., pp. 147, 169, 216–17.

3. Henry N. Blake, *Three Years in the Army of the Potomac* (Boston, 1865), p. 22; O.R., I, 2, p. 409.

4. Casler, *Four Years*, p. 29; Jackson, *Jackson*, p. 178; Samuel Seig to Carrie Davis, July 25, 1861, Samuel S. Seig Papers, Duke University; Opie, *Rebel Cavalryman*, pp. 25, 26, 29.

5. O.R., I, 51, pt. 1, p. 21; Lloyd Pendergast to friends, July 26, 1861, Lewis Harrington Family Papers, Fred ? to George ?, July 24, 1861, Charles E. Davis Papers, Minnesota Historical Society, St. Paul; Opie, *Rebel Cavalryman*, p. 29.

6. Allen, "Second Wisconsin," pp. 388–91.

7. Lusk, *Letters*, pp. 58–59; Todd, *Seventy-Ninth Highlanders*, p. 37.

8. O.R., I, 2, pp. 370, 372; Howe, *Home Letters*, pp. 207–10.

9. Beattie, *Road to Manassas*, pp. 174–75.

10. Heintzelman Diary, September 5, 1861, Heintzelman Papers; Marshall Phillips to his wife, July 24, 1861, Marshall Phillips Papers, Maine Historical Society, Portland.

11. Howard, *Autobiography*, I, p. 158.

12. Edward K. Gould, *Major-General Hiram G. Berry* (Rockland, Me., 1899), pp. 63–65; O.R., I, 2, p. 422.

13. Howard, *Autobiography*, I, p. 159; Howard to his mother, July 29, 1861, Howard Papers.

14. Henig, "Letters of George S. Rollins," p. 24; Howard, *Autobiography*, I, pp. 159–60.

15. Samuel W. Ferguson Memoirs, Samuel W. Ferguson Papers, Duke University.

16. C. P. Fisher to his sister, July 17, 1861, Hairston Papers; Benjamin White to J. J. Phillips, n.d. [August 1861], James J. Phillips Papers, North Carolina Department of Archives and History, Raleigh.

17. O.R., I, 2, pp. 518–19; C. P. Varner, "Third South Carolina Regiment," *Confederate Veteran*, XVIII (November 1910), p. 520; Shand, Incidents, p. 43; Melton to his wife, July 25, 1861, Melton Papers.

18. O.R., I, 2, p. 522; Alfred ? to E. M. Kennedy, July 25, 1861, Means-English-Doby Family Papers, South Caroliniana Library; Scarborough, *Ruffin*, p. 83.

19. O.R., I, 2, p. 522.

20. *Ibid.*, p. 522; William H. Murry to ?, July 1861, Maryland Historical Society, Baltimore; Randolph McKim, *A Soldier's Recollections* (New York, 1911), p. 34; Samuel D. Buck Memoir, Sam-

uel D. Buck Papers, Duke University; Arnold Elzey, Report, July 25, 1861, Johnson Papers, Duke University.

21. Howard, *Recollections*, p. 35; McKim, *Recollections*, pp. 34–35.

22. Johnston, *Narrative*, pp. 51–52; Nina Kirby-Smith, " 'Blucher of the Day' at Manassas," *Confederate Veteran*, VII (March 1899), p. 108; Johnson, "Memoir," p. 482.

23. Howard, *Recollections*, pp. 35–36; J. W. Lillard, "Events of 1861–65 Recalled," *Confederate Veteran*, XXI (January 1913), p. 18.

24. O.R., I, 2, p. 522; McKim, *Recollections*, p. 36; Howard, *Recollections*, pp. 36–37; Johnson, Memoir, January 1863, Johnson Papers.

25. Elzey, Report, Johnson Papers; O.R., I, 2, p. 482; Howard, *Recollections*, pp. 37–40; Johnson, "Memoir," p. 483.

26. Freeman, *Lee's Lieutenants*, I, pp. 71–72n.; Beauregard to Early, April 8, 1881, April 14, 1884, Early Papers.

27. O.R., I, 2, pp. 555–56; Early, *Memoirs*, pp. 16–19; Johnston, *Four Years*, p. 82; P. E. Ellis, "On that Hot Sunday Afternoon, July 21, 1861," *Confederate Veteran*, V (December 1897), p. 624.

28. Johnston, *Narrative*, p. 52.

29. Early, *Memoirs*, pp. 22–23; Johnston, *Four Years*, p. 86.

30. Phillips to ?, July 24, 1861, Phillips Papers; Howard, *Autobiography*, I, pp. 160–61.

31. O.R., I, 2, pp. 476, 496; *Battles and Leaders*, I, p. 191.

32. O.R., I, 2, p. 353; Tyler, "*Wooden Nutmegs*," pp. 68–75; Mitchell, *Tyler*, p. 60; C.C.W., p. 201; Erasmus D. Keyes, *Fifty Years Observation of Men and Events* (New York, 1884), pp. 434–35.

33. O.R., I, 2, p. 320.

34. *Ibid.*, pp. 476–77, 497, 519, 543–44; Longstreet, *Manassas to Appomattox*, pp. 51–52.

35. Chisolm, Notes on Bull Run, Chisolm Papers; Keyes, *Fifty Years*, pp. 434–35.

36. O.R., I, 2, pp. 524–25; Scarborough, *Ruffin*, pp. 88–90.

37. Alfred ? to Lizzie ?, July 25, 1861, Means-English-Doby Family Papers; Davis W. Aiken to his brother, July 30, 1861, Davis W. Aiken Papers, South Caroliniana Library.

38. Howard, *Recollections*, p. 42; C. W. Andrews to his wife, July 27, 1861, C. W. Andrews Papers, Duke University; Benjamin I. Scott to Fannie Scott, July 25, 1861, Scott Family Papers.

39. O.R., I, 2, pp. 424–25, 427, 429–31; C.C.W., pp. 25–27, 76, 179; Beattie, *Road to Manassas*, pp. 182, 185, 188.

40. Mitchell, *Tyler*, pp. 62–63.

CHAPTER 12

1. Johnston, *Narrative*, pp. 53–54; Beauregard, Incident relative to Mr. Davis' telegram announcing our victory, n.d., P. G. T. Beauregard Papers, Library of Congress; O.R., I, 2, p. 987.

2. Jefferson Davis, *Rise and Fall of the Confederate Government* (New York, 1881), I, pp. 352–56; Roman, *Beauregard*, I, p. 114.

3. O.R., I, 2, p. 328; Robert M. Johnston, *Bull Run*, p. 259.

4. O.R., I, 2, p. 503.

5. *Ibid.*, pp. 568, 570.

6. J. W. Pelot to Lalla Pelot, September 15, 1861, Lalla Pelot Papers, Duke University; Jackson, *Jackson*, pp. 177–78.

7. Thomas Nicholson to Mrs. A. C. Nicholson, July 27, 1861, Thomas A. Nicholson Papers, Duke University; James H. Langhorne to his mother, July 21, 1861, Langhorne Family Papers; Manning to his wife, July 21, 1861, Williams-Chesnut-Manning Papers; Melton to his wife, July 21, 1861, Melton Papers; Alfred ? to Mrs. E. M. Kennedy, July 25, 1861, Means-English-Doby Family Papers; Alexander to his wife, July 25, 1861, Alexander Papers.

8. Myers, *Children of Pride*, pp. 720–21.

9. Williams, *Diary from Dixie*, pp. 86–87; Jones, *Diary*, pp. 34–35; R. E. Lee to Mary Lee, July 27, 1861, Lee Family Papers, Virginia Historical Society; Myers, *Children of Pride*, pp. 726–27, 736.

10. O.R., I, 2, p. 747.

11. *Ibid.*, pp. 748–54.

12. Carl Sandburg, *Abraham Lincoln; The War Years* (New York, 1939), I, pp. 302–3.

13. William T. Sherman to John C. Draper, July 19, 1867, John C. Draper Papers, Library of Congress; Howe, *Home Letters*, p. 203.

14. C.C.W., p. 41; O.R., I, 51, pt. 1, pp. 17–19.

15. Sherman, *Memoirs*, I, p. 209.

16. Henig, "Letters of George S. Rollins," p. 23; Perry Mayo to his parents, July 23, 1861, Mayo Family Papers; Setright to his cousin, July 28, 1861, Setright Letters; Gregg to "Friend Heber," July 25, 1861, Schmitt Collection; Christopher Heffelfinger to his sister, July 24, 1861, Christopher Heffelfinger Papers, Minnesota Historical Society; James Carter to L. Goodnow, July 25, 1861, James W. Carter Papers, East Carolina University.

17. Allan Nevins, ed., *Diary of the Civil War, 1860–1865* (New York, 1962), pp. 169–70; J. Cutler Andrews, *The North Reports the Civil War* (Pittsburgh, 1955), p. 98.

18. Nevins, *Diary*, p. 169.

19. Jones, *Diary*, p. 37.

20. Alexander to his wife, August 1, 1861, Alexander Papers; Richard Taylor, *Destruction and Reconstruction* (New York, 1879), pp. 17–18; R. B. Lee to Jefferson Davis, July 29, 1861, R. B. Lee Collection, Chicago Historical Society.

21. Alexander to his wife, July 27, August 20, 1861, Alexander Papers; William L. Cabell, "True History of Our Battle Flag," *Confederate Veteran*, XI (August 1903), p. 339.

Bibliography

The literature on the First Battle of Bull Run, like that of many other Civil War battles, is legion. It is absolutely impractical to try to list every source which relates to the engagement, or even to include just the sources consulted, which would give a listing twice the size of that which follows. Instead, only those sources cited in the footnotes, and a very few other indispensable works, have been included.

MANUSCRIPTS

Aiken, Davis W., Papers, South Caroliniana Library, University of South Carolina, Columbia, S.C.

Alexander, E. Porter, Papers, Southern Historical Collection, University of North Carolina, Chapel Hill, N.C.

Andrews, Charles W., Papers, Duke University Library, Durham, N.C.

Armstrong, Ezekiel, Diary, Mississippi Department of Archives and History, Jackson, Miss.

Ballou, Sullivan, Letter, Civil War Letters Collection, Chicago Historical Society, Chicago, Ill.

Beauregard, P. G. T., Papers, Duke University Library, Durham, N.C.

Beauregard, P. G. T., Papers, Library of Congress, Washington, D.C.

Boham, Milledge L., Papers, Duke University Library, Durham, N.C.

Bonham, Milledge L., Papers, South Caroliniana Library, University of South Carolina, Columbia, S.C.

Bonney, Eli W., Papers, Duke University Library, Durham, N.C.

Brown-Ewell, Papers, Tennessee State Library and Archives, Nashville, Tenn.

Bryant Family Papers, Virginia State Library, Richmond, Va.

Buck, Samuel D., Papers, Duke University Library, Durham, N.C.

Burrill, John H., Papers, State Historical Society of Wisconsin, Madison, Wisc.

Carter, James W., Papers, East Carolina Manuscript Collection, East Carolina University Library, Greenville, N.C.

Chamberlayne Family Papers, Virginia Historical Society, Richmond, Va.

Chisolm, Alexander R., Papers, New-York Historical Society, New York, N.Y.

Dabney-Jackson Collection, Virginia State Library, Richmond, Va.

Davis, Charles E., Papers, Minnesota Historical Society, St. Paul, Minn.

Dawson, Nathaniel H. R., Papers, Southern Historical Collection, University of North Carolina, Chapel Hill, N.C.

Draper, John W., Papers, Library of Congress, Washington, D.C.

Early, Jubal A., Papers, Library of Congress, Washington, D.C.

Ferguson, Samuel W., Papers, Duke University Library, Durham, N.C.

Gardner, Amanda, Papers, Duke University Library, Durham, N.C.

Giddings, Allan M., Collection, Western Michigan University Library, Kalamazoo, Mich.

Griffin, James, Papers, in possession of Ronald Bransford, Fort Worth, Tex.

Haas, Clarrissa, and Stanley Oswalt, Collection, Western Michigan University Library, Kalamazoo, Mich.

Habersham Family Papers, Library of Congress, Washington, D.C.

Hairston, Peter, Papers, Southern Historical Collection, University of North Carolina, Chapel Hill, N.C.

Halpine, Charles G., Papers, Henry E. Huntington Library, San Marino, Cal.

Harrington, Lewis, Family Papers, Minnesota Historical Society, St. Paul, Minn.

Haydon, Charles B., Diary, Michigan Historical Collection, University of Michigan, Ann Arbor, Mich.

Heffelfinger, Christopher B., Papers, Minnesota Historical Society, St. Paul, Minn.

Heintzelman, Samuel P., Papers, Library of Congress, Washington, D.C.

Henry, Eleana H., Notes on Judith Henry, Virginia Historical Society, Richmond, Va.

Hollis, Rufus, Memoir, Tennessee State Library and Archives, Nashville, Tenn.

Hopkins, George W., Papers, Mississippi Department of Archives and History, Jackson, Miss.

Howard, Oliver O., Papers, Bowdoin College Library, Brunswick, Me.

Hundley, George J., Reminiscences of the First and Last Days of the War, Virginia Historical Society, Richmond, Va.

Hunter, Alexander, Four Years in the Ranks, Virginia Historical Society, Richmond, Va.

Jenkins, Micah, Papers, Duke University Library, Durham, N.C.

Johnson, Bradley T., Papers, Duke University Library, Durham, N.C.

Johnston, Joseph E., Papers, Henry E. Huntington Library, San Marino, Cal.

Johnston, Joseph E., Papers, William and Mary College Library, Williamsburg, Va.

Jordan, Thomas, Papers, Chicago Historical Society, Chicago, Ill.

Lane, John F., Collection, Western Michigan University Library, Kalamazoo, Mich.

Langhorne Family Papers, Virginia Historical Society, Richmond, Va.

Lee, Richard B., Collection, Chicago Historical Society, Chicago, Ill.

Lee Family Papers, Virginia Historical Society, Richmond, Va.

Lowndes, James, Papers, South Caroliniana Library, University of South Carolina, Columbia, S.C.

Mayo Family Papers, Michigan State University Historical Collections, East Lansing, Mich.

McKissick, James R., Papers, South Caroliniana Library, University of South Carolina, Columbia, S.C.

Means-English-Doby Family Papers, South Caroliniana Library, University of South Carolina, Columbia, S.C.

Melton, Samuel W., Papers, South Caroliniana Library, University of South Carolina, Columbia, S.C.

Miles, William Porcher, Papers, Southern Historical Collection, University of North Carolina, Chapel Hill, N.C.

Nicholson, Thomas A., Papers, Duke University Library, Durham, N.C.

North Family Papers, Cornell University Library, Ithaca, N.Y.

Pelot, Lalla, Papers, Duke University Library, Durham, N.C.

Perkins, Charles C., Diary, in possession of Frederick Clark, Marblehead, Mass.

Phillips, James J., Papers, North Carolina Department of Archives and History, Raleigh, N.C.

Phillips, Marshall, Papers, Maine Historical Society, Portland, Me.

Pitts-Craig Papers, Emory University Library, Atlanta, Ga.

Robbins, Jerome J., Diaries, Michigan Historical Collection, University of Michigan, Ann Arbor, Mich.

Schmitt, Peter, Collection, Western Michigan University Library, Kalamazoo, Mich.

Scott Family Papers, Virginia Historical Society, Richmond, Va.

Seig, Samuel S., Papers, Duke University Library, Durham, N.C.

Sessions, Joseph F., Papers, Mississippi Department of Archives and History, Jackson, Miss.

Setright, John T., Papers, Michigan Historical Collection, University of Michigan, Ann Arbor, Mich.

Shand, Robert W., Incidents in the Life of a Private Soldier, South Caroliniana Library, University of South Carolina, Columbia, S.C.

Sherman, William T., Papers, Library of Congress, Washington, D.C.

Solomons, M. J., Scrapbook, Duke University Library, Durham, N.C.

Squires, Charles W., Memoir, Southern Historical Collection, University of North Carolina, Chapel Hill, N.C.

Stuart, J. E. B., Papers, Duke University Library, Durham, N.C.

Vairin, A. L. P., Diary, Mississippi Department of Archives and History, Jackson, Miss.

Wells, George D., Letterbook, East Carolina Manuscript Collection, East Carolina University Library, Greenville, N.C.

Wells, William R., Papers, Southern Historical Collection, University of North Carolina, Chapel Hill, N.C.

Wheat, John T., Papers, Southern Historical Collection, University of North Carolina, Chapel Hill, N.C.

White, Benjamin F., Papers, North Carolina Department of Archives and History, Raleigh, N.C.

Wight, Charles C., Reminiscences, Virginia Historical Society, Richmond, Va.

Williams-Chesnut-Manning Papers, South Caroliniana Library, University of South Carolina, Columbia, S.C.

NEWSPAPERS

The only papers cited are the Charleston, South Carolina, *Mercury*, and the Staunton, Virginia, *Vindicator*. Of course, hundreds of papers North and South covered the campaign and battle, but such an abundance of firsthand materials is available that there is little need to use newspapers except for public reaction after the fight. Consequently, no full listing of papers containing coverage is thought necessary here.

GENERAL SOURCES

Andrews, J. Cutler. *The North Reports the Civil War.* Pittsburgh, 1955.

Beattie, Russell H., Jr. *Road to Manassas.* New York, 1961.

Cabell, William L. "True History of Our Battle Flag," *Confederate Veteran,* XI (August 1903), p. 339.

"Clark Leftwich's Coat," *Confederate Veteran,* V (June 1897), p. 298.

Cunningham, Horace H. *Field and Medical Services at the Battles of Manassas.* Athens, Georgia, 1968.

Davis, Jefferson. *Rise and Fall of the Confederate Government.* New York, 1881. 2 vols.

Freeman, Douglas Southall. *Lee's Lieutenants.* New York, 1943–44. 3 vols.

Hanson, Joseph Mills. *Bull Run Remembers.* Manassas, Virginia, 1953.

Hassler, Warren W., Jr. *Commanders of the Army of the Potomac.* Baton Rouge, 1962.

Johnson, Robert U., and Clarence C. Buel, eds. *Battles and Leaders of the Civil War.* New York, 1887. 4 vols.

Johnston, Robert M. *Bull Run, Its Strategy and Tactics*. Boston, 1913.

Sigaud, Louis A. "Mrs. Greenhow and the Rebel Spy Ring," *Maryland Historical Magazine*, XLI (1946), pp. 172–81.

Smith, Gustavus, W. *General J. E. Johnston and G. T. Beauregard and the Battle of Manassas, July, 1861* New York, 1892.

Stine, James H. *History of the Army of the Potomac*. Philadelphia, 1892.

U. S. Committee on the Conduct of the War. *Report of the Joint Committee on the Conduct of the War*. Washington, 1863.

U. S. War Department. *War of the Rebellion: Official Records of the Union and Confederate Armies*. Washington, 1880–1901. 128 vols.

Warder, T. B. *Battle of Young's Branch, or Manassas Plain*. Richmond, 1862.

"Work of a Confederate Woman," *Confederate Veteran*, IX (July 1901), pp. 321–25.

REGIMENTAL HISTORIES

Allen, Thomas S. "The Second Wisconsin at the First Battle of Bull Run." *War Papers Read Before the Commandery of the State of Wisconsin, Military Order of the Loyal Legion of the United States*. Milwaukee, 1896. Volume I, pp. 374–93.

Anderson, Keller. "Kentuckians Defend Their State," *Confederate Veteran*, XVI (November 1908), p. 597.

Barton, Randolph. "Stonewall Brigade at Louisville," *Confederate Veteran*, VIII (November 1900), pp. 481–85.

Bicknell, George W. *History of the Fifth Regiment Maine Volunteers*. Portland, Maine, 1871.

Brown, Maud. *The University Greys*. Richmond, 1940.

Chapman, J. A. "The 4th Alabama Regiment," *Confederate Veteran*, XXX (May 1922), p. 197.

Cudworth, Warren H. *History of the First Regiment Massachusetts Infantry*. Boston, 1866.

Daniel, Frederick S. *Richmond Howitzers in the War*. Richmond, 1891.

Dickert, D. Augustus. *History of Kershaw's Brigade*. Newberry, South Carolina, 1899.

Fairchild, Charles B. *History of the 27th Regiment N.Y. Vols*. Binghamton, New York, 1888.

Finch, George M. "The Boys of '61," *G.A.R. War Papers, Department of Ohio*. Cincinnati, 1891. pp. 237–63.

Goldsborough, W. W. *The Maryland Line in the Confederate Army*. Baltimore, 1900.

Haskin, William L., comp. *History of the First Regiment of Artillery*. Portland, Maine, 1879.

Haynes, Martin A. *A History of the Second Regiment, New Hampshire Volunteer Infantry.* Lakeport, New Hampshire, 1896.

Loehr, Charles T. *War History of the Old First Virginia Infantry Regiment.* Richmond, 1884.

Owen, William M. *In Camp and Battle with the Washington Artillery of New Orleans.* Boston, 1885.

Reid, Jesse W. *History of the Fourth Regiment of S.C. Volunteers.* Greenville, South Carolina, 1892.

Robertson, James I., Jr. *The Stonewall Brigade.* Baton Rouge, 1963.

Roe, Alfred S. *The Fifth Regiment Massachusetts Volunteer Infantry.* Boston, 1911.

Thompson, William M. *Historical Sketch of the Sixteenth Regiment N.Y.S. Volunteer Infantry.* N.p., 1886.

Todd, William. *The Seventy-Ninth Highlanders.* Albany, 1886.

Tyler, Elnathan B. "*Wooden Nutmegs*" *at Bull Run.* Hartford, 1872.

Varner, C. P. "Third South Carolina Regiment," *Confederate Veteran,* XVIII (November 1910). p. 520.

Wallace, Lee A., comp. *A Guide to Virginia Military Organizations.* Richmond, 1964.

Woodbury, Augustus. *A Narrative of the Campaign of the First Rhode Island Regiment.* Providence, 1862.

LETTERS, DIARIES, MEMOIRS

Alexander, E. P. *Military Memoirs of a Confederate.* New York, 1907.

Barnard, John G. *The C.S.A. and the Battle of Bull Run.* New York, 1862.

Barrett, Edwin S. *What I Saw at Bull Run.* Boston, 1886.

Basler, Roy P., ed. *The Collected Works of Abraham Lincoln.* New Brunswick, New Jersey, 1953. 9 vols.

Baylor, George. *Bull Run to Bull Run or Four Years in the Army of Northern Virginia.* Richmond, 1900.

Beauregard, P. G. T. *A Commentary on the Campaign and Battle of Manassas of July, 1861.* New York, 1891.

Bibbs, George A. "With a Mississippi Private in . . . the Battle of First Bull Run," *Civil War Times Illustrated,* IV (April 1965), pp. 42–43.

Blackford, William W. *War Years with Jeb Stuart.* New York, 1945.

Blake, Henry N. *Three Years in the Army of the Potomac.* Boston, 1865.

Bond, Natalie J., ed. *The South Carolinians. The Memoirs of Col. Asbury Coward.* New York, 1968.

Brown, Campbell, ed. *The First Manassas Correspondence Between Generals R. S. Ewell and G. T. Beauregard.* Nashville, 1885.

Casler, John O. *Four Years in the Stonewall Brigade.* Guthrie, Oklahoma, 1893.

Chittenden, Lucius E. *Invisible Siege*. San Diego, 1968.

Conrad, Daniel B. "History of the First Battle of Manassas and the Organization of the Stonewall Brigade. How It Was So Named," *Southern Historical Society Papers*, XIX (1891), pp. 82–92.

Cooke, John Esten. *Wearing of the Gray*. Bloomington, Indiana, 1959.

Coxe, John. "The Battle of First Manassas," *Confederate Veteran*, XXIII (January 1915), pp. 24–26.

Crockett, Cary I. "The Battery That Saved the Day," *Field Artillery Journal*, XXX (January–February, 1940), pp. 26–33.

Crotty, Daniel G. *Four Years Campaigning in the Army of the Potomac*. Grand Rapids, 1874.

Cummings, Arthur C. "Thirty-Third Virginia at First Manassas," *Southern Historical Society Papers*, XXXIV (1906), pp. 363–71.

Curtis, Newton M. *From Bull Run to Chancellorsville*. New York, 1906.

Douglas, Henry Kyd. "Stonewall Jackson and His Men," *Annals of the War*. Philadelphia, 1879, pp. 642–53.

Early, Jubal A. *War Memoirs*. Bloomington, Indiana, 1960.

Ellis, P. F. "On that hot Sunday Afternoon, July 21, 1861," *Confederate Veteran*, V (December 1897), p. 624.

Ewell, Richard S. *The Making of a Soldier*. Richmond, 1935.

Franklin, James. "Incidents at the First Manassas Battle," *Confederate Veteran*, II (October 1894), pp. 291–92.

Fry, James B. *McDowell and Tyler in the Campaign of Bull Run*. New York, 1884.

Gibbs, George A. "With a Mississippi Private," *Civil War Times Illustrated*, IV (April 1965), pp. 42–49.

Gordon, John B. *Reminiscences of the Civil War*. New York, 1904.

Greenhow, Rose O. *My Imprisonment and the First Year of Abolition Rule at Washington*. London, 1863.

Hall, Henry S. "A Volunteer at the First Bull Run," *War Talks in Kansas*. Kansas City, 1906. Vol. I, pp. 143–59.

Henig, Gerald S., ed. "The Civil War Letters of George S. Rollins," *Civil War Times Illustrated*, XI (November 1972), pp. 16–28.

Howard, James McHenry. *Recollections of a Maryland Confederate Soldier*. Baltimore, 1914.

Howard, Oliver O. *Autobiography*. New York, 1907. 2 vols.

Howe, M. A. De Wolfe. *Home Letters of General Sherman*. New York, 1909.

Hunter, Alexander. *Johnny Reb and Billy Yank*. New York, 1905.

Hunter, David. *Report of Military Service*. New York, 1892.

Jackson, Mary Anne. *Memoirs of Stonewall Jackson*. Louisville, 1895.

John, Samuel W. "The Importance of Accuracy," *Confederate Veteran*, XXII (August 1914), p. 343.

Johnson, Bradley T. "Memoir of the First Maryland Regiment," *Southern Historical Society Papers*, IX (1881), pp. 344–53, 481–88, X (1882), pp. 46–56, 97–109, 145–53, 214–23.

Johnston, David E. *Four Years a Soldier*. Princeton, West Virginia, 1887.

Johnston, Joseph E. *Narrative of Military Operations*. New York, 1874.

Jones, Charles T. "Five Confederates, the Sons of Bolling Hall in the Civil War," *Alabama Historical Quarterly*, XXI (1963), pp. 133–221.

Jones, John B. *A Rebel War Clerk's Diary*. New York, 1961.

Keyes, Erasmus D. *Fifty Years Observations of Men and Events*. New York, 1884.

Lee, Susan P. *Memoirs of William Nelson Pendleton*. Philadelphia, 1893.

Lightfoot, Thomas R. "Letters of the Three Lightfoot Brothers, 1861–1864," *Georgia Historical Quarterly*, XXV (1941), pp. 371–400, XXVI (1942), pp. 65–90.

Lillard, J. W. "Events of 1861–65 Recalled," *Confederate Veteran*, XXI (January 1913), p. 18.

Longstreet, James. *From Manassas to Appomattox*. Philadelphia, 1896.

Lusk, William T. *War Letters*. New York, 1911.

Lyster, Henry F. "Recollections of the Bull Run Campaign," *War Papers Read Before the Michigan Commandery of the Military Order of the Loyal Legion of the United States*. Detroit, 1888, I.

McKim, Randolph H. *A Soldier's Recollections*. New York, 1911.

McWhorter, J. K. "Caring for the Soldiers in the Sixties," *Confederate Veteran*, XXIX (October 1921), pp. 409–11.

Metcalf, Lewis H. "So Eager Were We All," *American Heritage*, XVI (June 1965), pp. 32–41.

Mitchell, Donald. *Daniel Tyler, A Memorial Volume*. New Haven, 1883.

Morgan, William H. *Personal Reminiscences of the War of 1861–5*. Lynchburg, Virginia, 1911.

Myers, Robert Manson, ed. *The Children of Pride*. New Haven, 1972.

Nevins, Allan, ed. *Diary of the Civil War, 1860–1866* New York, 1962.

Noyes, Henry E. "A Few Guns Before the First Gun at Bull Run," *Journal of the Military Service Institution of the United States*, XLIX (1911), pp. 413–18.

Opie, John N. *A Rebel Cavalryman with Lee, Stuart and Jackson*. Chicago, 1899.

Parker, Dangerfield. "The Regular Infantry in the First Bull Run Campaign," *United Service*, XII (1885), pp. 521–31.

Patterson, Robert. *A Narrative of the Campaign in the Valley of the Shenandoah in 1861.* Philadelphia, 1865.

Russell, William H. *The Battle of Bull Run.* New York, 1861.

Scarborough, William, ed. *The Diary of Edmund Ruffin.* Baton Rouge, 1977. Vol. II.

Sherman, William T. *Memoirs.* New York, 1875. 2 vols.

Smith, William. "Reminiscences of the First Battle of Manassas," *Southern Historical Society Papers,* X (1882), pp. 433–44.

Sorrel, G. Moxley. *Recollections of a Confederate Staff Officer.* New York, 1905.

Suddath, James Butler. "From Sumter to the Wilderness," *South Carolina Historical Magazine,* LXIII (1962), pp. 1–11, 93–104.

Taylor, Richard. *Destruction and Reconstruction.* New York, 1879.

Williams, Ben Ames, ed. *A Diary from Dixie.* Boston, 1949.

Winder, J. R. "Second South Carolina at First Manassas," *Confederate Veteran,* XVII (January 1909), p. 28.

Zettler, Berrien M. *War Stories and School-day Incidents for the Children.* New York, 1912.

BIOGRAPHIES

Coxe, John. "Wade Hampton," *Confederate Veteran,* XXX (December 1922), pp. 460–62.

Gould, Edward K. *Major-General Hiram G. Berry.* Rockland, Maine, 1899.

Govan, Gilbert E., and James W. Livingood. *A Different Valor, The Story of General Joseph E. Johnston.* Indianapolis, 1956.

"Joe P. Angell," *Confederate Veteran,* XVIII (March 1910), p. 133.

Johnson, Bradley T. *A Memoir of the Life and Public Service of Joseph E. Johnston.* Baltimore, 1891.

Kirby-Smith, Nina. "'Blucher of the Day' at Manassas," *Confederate Veteran,* VII (March 1899), pp. 108–9.

Klein, Maury. *Edward Porter Alexander.* Athens, Georgia, 1971.

"Major Chatham Roberdeau Wheat," *Confederate Veteran,* XIX (September 1911), pp. 425–28.

Roman, Alfred. *The Military Operations of General Beauregard in the War Between the States.* New York, 1884. 2 vols.

Sandburg, Carl. *Abraham Lincoln: The War Years.* New York, 1939. 4 vols.

Thompson, Magnus H. "The Strategy of Stonewall Jackson," *Confederate Veteran,* XXX (March 1922), pp. 93–96.

Wellman, Manly Wade. *Giant in Gray! A Biography of Wade Hampton.* New York, 1947.

Williams, T. Harry. *P. G. T. Beauregard, Napoleon in Gray.* Baton Rouge, 1957.